RETURN TO PROSPERITY

How America Can Regain Its
Economic Superpower Status

Arthur B. Laffer, Ph.D.
Stephen Moore

THRESHOLD
EDITIONS

New York London Toronto Sydney

Threshold Editions
A Division of Simon & Schuster, Inc.
1230 Avenue of the Americas
New York, NY 10020

First Threshold Editions hardcover edition February 2010

THRESHOLD EDITIONS and colophon are trademarks of Simon & Schuster, Inc.

For information about special discounts for bulk purchases,
please contact Simon & Schuster Special Sales at 1-866-506-1949
or business@simonandschuster.com.

The Simon & Schuster Speakers Bureau can bring authors to your live event.
For more information or to book an event contact the Simon & Schuster Speakers
Bureau at 1-866-248-3049 or visit our website at www.simonspeakers.com.

Manufactured in the United States of America

10 9 8 7 6 5 4 3 2 1

Library of Congress Cataloging-in-Publication Data

Laffer, Arthur B.
      Return to prosperity : how America can regain its economic superpower status /
by Arthur B. Laffer and Stephen Moore
          p.   cm.
      1. United States—Economic policy—2009–   2. United States—Economic
conditions—2009–   3. United States—Foreign economic relations.   I. Title.
      HC106.84.L34 2010
      330.973—dc22   2009038255

ISBN 978-1-4391-5992-7
ISBN 978-1-4391-6938-4 (eBook)

To our friends who are no longer with us.

While we mention names in trepidation for fear of not including someone we should have, we dedicate this to Bill Steiger, Justin Dart, Fischer Black, Norman Ture, Bob Bartley, Ronald Reagan, Jude Wanniski, Milton Friedman, Bill Buckley, Jack Kemp, Bob Novak, Irving Kristol, and all those who made the supply-side movement possible.

Contents

PART TWO: FISCAL POLICY

PART THREE: MONETARY AND TRADE POLICIES: INTEREST RATES, EXCHANGE RATES, AND INFLATION

Return to Prosperity

INTRODUCTION

This book is all about the political economy in the old sense of the phrase—a melding of economics and politics. Economics by itself has little meaning unless applied, and when applied by governments it's always political.

Even though this book is by its very nature political, it will not be partisan. Good political economics is neither left wing nor right wing; it's not liberal, it's not conservative; and goodness knows it's not Republican or Democrat; it's just plain, straightforward economics. To a casual observer it would seem that practitioners of economics cover a broad spectrum of views and widely diverse fields. But economics is economics, and this book will always be strictly about economics and the application of basic economics through the political process. It is my belief that good economics always turns out, ultimately, to be good politics.

Barack Obama, the current president of the United States, represents an American success story as much as any person whom I've ever seen. He is the essence of the melting pot that is America.

President Obama went to Occidental College, where he proved himself to be an extraordinary student and a bigger-than-life personality. Given the opportunity, Barack transferred to Columbia University, where his record was once again first-class. After graduating from Columbia University he attended Harvard Law School, where he became editor of the *Harvard Law Review*. A person becomes editor of the *Harvard Law Review* only because of excellence.

He then went on to teach at the University of Chicago, where I was on the faculty from 1967 to 1976 and taught for much of my academic life. I can assure you that only the very best and the very

1

brightest are ever even considered for appointments at the University of Chicago. (Just kidding.)

Barack's political record speaks for itself. There is no higher achievement possible than being the president of the United States of America. He achieved all of this by the age of forty-seven.

His personal life is equally exceptional. If we were to go to central casting and ask for an American hero, Barack Obama would undoubtedly be one of the top five choices.

But that having been said, as shown by his economic policies, President Obama has adopted a view of economics that is as wrong in every single dimension as it can be. The mistakes that he and his administration are making are basic Econ 1 mistakes. These mistakes will not only doom his presidency, they will do enormous damage to the U.S. economy.

Good man, bad president.

Over the full span of my career I have spent a great deal of time directly and indirectly involved with government. My first stint in Washington, D.C., was during the years 1967 and 1968, when I worked at the Brookings Institution, a well-respected liberal think tank. I was appointed the chief economist of the newly formed Office of Management and Budget (OMB) in late 1970, under my mentor and OMB director George P. Schultz. My first official task was traveling to Japan, China, and Vietnam in *Air Force II* with both George Schultz and John Ehrlichman, then head of President Nixon's domestic council. Thereafter I became integrally involved in the domestic economy of Vietnam and U.S. relations with China.

After returning to the University of Chicago in 1972 I stayed on as a personal consultant two days a week for George Schultz when he was secretary of the treasury, and later on with Casper Weinberger when he was secretary of health, education, and welfare, and William Simon when he was secretary of the treasury. After Nixon's resignation and Gerald Ford's ascendance to the presidency, I was a personal consultant to Donald Rumsfeld as chief of staff for the president, and his deputy Dick Cheney, and later on to Cheney as chief of staff, and Rumsfeld as secretary of defense.

My role with President Reagan was initially as an economic advisor in his campaigns of 1976 and 1980. In 1980 I was one of a handful of original members of Governor Reagan's executive advisory committee, along with Justin Dart, Holmes Tuttle, William French Smith, Bill Wilson, Earl Jorgenson, Ben Biagini, Jack Wrather, Charles Zwick, Alfred Bloomingdale, Judy Israel, Ted Cummins, and others. I was the young kid on the block, if that's even conceivable now.

Later on I was a member of President Reagan's Economic Policy Advisory Board for his full eight years in office. Then during the Clinton years, I was on the Congressional Policy Advisory Board, which consisted of some twenty-five people who advised the Republican congressional leadership at that time.

The reason I drag the reader through this tedious litany is to give weight to one generalization that in my opinion is critical to understanding policy-making in Washington, D.C., or anywhere else, for that matter: Whenever people make hasty decisions when panicked or drunk, the consequences are almost always ugly.

I do not believe there ever needed to be a stimulus program in 2008, or any spending package, for that matter, to save the economy. When Secretary Paulson went to Congress with a one-page piece of legislation allocating to him and him alone $700 billion, to spend as he chose, without any hearings, without any oversight whatsoever, I knew that our government had lost its senses. My view then and now is that Secretary Paulson's decision was a classic panic decision, and the consequences have been ugly.

And nothing has changed. The politicians are still running around grabbing at this straw or that straw, trying to save the economy.

You should be scared.

When I was the chief economist in the White House Office of Management and Budget in August 1971, Richard Nixon assembled his key economic advisors for a panicked weekend retreat at Camp David. On August 14, 1971, President Nixon brought down from the mountain a series of decisions reflecting radical change in economic policy. The impetus for the Camp David meeting in 1971 was a bad inflation number; I think the number came in one month at a 4.6 percent annualized rate, which was a little blip by the standards of the very early 1970s, and well below the uptick in early 1970 (see Figure 1). The economic proposals brought down from Camp David were President Nixon's solution to the inflation and unemployment problems.

Figure 1 12-Month Rates of Inflation by Month
(January 1968–December 1974)

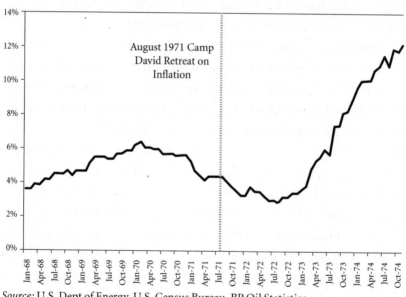

Source: U.S. Dept of Energy, U.S. Census Bureau, BP Oil Statistics.

In summary, President Nixon devalued the U.S. dollar and took the dollar off the gold standard. He imposed a tax surcharge up to 10 percent on products imported into the United States. He also proposed something called the Job Development Credit, which was an investment tax credit that applied only to American-made investment goods. And last, but not least, President Nixon imposed severe price controls on a huge cross-section of U.S. products, and wage controls on U.S. labor. Diocletian, the ancient ruler of Rome, who is reputed to have first imposed wage and price controls in his Edict on Maximum Prices in A.D. 301, would have been proud.[1]

The 1971 Camp David edict was a perfect example of a panic decision made in haste with far-reaching deleterious consequences that would last for years to come—inflation surged and unemployment rose as output fell. And all for what? A silly one-month inflation number. Seriously! Do you think it was worth it?

In 1972 another bad Nixon decision was made in a state of panic. There was a break-in at Democratic National Committee chairman Larry O'Brien's office in the Watergate. Three men were caught red-handed, each linked in one way or another to the Committee to Re-elect the President (CREEP).

The obvious response of the Nixon administration would have been to acknowledge who those caught in the break-in were and admit that they were collecting counterintelligence against the Democrats but, in the same breath, state that they were not authorized to break the law. Let the chips fall where they might but then be done with it.

But, oh, no, President Nixon met with his advisors H. R. Haldeman, then chief of staff; John Ehrlichman, head of the U.S. Domestic Policy Council in the White House; and John Mitchell, attorney general of the United States, among others. And from this panicked meeting, a plot to cover up the crime was hatched, with consequences that were fifty thousand times more damaging than they ever would have been with immediate full disclosure.

And then there was President Ford's "Whip Inflation Now"

---

1. "Edict on Maximum Prices," *Wikipedia*, http://en.wikipedia.org/wiki/Edict_on_Maximum _Prices (August 11, 2009).

(WIN) plan with its 5 percent tax surcharge on "corporate and upper-level individual incomes" to bring inflation under control.[2] It was at this time in a discussion of President Ford's WIN program that I drew my curve on a napkin for then chief of staff Don Rumsfeld and his deputy, and my Yale classmate, Dick Cheney. The tax surcharge was put into law, and again, far more damage was done to the economy by these panic-driven policies than could ever have been caused by events at the time.

Yet of all the 1970s' panicked decisions, Jimmy Carter's National Energy Plan took the cake. Threatened by OPEC, President Carter imposed well-head price controls on U.S. oil producers— guaranteeing that U.S. producers would reduce production. He also put an excess-profits tax on U.S. oil companies, which had the effect of reducing supplies of refined oil products. In addition, President Carter put on gas price ceiling controls, which artificially increased U.S. demand for gas.

As if all the policies enumerated above weren't bad enough, President Carter also mandated temperature controls in government buildings and required airlines to recirculate the air in planes to save on fuel costs. Gadzooks! Panicked decisions and drunk decisions invariably lead to ugly results.

The Obama administration and its predecessor have been acting in panic mode nonstop. Their behavior is the antithesis of good governance and good economics. My fear is that their decisions will do even more damage in the future than they have already done. Cap and trade and health-care reform are only two of the many scary policies being proposed. Just imagine the consequences of "Card Check" for unions, which would deny union members their right of a secret ballot.

The best solution to make government work for the people and institute good economic policy is really straightforward and

---

2. Gerald Rudolph Ford, " 'Whip Inflation Now' Speech," Miller Center of Public Affairs, October 8, 1974, http://millercenter.org/scripps/archive/speeches/detail/3283 (September 24, 2009).

so obvious it is one of Jackie Mason's standard jokes.[3] Politicians should be put on commission just like the rest of us. If they do a good job they should be paid a lot, and if they do a bad job they either should not be paid at all or they should be fined. If politicians had to bear the consequences of their own actions, they would vote and act very differently. But alas, such a simple and direct solution to our problems seems out of reach. Nonetheless, there are three simple provisions to the legislative process that should always apply.

First, Congress and all government employees should be required to live by the letter of the law and all the provisions that apply to other citizens for whom the laws apply. They should be required to retire on Social Security like everyone else and have no other retirement benefits provided separately by the government. They should be provided with health care and other perquisites commensurate with those given to other citizens. All laws should be applicable to all politicians.[4]

Second, Congress should not be allowed to place earmarks on legislation and thereby circumvent the congressional vetting process.[5] For a sufficient period of time to elapse to allow Congress to fully understand and assess the implications of legislation, a bill in its final form should be allowed to be voted on only after two full weeks.

Last, the president should be granted the authority for a line item veto that would require a 60 percent vote in the Senate to override.

The above three provisions would materially change the spending culture of Washington, D.C.

---

3.   One of Jackie Mason's stock political jokes about Congress goes something like, "If we want them to be successful, put them on commission and don't pay them until they show a profit." For a biography of Jackie Mason, see http://www.playbill.com/celebritybuzz/whoswho/biography/6553.

4.   This is equivalent to the Shay Amendment of 1994.

5.   "The federal Office of Management and Budget defines earmarks as funds provided by Congress for projects or programs where the congressional direction (in bill or report language) circumvents executive branch merit-based or competitive allocation processes, or specifies the location or recipient, or otherwise curtails the ability of the executive branch to manage critical aspects of the funds allocation process." Wikipedia. September 25, 2009.

• • •

As for content, this book is intended to help the reader understand the logical policy implications of basic economics. The fundamental tenet of economics is that people respond to incentives. As a result the policies most adept at achieving prosperity have to be consistent with basic human behavior. All economic policies fall into one of the four grand kingdoms of macroeconomics.

The first grand kingdom is fiscal policy. Fiscal policies comprise all the revenue and expenditure policies of the federal government. This is a grandiose kingdom that includes all federal taxes, including personal income taxes, payroll taxes, corporate income taxes, capital gains taxes, estate taxes, and sin taxes. Also included in the fiscal policy kingdom are the government's expenditure decisions, including defense, highways, welfare, unemployment compensation, and Social Security payments.

As we will see, the fiscal policy kingdom has made a significant turn for the worse. Taxes are increasing and becoming more progressive. Expenditures are growing at an astronomical rate, wasting money on corporate bailouts and ineffective tax rebates.

In contrast, the ideal tax policy, a flat-tax rate, is one that imposes the lowest possible tax rate on the broadest possible tax base. As a result people will have the least incentive to evade, avoid, or otherwise not report taxable income, and they will have the fewest places in which they can escape taxation. In Part Two we dive headfirst into the details of my complete flat-tax proposal.

Sin taxes should be separate, for their purpose is not so much to raise revenue as to discourage the taxed activity. In our proposal we leave open the question of whether there should be a carbon emissions tax. But if there is a carbon emissions tax, then the flat-tax rate should be reduced in such a way as to be static revenue neutral. Without a carbon emissions tax the revenue-neutral flat-tax rate would be approximately 13 percent on business net sales (VAT) and personal unadjusted gross income—the two tax bases.

The ideal tax policy also creates a more stable revenue source. Stability in revenues improves the government's ability to budget and thereby improves the level and composition of expenditures.

Monetary policy is the second grand kingdom of economics. Monetary policy's specific purpose should be to provide a stable valued currency both now and far into the future. As we demonstrate in the monetary policy chapter in Part Three, the current policy of the Federal Reserve is failing to meet this basic goal. The result will be a growing inflation problem in the United States, rising interest rates, and a falling dollar on foreign exchange markets.

To ensure a stable dollar, the Federal Reserve should operate on a price rule whereby reserves should be added to the banking system when prices are under downward pressure and should be taken out of the banking system when prices face upward pressure. Spot commodity prices, interest rates, exchange rates, and the price of gold are good indicators of inflationary pressures. Most of all, good monetary policy is one whereby decisions are made on a deliberative and purposive basis devoid of erratic, rapid changes. Monetary policy is like driving a huge tanker full of highly flammable materials over a narrow bridge spanning a deep and wide rocky gorge. Minute adjustments of steering and speed are essentials. Steady as she goes is the key to good monetary policy.

Trade policy is the third grand kingdom of economics. Trade policy encompasses all those policies related to the exchange of goods, services, and capital flows across international boundaries. Trade policy in an optimal economic environment has as its basic rule free trade unencumbered by impediments on the free flow of goods and services and people across national boundaries. Obvious exceptions include strategic materials and high-tech products useful in weaponry. But the lessons of free trade are clear. If you find a store that sells you high-quality products at low prices, is your first thought, How can I boycott that store? The answer is a resounding no. Free trade is a huge source of economic strength.

Our concern about current trade policy is the antitrade rhetoric of the Obama administration. This rhetoric against trade diminishes the possibility that any further international trade agreements (either bilateral or multilateral) will become ratified and even threatens to change the terms of current trade agreements such as NAFTA. As we show in Part Three, all these developments will diminish the gains in productivity and welfare that the U.S. economy has experienced over the past thirty years.

Incomes policies is the final grand kingdom of economics. Incomes policies encompass all the rules, regulations, and other restrictions mandated by the government. No one in his right mind would ever want to abolish incomes policies or regulations. Surely we shouldn't have the free choice to wake up in the morning and decide which side of the road we wish to drive on today. But regulations should not go beyond the purpose for which they were intended and thereby do collateral damage to the economy. The key function of good incomes policies is one of limitations to avoid unintended detrimental consequences. Here the Latin phrase *primum non nocere* ("First, do no harm") should be the guide. Simple, clear, and narrowly focused are the appropriate adjectives for good incomes policies.

Whether it is financial regulations, government-run health care, or cap and trade, the Obama administration is showing a penchant for over-regulating. The potential for collateral damage to the economy is tremendous.

The current course in all four of the grand kingdoms of economics is moving us further and further away from the ideal policy environment. Our policy suggestions are designed to reverse course and move our economic policies closer to the ideals. Such a fundamental change in our economic direction is the precondition for returning our economy to prosperity.

Part One

REACTIVE POLICIES

1

ENERGY INDEPENDENCE
AND PROTECTIONISM

To illustrate this government's inability to understand economics I'll start my journey with the president's environmental and energy policies. I was asked by Fox News to be a guest correspondent to discuss the appointment of President Obama's Energy and Environment team along with the administration's policies on energy and the environment. Berkeley Professor Steven Chu was chosen by the president to be the secretary of energy and to head Obama's team.

Professor Chu is a Ph.D. physicist with a Nobel Laureate and formerly a professor and chairman of the department of physics at Stanford University, where I received my Ph.D. in economics. This man has a résumé a mile long. Nobody is more qualified or more highly recognized in his or her chosen field than is Professor Chu.

In the course of introducing Professor Chu, President Obama described his administration's first priority for energy policy as securing U.S. energy independence. "It will be the policy of my administration to reverse our dependence on foreign oil while building a new energy economy that will create millions of jobs."[1] President Obama also emphasized, as he did in his inaugural address, that

---

1. "Obama Announces Plans to Achieve Energy Independence," *Washington Post*, January 26, 2009; http://www.washingtonpost.com/wodyn/content/article/2009/01/26/AR2009012601147.html.

his administration will "restore science to its rightful place."[2] And when he said the word "science," there was a slight hesitation, and the word was uttered with a bit of reverence, leaving the impression that his was the first administration in a long time that actually relied on science.[3]

When Professor Chu took the podium he reiterated the importance of energy independence for America and said that this administration would use science, and that he, by example, was literally a man of science.

Whenever people say that they want the United States to be energy independent they demonstrate that they simply don't understand Econ 1. In fact, the notion of legislated or politically driven self-sufficiency with respect to any product—oil included—is one of the worst mistakes politicians can make, and yet they do it all the time.

When I look at this planet, I see one group of people that has lots and lots of oil, and they basically don't know what to do with it. And then when I look at the United States I see another group of people that knows what to do with oil and could always use more. Venezuela, Russia, Canada, Nigeria, Mexico, and the Middle East selling oil to the United States is a win-win situation for both the United States and those oil-producing countries. Oil producers benefit by getting paid for selling their oil to us, which allows them to buy products they otherwise could not have acquired, and we benefit by purchasing that oil and using it better than they would use it.

The idea of politically motivated energy independence violates the precepts of David Ricardo's concept of comparative advantage and the gains from trade.[4] Ricardo was a late-eighteenth- and early-nineteenth-century English economist whose work is still revered

---

2.   Quoted from William McGum, "The Health Care Grail," *Wall Street Journal*, A15, 8/11/09.
3.   "President-elect Barack Obama announces key members of energy and environment team," Change.gov: The Office of the President-Elect, http://change.gov/newsroom/entry/president_elect_barack_obama_announces_key_members_of_energy_and_environment/. (August 20, 2009).
4.   David Ricardo, "The Principles of Political Economy and Taxation," New York: Prometheus, 1996, pp. 94–98; originally published 1817.

today for showing that both countries involved in a trade arrangement can gain from trade even if one of the countries has an absolute advantage in production of all of the traded goods. Trade in oil is a classic example of Ricardo's principle that gains from trade result from comparative advantage. The example of Ricardo's comparative advantage that I was taught used cloth and wine, where Portugal had a comparative advantage in producing wine and Britain had a comparative advantage in producing cloth. In this example Britain can produce cloth more efficiently, comparatively, than can Portugal, and Portugal can produce wine more efficiently, again, relatively speaking, than can Britain. Both Portugal and Britain would be winners if Britain sold Portugal its cloth and in exchange bought wine from Portugal.

To bring Ricardo's example of comparative advantage to the present, we Americans make some things comparatively better than foreigners, and foreigners, in turn, make other things comparatively better than Americans. We and foreigners would both be foolish in the extreme if we didn't sell to foreigners those things we make better than they do, and they sell to us, in return, those things they make better than we do. It's a win-win relationship.

The proceeds from U.S. purchases of products from foreigners provide foreigners with the wherewithal to buy goods from us. Our exports are their imports. This administration simply doesn't get it. U.S. imports don't mean job losses for Americans. U.S. imports are the means by which foreigners earn the income to buy products from us. Without U.S. imports there are no U.S. exports.[5]

And while I use energy independence and oil as the example of this administration's isolationist and protectionist tendencies, it's by no means an isolated example. President Obama's policies are riddled with protectionism. It was after all candidate Barack Obama who denounced NAFTA, and he has not changed that position.

---

5.   This is the essence of Abba P. Lerner's Symmetry Theorems; "The Symmetry Between Import and Export Taxes," *Economica*, New Series, Vol. 3, No. 11 (1936), pp. 306–13.

In April 2009, Congress effectively banned Mexican trucks from U.S. highways, and the Mexican government responded with tariffs on roughly $2 billion worth of American exports to Mexico. Similarly, Paragraph (a) of Section 1605 of the stimulus package states:

> *None of the funds appropriated or otherwise made available by this Act may be used for a project for the construction, alteration, maintenance, or repair of a public building or public work unless all of the iron, steel, and manufactured goods used in the project are produced in the United States.*[6]

In 1929 and 1930 the United States passed a trade bill called the Smoot-Hawley tariff, named after the chief Senate sponsor and the chief House sponsor. The bill was signed into law by President Herbert Hoover, and in my opinion was the catalyst for what we now call the Great Depression.[7] The Smoot-Hawley tariff raised duties (read taxes) on imported products to levels rarely seen in modern economies. Since the imposition of the Smoot-Hawley tariff, the United States has systematically been lowering tariffs and duties on imports. In Figure 1-1, a straightforward measure of the bipartisan progress is readily apparent. It is my fear that the Obama administration and its hostility toward NAFTA and free trade in general will reverse this trend.

The idea of the United States being energy independent, or independent with respect to any other product, for that matter, makes no sense whatsoever. Imagine if Minnesota tried to ban the importation of bananas into the state to achieve "banana independence." If Minnesota refused to buy bananas from Costa Rica, it wouldn't be able to sell Costa Rica iron ore. In fact, Minnesotans would have to build greenhouses in the frozen tundra to grow bananas in the winter. Ignoring the gains from trade is absolutely foolish.

---

6.   American Recovery & Reinvestment Act, Section 1605 (a).
7.   Jude Wanniski, *The Way the World Works*, Washington, D.C., 1978; Arthur B. Laffer, "Texas, Depression, and our Current Troubles," *Wall Street Journal*, September 22, 2009.

Figure 1-1 Average U.S. Tariffs, Duties Collected as a % of All Imports

(through 2008)

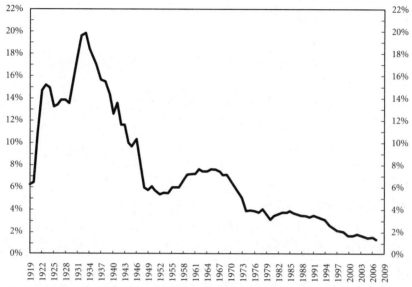

Source: "Value of U.S. Imports for Consumption," *U.S. International Trade Commission,* http://dataweb.usitc.gov/scripts/AVE.PDF.

Prohibiting banana imports makes Minnesota worse off, and the United States' prohibiting imports of oil also makes the United States worse off. In the Minnesota example, Costa Rica will be worse off as well, because it has less iron ore than it needs and too many bananas. If they don't sell us their oil, oil-producing nations will also be worse off. While Professor Chu may be very good at high-energy physics and manipulating Feynman diagrams and all of that, both he and President Obama clearly don't understand Econ 1 when it comes to the gains from trade.

The economic consequences of energy independence for the United States would be catastrophic for us and the rest of the world. The United States is the world's third-largest producer of oil.[8] We

---

8.   Source: Energy Information Administration.

fall slightly behind Saudi Arabia and Russia. The number-four producer is way below the United States. But in spite of being a major producer of oil, the United States is the number-one consumer of oil. We import about 50 percent of the oil we use currently in the United States (see Figure 1-2).

Figure 1-2 Oil Imports as a % of Total Oil Consumption
(annual, through 2008)

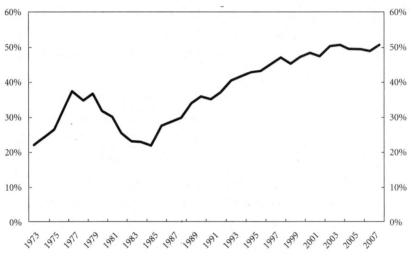

Source: U.S. Dept. of Energy, U.S. Census Bureau, BP Oil Statistics.

Can you imagine what the U.S. economy would look like today if President Obama were to successfully stop the importation of oil? The U.S. economy would be in even worse shape than it already is. If we had to make do with only half the oil we currently use, what would be the price of a gallon of gas or an airplane ticket? People would have to suffer the cold in the winter and heat in the summer. The economic results would be catastrophic, pure and simple. And yet the words "energy independent" roll off the lips of the physicist and the Harvard-educated lawyer with ease.

Oil Imports/Total Oil Consumption

Now, President Obama is not alone among today's politicians in espousing energy independence, and the concept of energy independence is surely not unique to this day and age. The espoused goal of U.S. energy independence was alive and well when Dwight David Eisenhower was president of the United States. Eisenhower was elected way back in 1952. In 1959, in the never-ending quest for energy independence, President Eisenhower imposed strict oil import quotas, which remained in force for many years, until 1973.[9] As a result of those quotas and other targeted taxes, regulations, and restrictions, crude oil prices, as received by U.S. oil suppliers, deviated substantially from their rest-of-world counterparts even though wholesale prices of retail products were roughly similar.

But the idea of energy independence was just as silly back in Eisenhower's day as it is today. Since the days of President Eisenhower, every president has at least paid lip service to the idea of energy independence. But frankly, year after year the United States has become more and more dependent on foreign oil (see Figure 1-2). Economics has until now triumphed over nonsensical politics. However, with his proposed "cap and trade" legislation, President Obama intends to change all of that. Cap-and-trade legislation not only entails a $600 billion–plus tax increase but also is about as protectionist a piece of legislation as can be found.

As drafted, the "Clean Energy and Security Act" (the "Waxman-Markey" Cap and Trade bill) would subsidize companies that pay higher costs than their international competitors. This subsidy is currently considered an "illegal state aid" program and violates our commitments under World Trade Organization (WTO) rules. Waxman-Markey also empowers the president to impose a border

---

9.   "1959 U.S. Quota on Foreign Oil Imports," County of Santa Barbara Planning and Development Energy Division, http://www.countyofsb.org/energy/information/1959Quota.asp (September 25, 2009).

adjustment that is essentially a tariff on foreign companies to pay for the cost of carbon.

My final point on the follies of protectionism has to do with re-taliation. While one restrictive measure by itself may not do all that much harm, what a protectionist move by the United States does do is incite foreign governments to retaliate against U.S. exports into their countries. The aforementioned recent example of Mexico's putting tariffs on some imports from the United States in retali-ation for U.S. prohibitions on Mexican trucks entering the U.S. is a case in point. Perhaps more ominously, this is exactly what hap-pened in the 1930s after the United States began the protectionist war with the Smoot-Hawley tariff. In my opinion, it was in part the trade war brought on by the Smoot-Hawley tariff legislation that created the preconditions for World War II.

2

ENERGY INDEPENDENCE
AND FOREIGN POLICY

When confronted by the obvious economic lunacy of the concept of energy independence, proponents of energy independence respond that in fact, while David Ricardo's concept of the gains from trade (which we cover shortly) is all well and good, it doesn't apply today in the United States. The leaders of the oil-producing countries are really just one step removed from being declared enemies of the United States. They are truly terrible people and we cannot allow the U.S. economy to be held hostage by them. Putin, Chavez, Ahmadinejad, and the like hate us and at the same time control the market for oil. They can't be trusted, because in times of great need they just might cut us off from their oil.

On the face of it, such an argument for protectionism is ridiculous. The people who advocate enforced U.S. energy independence want us to stop importing oil from foreigners because these foreigners might stop selling oil to us. Huh? This is the perfect example of the old saying "Cut off your nose to spite your face."

We stop buying because we're afraid that they might stop selling! Now, there's an example of why logic should be a required course at every law school. It's like the person who at age twenty-two realizes he, like everyone else, will someday die and as a result becomes so depressed that he commits suicide.

Now let me stipulate at this juncture that I agree that the leaders of many of the oil-producing countries are not good guys. In

21

fact, they really are bad guys. There are, however, a number of major exceptions to the bad-guy rule when it comes to oil suppliers—Canada, Mexico, the United Kingdom, Norway, and Denmark to mention just a few.

But that a leader of a foreign country is a bad guy does not mean that we should not trade with that country. Far from it.

Refusing to buy products from countries run by bad guys does not convince those countries or their leaders to become good guys. If embargoes caused people to rethink their politics and see the light, then North Korea sixty years ago would have become a free-market, progrowth, democratic, capitalist nation. We have embargoed North Korea for sixty years, since the Korean War, and as you can see, not only does it not see the light, it is as bad, if not worse, than ever.[1] Just picture Kim Jong Il in your mind's eye and you can see the product of economic embargoes and isolation.

The same lesson is equally true for Cuba. Shortly after Fidel Castro took over Cuba, the United States put an embargo on virtually all U.S.-Cuban trade. The Cuban embargo has not changed Cuban minds one iota. Fidel and his brother Raul Castro are as much in charge today as ever. Embargoes do not work.

That embargoes fail so miserably is not solely a consequence of Ricardo's gains from trade (a subject often taught in Econ 1). The failure of embargoes also results from the principles underlying core trade policy theory usually taught in more advanced econ classes.[2] But alas, if our country's current leaders don't get Econ 1, they surely won't understand trade theory.

Using trade as a political weapon is about as silly a policy as is imaginable. As shown by Ricardo's gains from trade, when you embargo a country, you not only do damage to the country you're

---

1.   "Embargoes and Sanctions," *Encyclopedia of American Foreign Policy,* http://www.american foreignrelations.com/E-N/Embargoes-and-Sanctions-Cold-war-sanctions.html (August 11, 2009).
2.   These include the Stolper/Samuelson Theorem, the Samuelson Factor Price Equalization Theorem, and the Samuelson/Rybczynski theorem; see Arthur Laffer and Marc Miles, *International Economics in an Integrated World,* Scott Foresman and Company, 1982, pp. 62–66.

embargoing, but you also do damage to yourself. Now, what's the benefit of hurting yourself? Both countries are worse off. And that is what our current Congress and the Obama administration do not understand. By the way, legislators from both sides of the aisle are equally ignorant when it comes to outsourcing and immigration. Detrimental unintended consequences from embargoes and other protectionist trade legislation are the rule, not the exception. Embargoes and trade protection also don't create domestic jobs and most definitely don't lead foreigners to see our point of view. Energy independence and other protectionist embargoes are a lose/lose for the United States.

For example, look at what's happening with the embargo and sanctions on Zimbabwe right now. Isolating Zimbabwe and the nation's tyrannical dictator, Robert Mugabe, obviously does not work. In fact, if anything, cutting Zimbabwe off from the rest of the world solidifies Robert Mugabe's leadership, by assuring his place as the lone leader looking out for the well-being of Zimbabwe. Trade embargoes and sanctions are not good political tools, no matter what people may tell you. In addition, putting energy independence and embargoes in place shows that Congress and the Obama team simply don't understand the basic economics of the Bhagwati theorems.[3]

The Bhagwati theorems, which are taught in most international trade courses, are named after Jagdish Bhagwati, an economics professor at Columbia University, who demonstrated mathematically that a country should always use direct cures for problems, never indirect cures, because indirect cures have detrimental unintended consequences. Indirect cures such as embargoes also often don't achieve the objectives the embargoing country seeks. And, if embargoes do happen to achieve the embargo-imposing country's objectives, they do so at great inefficiency cost. But all these

---

3.   Jagdish Bhagwati and V. K. Barnaswami (1963) "Domestic Distortions, Tariffs and the Theory of Optimum Subsidy," *Journal of Political Economy*, Vol. 71, No. 1 (February), pp. 44–50.

inefficiencies and impediments to using trade as a weapon against misbehaving countries do not mean we don't have tools at our command that can deal with bad governments.

The United States does have political tools available that directly deal with our national political objectives. For example, if the United States wanted to subtly influence another country and produce only a small political effect, there is always the bully pulpit of the White House. The president can bring public attention to bad behavior in order to sway public opinion to get a foreign leader to see the error of his ways. If the bully pulpit doesn't work, we always have slightly heavier policy tools, which come out of the State Department with its attachés, ambassadors, the Agency for International Development, and other formal relationships with other countries. The use of the State Department is usually a slightly heavier dose of political pressure that goes above and beyond the bully pulpit of the White House. And then there's always the United Nations, the International Monetary Fund (IMF), the Organisation for Economic Co-operation and Development (OECD), and the Organization of American States.

Last, we have the very heavy dose of political pressure that comes from departments such as the CIA, the Department of Defense, and international military organizations such as NATO and SEATO, and from the United Nations. If a country is behaving sufficiently badly and not responding to softer means of persuasion, there is always the military option, much as President Obama is using it in Afghanistan today.

That a country is headed by a bad person does not mean that the United States should not trade with that country. In fact, just the reverse is true. The tools that should be used to deal with bad governments are political tools, not economic tools, which have only indirect effects and often just solidify the bad person's position of power in that country. Hugo Chavez and Fidel Castro explicitly use U.S. trade sanctions against their respective countries as examples of U.S. belligerence and a reason for them to stay in power. Without the threat of a bellicose United States neither dictator could stay in power.

Many experts argue that trade with a potentially hostile country is, in fact, the best way to get that country to take our views seriously and to consider us a friend. Trade opens a country up to the rest of the world and allows it to see our point of view and share in our affluence. Goodness knows trade may help us get a better perspective on the rest of the world, too! The old saying goes that if China owns lots of assets in the United States it will be less likely to bomb us. There's a lot of truth to that saying. Does anyone still really believe that the embargo of Cuba has actually helped? I sure hope not.

It's ironic that the very people who want the United States to be energy independent argue their case by saying that being energy independent will prevent other countries from harming the United States by withholding their oil from us. Yet even if we go full tilt for free trade and import oil freely into the United States, there are many ways to protect the U.S. economy from a sudden shut-off of oil imports. We could always expand our strategic oil reserve, for example, or allow private users to store more oil. Emergency allocation plans, like those used in wartime, also work remarkably well.

The research of Professor Mancur Olson on the German and French embargoes of food supplies to Britain during the Napoleonic Wars, World War I, and World War II is a classic study of the economic and social impact of wartime blockades. The wartime blockades of food shipments into Britain by the belligerents were, if measured by the amount of food imports into Britain, highly successful. Food imports declined drastically.[4]

But while the embargoes reduced food imports into Britain, Britain was able to quickly adjust to the embargoes with "victory gardens" and other conservation and production measures. The British won each of these wars with well-nourished citizens. According to Mancur Olson:

---

4.   Mancur Olson, *Economics of the Wartime Shortage*, Duke University Press, 1913, p. 16.

*Because of the possibilities for substitution, advanced indus-
trial economies are not as inflexible in the face of shortages
as might be supposed. They have a considerable capacity to
substitute for anything in short supply. . . . This substitution
is not only—not even mainly—of the obvious kind, where
something ersatz, something that is obviously a "substitute,"
takes the place of what is in short supply. People may often readjust their patterns of production and consumption
in ways such that no one thing, but rather many different
things, take the place of what is scarce.*[5]

It is truly amazing how flexible and adaptive a free-market economy can be in its time of greatest need. In their ultimate objective
of bringing Britain to its knees, the embargoes were a total failure.

A quick digression to look at the Clinton administration's support for NAFTA provides a demonstration that good economics is
not partisan. Going against many in his own party and especially
going against unions, President Clinton, with the help of a number of Republican legislators, to be sure, was able to get Congress to
pass NAFTA. The passage of NAFTA was a major move toward freer
global trade, as it created one of the largest trading blocs in the world.

In addition to his performance on NAFTA, President Clinton reappointed Reagan's Fed chairman, Alan Greenspan, twice; removed
the retirement test for Social Security recipients, thereby increasing incentives for older Americans to work; reduced Social Security
benefits by subjecting 85 percent of those benefits to the income tax;
signed welfare reform into law, whereby welfare recipients actually
have to be looking for work to receive welfare; cut the capital gains
tax rate; and cut government spending as a share of GDP by more
than the next four best presidents combined. Yes, he did raise the
highest personal income tax rate, but then again, nobody's perfect.
I voted for President Clinton twice and I'm glad I did.

---

5.   Mancur Olson, *Economics of the Wartime Shortage*, Duke University Press, 1963.

• • •

My first reactive policy measure would be a unilateral reduction in all U.S. tariffs and the elimination of all unnecessary secondary restrictions on U.S. imports, which rely on ruses such as safety, health, or unfair practices. The determination of just what should be sanctioned should be left up to a nonpartisan panel of economists and trade specialists. Exports of certain military products should definitely be screened carefully so that military technology does not fall into the wrong hands. Otherwise the United States should live up to the letter of WTO agreements and should aggressively push for the signing of the Doha Round of tariff reductions.

3

OFFSHORE DRILLING

A nother part of the discussion at Obama's press conference on the environment and energy had to do with offshore drilling and the promise made by the Obama administration to safeguard the environment and to preserve Earth's heritage for future generations. Again we can all agree with the stated objectives of the Obama administration when it comes to respect for the environment, the heritage of future generations, and safeguarding life on Earth. But what President Obama et al. have decided to do is to persist in prohibiting offshore drilling, which, as I will show, will achieve just the opposite of the effect they wanted.

An oil spill, especially in water, does enormous damage because it is extraordinarily difficult to confine. Oil damage spreads quickly through diverse ecosystems with lethal consequences for most forms of life. In March 2009, there was a major oil spill off the coast of Queensland, Australia, that did extensive damage to about thirty-five miles of pristine Australian coastline. That oil spill alone killed many plants and animals, and it degraded the environment for a long time to come. It was a disaster.[1]

Also, if you can remember back several years ago, there was the *Exxon Valdez* oil spill in Alaska. Again, it took years and years to clean up the damage done by that ecological disaster. The toll on

---

1. "Australia Oil Spill '10 times worse,' " BBC News, March 14, 2009, http://news.bbc.co.uk/2/hi/asia-pacific/7943392.stm (August 10, 2009).

the environment was enormous, and the expense as measured in dollars was enormous as well. I don't want in any way, shape, or form to downplay the importance of preserving the environment; far from it. I think we ought to be very, very careful when it comes to offshore drilling and the transportation of oil over water. I have every desire for my children and grandchildren to enjoy a beautiful Earth as much as I have.

But reviewing global records of individual countries' national efforts to make the world a safer and better place for all to live, I've got to tell you that I'm excited and extremely proud of the United States. We as a nation have taken the environment seriously. I was raised in Cleveland, Ohio, in the 1940s and 1950s. Back then the joke was that if the Christ were to come back to Earth in Cleveland, to prove that, in fact, He was the Christ, He wouldn't have to walk on the water of Lake Erie—anyone could do that—He would have to sink in the water. That's all changed now. Lake Erie is clean.

When you see how much the United States has improved environmentally, from the Hudson River to the air quality of Los Angeles, it's an incredible success story. Our past success, however, is not an excuse for current laxity; far from it. We still have to move forward as diligently as ever. But there's a lesson to be learned here. The United States is about as good as it gets when it comes to the environment in today's world.

The problem with this administration is it believes that if the United States doesn't allow offshore drilling, Indonesia and other such countries won't allow offshore drilling either. And in fact, that's just plain not true. If we don't allow offshore drilling, the natural response from the rest of the world will be that they have a gap to fill, and countries such as Indonesia will drill offshore as if there were no tomorrow. And if Indonesia drills offshore there may well be no tomorrow for many life-forms living off the shore of Indonesia! If we in the United States are careless with regard to the environment, other countries are a thousand times more careless. Their offshore drilling would do far more damage than U.S. offshore drilling would ever do.

As an aside, there have been almost no spills from U.S. offshore drilling. When spills have occurred, they usually have happened when oil was transported over water. Prohibiting offshore drilling is pretty much a feel-good solution to a nonproblem.

Offshore drilling isn't an isolated example of this administration's inability to think dynamically. An equally apropos example is air pollution standards. Prohibiting mildly polluting U.S. producers from producing certain products here in the United States creates a whole new industry of heavy polluters abroad. When polluters aren't operating their facilities here in the United States we can't oversee their activities very well, and when there's an absence of oversight, that's when the real problems emerge. And again, President Obama's cap-and-trade legislation will have the effect of reallocating businesses that pollute out of the United States. U.S. cap-and-trade won't eliminate polluters; it will just redistribute them.

This administration and Congress just don't understand the idea of dynamic complex systems, which are basic to economics.

U.S. offshore drilling should not only be allowed, it should be actively encouraged, under strict safety and environmental standards. The standards should be set by a diverse panel of environmental experts from industry and other sectors of the economy. Offshore drillers should be held fully accountable for any damage done to the environment, as should global oil transporters. But on the other side of the ledger, there is nothing wrong with their profiting handsomely.

4

Cap-and-Trade Regulations

Political and scientific consensus appears to be coalescing on two closely related hypotheses. The first hypothesis is that planet Earth is facing a global warming crisis the environmental consequences of which will be disastrous. The second hypothesis is that man is a primary cause of global warming.

Even after spending considerable one-on-one time with former vice president Al Gore, I'm still not an expert on the question of whether either of the above statements is correct. But as we'll see in the next chapter, their literal veracity doesn't matter.

Scientists have changed their collective minds 180 degrees on global warming in the past thirty-six years. But this does not mean that the current consensus on global warming is not correct. And it also, for sure, does not mean that the global warming threat is not serious. As a safeguard against future ecological damage to the planet, we may well want to reduce carbon emissions.

But the costs of reducing carbon emissions are by no means trivial, and therefore it's not enough to simply press forward in the name of combating global warming and ignore the consequences. Global warming may well be serious, but so are the consequences of combating global warming. What we can say with a high degree of certainty is that a higher overall tax rate on carbon emissions per se will have a devastatingly negative impact on the long-term growth of America and the world.

Prior episodes of drastic reduction in oil supply illustrate the possible economic consequences in the United States if economic considerations are not carefully incorporated into a prudent plan to reduce carbon emissions. The devastating economic consequences of oil shortages as witnessed in the 1970s, 1980s, and 1990s were not preordained, but they will recur if politics as usual supplants economic reasoning.

Cap-and-trade regulations as contained in the Waxman-Markey Cap and Trade bill establish an aggregate constraint, the cap, on the amount of carbon that can be legally emitted. Typically this constraint is benchmarked to the carbon emissions from a base year—for instance, the Kyoto Protocol establishes a carbon emissions cap that is 7 percent below 1990 levels.

The aggregate constraint is then subdivided into emission allowances that are allocated to manufacturers. Constrained by the overall cap, all manufacturers face a choice—comply with their emissions allocation or purchase more emission allowances from other emission allowance holders.

Cap and trade forces the price of carbon emissions higher (taxes carbon emissions) but without correcting for the negative impact on the long-term growth rate.

Cap and trade is billed as a market-based approach to managing carbon emissions. As the theory goes, there is an efficient division of labor: The government establishes how much carbon may be emitted while the market sorts out who earns the right to produce the carbon emissions. The products that are in greater demand will be able to pay a higher price for the right to emit carbon. As a consequence, the manufacturers of the products in high demand will outbid other users for the right to emit carbon, while the manufacturers of the less-valued products either will have an incentive to sell these rights to the manufacturers of the products in high demand or will not be able to purchase these rights in the first place. Either way, only the producers of the products that consumers value the most will end up with the right to emit carbon. In this manner, the market is allocating the scarce right to emit carbon based on its most valued use.

The problem is that policies that control quantity (Waxman-Markey is controlling the quantity of carbon emissions) are less efficient than those policies that tax carbon emissions directly. A carbon tax is far preferable economically than is a quantity cap. The Congressional Budget Office correctly raised these precise concerns in a 2003 paper:

> *When costs and benefits are uncertain, as they are in the case of climate change, a system that raises the price of emissions—for example, a tax or a permit system with a set permit price—can have significant advantages over one that establishes an emissions quota. Tightening restrictions on emissions is likely to raise the incremental cost of mitigation much more quickly than it lowers the incremental benefit. As a result, the cost of guessing wrong and imposing an overly restrictive quota could be relatively high. In contrast, the cost of guessing wrong about the appropriate tax level—and perhaps failing to reduce emissions enough in any given year— will probably be relatively low.*[1]

The cap-and-trade system also requires an initial distribution of carbon emission allowances. One possibility is for the government to auction off the emission allowances. However, as implemented in Europe and as currently proposed here in the United States under Waxman-Markey, the vast majority of the initial carbon emissions allowances are simply allocated to different private individuals and companies—often referred to as "grandfathering." A cap-and-trade system implemented with a grandfathering distribution of carbon

---

1.   "Addressing the Uncertain Prospect of Climate Change," *Congressional Budget Office: Economic and Budget Issue Brief*, April 25, 2003.

emission allowances limits the government's options to offset the impact on the economy of the carbon reduction policy.

Urban experiences with taxi medallions exemplify many of the aforementioned difficulties of quantity constraints in general, and the cap-and-trade system in particular. Many cities, most famously New York City, constrain the number of taxis by requiring all taxi drivers to acquire a "taxi medallion." The supply of taxi medallions is constrained with the purpose of capping the total number of taxis operating within the city. The constrained quantity leads to higher prices; supply shortages during times of peak usage (especially during rush hour or rainstorms); and inflated and volatile values for taxi medallions, depending on changing market dynamics and regulatory response.[2] Ultimately, taxi services are compromised as the taxi medallions reduce the taxi market's efficiency. It would be far preferable if New York City just taxed taxis on miles driven at peak hours rather than issuing medallions.

As implemented, cap-and-trade regimes also limit the government's options for implementing policies that can offset the adverse economic impact of creating a carbon emissions shortage. A carbon tax is a more direct and effective policy instrument to reduce overall carbon emissions.

Effectively addressing global warming concerns requires both a reactive and a proactive policy response. Reactively, any cap-and-trade legislation that might be passed (e.g., Waxman-Markey) should be immediately repealed. This economy can ill afford the net tax increase contained in the current legislation. However, the issue of global warming should be addressed and will be addressed in the next chapter. Repeal requires the government to repurchase all carbon emission allowances from the current owners of those rights,

---

2.   See, for instance, Robert Cervero, "Deregulating Urban Transportation," *Cato Journal*, Vol. 5, No. 1 (Spring/Summer), 1985.

regardless of whether the original emission allowance was sold or given away. Due to government mandate, companies and individuals would be holding an asset with market value. The government should not expropriate assets without paying proper compensation. A time frame that is sufficiently long to allow for the repurchase of these allowances should be established. After that date, all carbon emission allowances would be worthless.

I will discuss the appropriate policy to address global warming in the proactive-policies section as part of the overall tax system. The main point to take away is that a carbon tax is vastly superior to a cap-and-trade allocation system. Also, any carbon tax must be matched with equivalent supply-side, progrowth tax cuts.

5

Nuclear Power

Another perfect example of just how clueless this Congress and this administration are is their stance against nuclear power. Nuclear-generated power is a proven, environmentally friendly way of producing clean energy that does a great job for virtually every objective you can think of. Nuclear-generated power, if administered correctly, is an amazingly cost-effective way to produce energy.

Nuclear energy also creates jobs in the United States and reduces energy dependence in a Ricardo-appropriate way. It's a win-win for everyone. Nothing is wrong with achieving energy independence per se if it is accomplished in an economically appropriate manner. Look at the years 1981 through 1986 when President Reagan decontrolled oil, removed the excess-profits tax off oil companies, and eliminated well-head price controls. Even though there was an economic boom, which increased the demand for oil in the United States, the price of oil fell and oil imports as a share of total consumption fell as well. U.S. suppliers were freed from government constraints and U.S. production of oil increased naturally.

However, this administration is against nuclear power ostensibly because it is worried about the safety of nuclear power plants.

My personal knowledge of the physics of nuclear power generation is limited, to say the least. I don't know a safe facility from an unsafe facility, except, of course, after the fact. But there are people who do. And as a result I do know how to create a safe nuclear power plant at least hypothetically. I would allow any nuclear power plant to exist and to produce energy as long as the board of directors and the officers of the corporation live on premise, and send their children to school on premise.

Proper government policy is all about aligning public and private incentives correctly. And this administration not only doesn't use incentives, it seems to actually be hostile to the use of incentives to induce people to behave in a socially appropriate manner. And if economics is about anything, it's about the use of incentives to maximize our collective welfare.

In order for a nuclear plant to function efficiently and safely, a country must understand how to internalize externalities through the use of incentives and make nuclear power generation facilities safe. You should never fly in a plane when the pilot has a parachute and you don't. It makes no sense whatsoever. You want the pilot of the plane to be personally responsible for and to bear the consequences of his or her own actions. It's the same for a company. Those who make the decisions should first and foremost bear the consequences of those decisions, be they good or bad.

Nuclear facilities have been operated safely the world over. It is true that Chernobyl was a major catastrophe, the effects of which are still felt. But then again, everything the Soviet Union did in those days of the Cold War was horrible, and we still feel the effects to this day. The United States of the early twenty-first century is not the Cold War–era Soviet Union. In today's France some 79 percent of all power is nuclear power, and the country is safe and has the cleanest air in Europe.[1] The lights work in France, there have been no nuclear disasters, and no nuclear disasters appear imminent. And yes, we in the United States can do better than France if we set our minds to it.

Professor Chu's team and political leaders today don't under-

---

1.   "International Electricity Generation," *Energy Information Administration*, http://www.eia.doe.gov/emeu/international/electricity/generation.html (August 10, 2009).

stand the role of incentives when it comes to the U.S. economy. A long-standing joke about physicists like Chu is that they may be able to invert matrices over Banach spaces, but they don't know how to tie their shoes.[2] Their policies, while sophisticated, fancy, and high-brow, fail at the test of basic Econ 1. Professor Chu and his team are choosing complex error over simple truth.

Restrictions on nuclear power generation should be greatly reduced as the United States prepares for a major expansion of nuclear power generation. Nuclear power plant owners and operators should be held fully accountable for any damage their actions may cause to the environment. In nuclear power generation, as with offshore drilling, holding the producers responsible for untoward consequences is essential, as is allowing them to profit fully from their successes.

---

2.   "Banach space," *Wikipedia*, http://en.wikipedia.org/wiki/Banach_spaces (August 10, 2009).

6

FISCAL STIMULUS

The criticism of failing to understand basic economics, of course, doesn't just apply to President Obama and his team. In many ways President George W. Bush wasn't much better. Not understanding Econ 1 and the role played by incentives represents a breakdown of the entire system in Washington, D.C. Too many politicians espouse policies that claim to get something for nothing, in order to reap political benefits from what they believe is an ignorant public.

I can't think of any example that more fits the mistaken notion of something for nothing than the series of stimulus packages currently in vogue.

To illustrate the conceptual error embedded in the latest batch of stimulus packages, I'm going to use the example that was put forth by Larry Summers[1] when he was lobbying for the stimulus package that was passed by Congress in March 2008.[2] Summers's package called for a $600 per capita stimulus check to be given to every individual who filed a tax return or, for couples filing jointly, $1,200.[3] The total cost of the stimulus package was $170 billion.

Let's focus for a moment on the eligibility requirements. In order

---

1. Larry Summers was a former secretary of the treasury under President Clinton, former president of Harvard University, and currently is the director of the National Economic Council.
2. 2008 American Recovery and Reinvestment Act (ARRA).
3. Now, that's not quite true, according to the initial legislation, because those who made more than a certain sum where ineligible to receive the stimulus checks. In other words, the stimulus check was "means tested."

to receive a stimulus check a person doesn't have to do anything. You can be sitting in your favorite armchair, watching *American Idol* and drinking a silver bullet, and the transfer payment check comes rolling in. The recipient doesn't have to work for the check or mortgage the house for the check. The recipient gets the transfer payment check just for being there. The stimulus check was technically a payment to people based upon something other than work effort.

According to the logic espoused by Larry Summers, the person who receives the transfer payment check of $600 will spend more than he would have spent had he not received that transfer payment check. The next step in the logic is that the additional spending by the people who receive the transfer payment checks will create jobs for people who supply the additional goods that otherwise would not have been purchased. The people who supply the additional goods and services will have higher incomes and thus they, too, will spend more. And there will be a chain, a cascading effect if you will, of demand trickling down, which creates a multiplied stimulus of aggregate demand in the overall economy from the initial stimulus check.

The Summers logic is simply an example of the Keynesian concept of a multiplier, where the numerical value of the multiplier in Keynesian terminology is one divided by one minus the marginal propensity to consume ($1/[1-MPC]$). Real GDP therefore is equal to total autonomous expenditures times the multiplier. The additional output created by the stimulus is the value of the stimulus times the multiplier. Pretty slick, eh?[4]

This was the logic used by Jared Bernstein and Christina Romer in their January 2009 white paper on the economy titled "The Job Impact of the American Recovery and Reinvestment Plan."[5] In that

4.   Robert H. Frank and Ben S. Bermanke, *Principles of Macroeconomics*, 2nd ed., Boston: McGraw Hill, 2004, pp. 345–46; Mankiw, N. Gregory, *Principles of Macroeconomics*, 4th ed., Mason: Thomson, 2007, pp. 483–86; Roger A. Arnold "Economics," New York: West, 1969, pp. 229–231; Bradley R. Schiller, *The Economy Today*, 10th ed., Boston: McGraw-Hill, 2006, pp. 212–14; Boyes I. Melvin, *Economics*, 6th ed., Boston: Houghton-Mifflin, 2005, pp. 255–63.
5.   Christina Romer and Jared Bernstein, "The Job Impact of the American Recovery and Reinvestment Plan," January 10, 2009, http://otrans.3cdn.net/45593e8ecbd339d074_13m6bt1te.pdf (August 10, 2009).

paper they evaluated the prospective total stimulus packages that have since been enacted. Bernstein and Romer, as is appropriate for professional economists, forecast what the economy would look like with and without the stimulus package. Naturally, they predicted that the economy would perform a lot better with the stimulus package than it would without the stimulus package. Their logic was based exclusively on the concept of the multiplier and the autonomous expenditures provided by the stimulus.

> *For the output effects of the recovery package, we started by averaging the multipliers for increases in government spending and tax cuts from a leading private forecasting firm and the Federal Reserve's FRB/US model. The two sets of multipliers are similar and are broadly in line with other estimates.*[6]

The Bernstein/Romer numerical estimates of the multiplier were in the range of .1.0 to 1.6. They specifically did not evaluate whether the concept of the "multiplier" type of analysis was appropriate or made any sense in this instance but instead dropped right into the details of the calculations.

The concept of a multiplier, i.e., the effect a given stimulus will have on the overall U.S. economy, doesn't just refer to one specific stimulus package such as the one in March 2008. The multiplier effect would naturally include all government spending and the stimulus spending packages that have occurred from March 2008 on: the purchase of AIG; supplements to the Farm Bill; the government guarantee of the loans of Fannie Mae and Freddie Mac; additions to the Housing Bill; Treasury Secretary Henry Paulson's bank bailout plan; the $787 billion stimulus package of the Obama administration; and the additional sums included in the projected deficit for

---

6.   Taken from Appendix 1, Multipliers for Different Types of Spending of "The Job Impact of the American Recovery and Reinvestment Plan."

fiscal year 2010. These stimulus amounts are very, very large. If the logic of the multiplier were correct we should see a huge impact on output, employment, and production. Just think of it, how wonderful would it be if we really could solve the economic problem by giving people money for not working? Well, this is exactly what this Congress and the former and current administration believe.

A careful review of economic theory shows that the Keynesian multiplier under current circumstances is little more than wishful thinking and makes no sense whatsoever as a basis for economic policy. It's all pie-in-the-sky theory with ugly consequences in the real world. These stimulus policies, in fact, will lead to greater unemployment, more poverty, and greatly diminished futures for most Americans. As is so often the case, reliance on false hopes means that politicians don't really make the hard choices that actually can restore prosperity. Whoever heard of a poor man spending himself into prosperity? It doesn't happen!

What Larry Summers said about the stimulus package is true as far as it goes. If the federal government gives a person $600 and doesn't require that person to do anything for the money, such as work, that person will spend more than he or she would otherwise have spent. That additional spending, in turn, will create jobs, output, and employment for people who otherwise would not have been employed. That is all true. And there also will be a trickle-down effect of spending throughout the economy. But this chapter of the story, while true, isn't the whole truth.

In fact, there are two missing chapters to the story. While it's true that the transfer recipients will spend more, unfortunately, in this world of ours, the federal government has yet to discover the tooth fairy. Or as my former colleague and friend Milton Friedman used to describe it, "There ain't no such thing as a free lunch."

Whenever resources are transferred to people based upon some characteristic other than work effort, those resources have to come from transfer payers. Resources don't miraculously materialize out of thin air, and there is no free lunch. You can't have a transfer recipient without having someone who is a transfer payer. What one person receives without working for, another person must work for without receiving.

If society produces 100 apples, and 10 of those apples are given to people gratis, then someone has to lose those 10 apples. As economists, we say that the income effects in an economy always sum to zero. Literally, they always sum to zero. The government cannot give to anybody anything that the government does not first take from somebody else.

While transfer recipients will spend more, transfer payers will spend less. Those people from whom the resources are taken will be poorer, and as a result, will reduce their purchases of goods and services. The reduced spending from the transfer payers, in turn, will disemploy people who had heretofore been supplying those people with goods and services that now are not being purchased. The disemployed suppliers will have lower incomes, and they, in turn, will spend less, leading to a cascading effect of reduced demand in the whole economy.

The positive income effects of the transfer recipients, which will boost the economy, will be exactly offset by the negative income effects of the transfer payers. The two income effects will offset each other, dollar for dollar. When it comes to government deficit spending, there is no stimulus in the stimulus package. There is no tooth fairy or free lunch.

Now, the specific concept of offsetting income effects from a transfer payment (or tax rate change, for that matter) is not new to economics and was brought into macroeconomics long ago by the French economist Léon Walras.[7] Walras's research was in turn brought into the English language by Lord Hicks in his book *Value and Capital*.[8]

My favorite example of Walras's point is that if the price of apples

---

7.   Léon Walras, *Elements of Pure Economics*, 1874.
8.   John Hicks, *Value and Capital: An Inquiry into Some Fundamental Principles of Economic Theory*, Oxford: Clarendon Press, 1939.

rises, apple growers will be wealthier, they will have higher incomes, and they will spend more on goods and services. But if the price of apples rises, apple consumers will be poorer, their incomes will be lower, and they will spend less. The income effects for apple growers and apple consumers literally offset each other to the 5,676th decimal place, by the hour, by the day, by the week, by the month, and by the year. It's basic math and accounting. There are no lag effects where one group happens to respond faster than another. It just doesn't happen that way.

The income increases for those who receive the transfer payment checks are thus exactly offset by the reductions in income for those who are liable for paying those transfer checks.[9] And remember, ultimately it is people who are responsible for funding the transfer payment, not the government.

Tax-rate reduction, which is the precise opposite of this administration's stimulus package, is another area where politicians and many economists as well simply don't get it. Professors Gwartney and Stroup in a 1983 article in the *American Economic Review* analyze the concept of income effects in great detail with respect to tax-rate reductions.[10] They find that income effects from tax changes across an economy, incorporating the impact from reduced government spending, offset one another. Therefore, a "tax cut will increase the quantity supplied of labor" and a tax increase "will decrease the quantity supplied of labor."

The income effects from government spending also sum to zero. Harvard University Professor Bob Barro estimated that "the multiplier associated with peacetime government purchases . . . [is] insignificantly different from zero."[11] The title of his *Wall Street*

---

9.   In microeconomics, the income effects of a price change and the substitution effects of a price change are contained in what economists call the Slutski equations. When the Slutski equations are aggregated over a full economy, it is easy to see that all the income effects sum to zero. For everyone who has an income effect that is positive, there is always someone else with a negative income effect.

10.   James Gwartney and Richard Stroup, "Labor Supply and Tax Rates: A Correction of the Record," *American Economic Review*, 1983.

11.   Robert Barro, "Government Spending Is No Free Lunch," *Wall Street Journal*, January 22, 2009.

Journal article says it all: "Government Spending Is No Free Lunch." Barro's seminal work, "Are Government Bonds Net Wealth?"[12] shows why. Government bonds aren't net wealth.

To the person who owns a government bond, the value of that bond is the discounted present value of all interest and principal payments. To the person who has to pay the taxes to fund those interest and principal payments, the value of the bond is the discounted present value of the future taxes needed to fund the interest and principal, which is exactly equal to minus one times the discounted present value of the interest and principal payments to the holder of the bond.

Imagine you're a one-person economy. How much wealthier would you be and how much more would you spend if you wrote yourself an IOU? It's dumb! Government bonds are not net wealth and there is no stimulus from increasing net debt, period. That just doesn't happen no matter how much you want to believe in the tooth fairy, Father Christmas, or free lunches.

So that's the second chapter of the three-chapter stimulus story.

Unfortunately, the full story of the stimulus doesn't end with the second chapter. While the income effects in an economy always sum to zero, the substitution effects do not.[13] All substitution effects resulting from a stimulus are in the same direction for every participant and therefore accumulate. In the example I used to illustrate Léon Walras's principle, if the price of apples rises, the higher apple prices will incentivize growers to produce more apples and apple consumers to consume fewer apples. Both groups are incentivized to bring apple prices back to where they had been.

It is these substitution effects that assure us that the stimulus plan à la President Obama actually hurts the economy. Substitution

---

12. Robert Barro, "Are Government Bonds Net Wealth?" *Journal of Political Economy,* Vol. 82, No. 6, November–December, 1974.

13. Here again the Slutski equations of microeconomics are instructive. When aggregated over all people, the substitution effects all move in the same direction. They don't cancel each other out like the income effects, they accumulate.

effects in the case of the stimulus plan really are as simple as the following: If you pay people not to work and tax people who do work, don't be surprised if lots of people aren't working.

If a government stimulus program gives people money only if their income is below a certain threshold, those people are incentivized to stop supplying work effort as they approach the income limit. At the same time, those people who are supplying the goods and services in order for the government to provide the stimulus now find that their work effort is worth less because there are fewer goods and services available to them at any given income. The higher-income earners are thus also incentivized to substitute away from supplying work effort. Because the substitution effects for those receiving the stimulus and those supplying it move in the same direction, they accumulate, ensuring that the stimulus program actually hurts the economy.

In the case where the government taxes the producers to transfer the goods and services to nonproducers, the disincentive for both groups is obvious. But even when the government transfer of goods and services to nonproducers is financed by government debt, the effect is the same on producers, only spread over a longer time period.

Free-lunch programs pop up all the time in the history of political economy, and they know no specific allegiance to any political party. They are equal-opportunity destroyers. Politicians of both parties want to get something for nothing. They always want a free lunch. No matter how many times silly ideas like these are put down, they keep coming back. The lure of something for nothing is just too great for politicians to resist. It's like hitting a gopher on the head with a shovel. You whack it over here and it soon pops up somewhere else. These examples right now are nothing other than the debunked theories of long, long ago. Get-rich-quick schemes are a constant favorite for politicians, including our current group in Washington, D.C.

I had a very hard time explaining the concept of substitution effects back in the early 1970s when I was testifying before Congress on President Gerald Ford's tax-rebate plan. While the conceptual error underlying President Ford's tax-rebate plan was the same conceptual error as that underlying both President George W. Bush's and President Barack Obama's stimulus packages, it was proportionally a whole lot smaller than either President Bush's or President Obama's plan.

Struggling to explain the substitution effects of government transfer payments in plain English, I finally said that if my esteemed colleagues on the stand with me who thought the tax rebate would stimulate the economy were correct, then what is wrong with Congress for proposing only a $600 per-capita tax rebate? Why just try to boost the economy a little bit? Let's go for the gold! Let's create an economic boom. Why not make the tax rebate $1,000 per person? $6,000? $60,000? $1 million? In fact, why don't we transfer 100 percent of GDP? "Senator," I asked, "can you imagine what would happen to GDP, if all those people who didn't work and didn't produce received everything, and all those people who did work and did produce received nothing? Obviously, GDP for the economy would fall to zero." Unfortunately, the illustration I used back in the early 1970s is perilously close to what is actually happening today.

During the 2008 presidential campaign, when University of Chicago professor Austan Goolsbee called President Obama's plan a tax cut for consumers and a tax increase on income earners, he fell right into the something-for-nothing trap. The substitution effects resulting from a transfer payment in an economy accumulate and they cause output to fall, not to rise.

Again, if an economy produces 100 apples, and 10 of those apples are given to people based on some characteristic other than work effort, then the producers of those 100 apples will now receive 10 fewer apples for producing 100 apples. Their incentives for producing 100 apples will be reduced and they will produce fewer apples. How someone can theorize that more apples will be produced is beyond me.

To reiterate the three chapters that Larry Summers should have covered: Chapter one, which he did cover, the transfer of resources and spending power to the transfer recipients will stimulate their demand for goods and services. Transfer recipients will spend more. But in chapter two the transfer payers will reduce their demand for goods and services. The increase in the demand for goods and services of the transfer recipients will be exactly offset by the reduction in the demand for goods and services by the transfer payers. There will be no net stimulus to the economy from a transfer payment. And finally, in chapter three, the substitution effects will reduce the incentives for people to work and produce, and output will fall. C'est ça!

I know the typical talking point from the government and much of the media is that the stimulus has saved the U.S. economy from the next Great Depression. We'll talk more about whether that is true a few chapters later, but for now let us wrap up this discussion by saying the economics behind the stimulus and the bailouts does not pass the smell test. The decisions made were panic decisions, pure and simple. While this view is pilloried by the mainstream consensus, that doesn't make it any less true. For what it's worth, I'm not alone in this viewpoint either. Nobel laureates Joseph Stiglitz and Ed Prescott have made similar comments.[14]

. . .

---

14.   Joseph Stiglitz commented in an SEC Historical Society webcast on regulatory reform, "We've really extended the safety net beyond too big to fail, and my view is that there's been no convincing argument that any of this was ever needed. It was based on the notion of fear—that if you didn't do it, the whole financial set of markets would fall. . . . But those who saw an opportunity to use scare tactics to get what they wanted did use those scare tactics, and it worked" (Bingham Presents: New World of Financial Regulation, originally broadcast September 24, 2009; http://connective. com/events/sechistorical). Meanwhile, Ed Prescott opined during a Bloomberg Radio interview with Tom Keene, "I think the financial crisis has been greatly overstated as a problem. . . . The press scared people. People running for office scared people. Bernanke scared people; Paulson scared people. . . . [P]eople began not to know what was going to happen" (March 30, 2009, interview on Tom Keene of Bloomberg's "On the Economy"; quoted from Brad DeLong's blog posting, "Do Chicago Economics Nobel-Prize Winners Live in the Consensus Reality?" September 27, 2009; http://delong.typepad.com/ed/2009/09/do-chicago-economics-nobel-prize-winners-live-in-the -consensus-reality.html).

All stimulus and bailout funds that have not been spent should immediately be impounded. Any ownership rights government has acquired in private companies via bailouts should be sold as quickly as is feasible, and the government should refrain from any exercise of control over those companies. Fannie Mae, Freddie Mac, and Ginnie Mae should stop buying and guaranteeing mortgages immediately and should develop a plan to sell their current inventory of mortgages they own in the private market. The Federal Reserve should be admonished not to acquire any major stakes in private firms save for very short-term stabilization reasons.

7

THE INCREASE IN PUBLIC DEBT

I wouldn't have gone through the analysis of transfer payments and government spending in such detail if this administration's and Congress's stimulus package were small. But frankly, government stimulus spending over the past several years is not small, and worse, there's no sign that it's over yet. The Bush administration and the Obama administration, along with Congress, have gone crazy, and I mean crazy, on government spending and on transfer payments. Take a look at some of the numbers and their implications, as shown in Figure 7-1.

But the official federal government spending numbers in Figure 7-1 grossly understate the true amount of federal spending. The stimulus package in March 2008 was along the lines of $170 billion and is included in the spending number. But the equivalent of the spending bailout of AIG on a cumulative basis came out to a transfer payment of about $185 billion and is not in the spending numbers. And even before the bailout of AIG there were massive supplements to the housing and agricultural bills. Additionally, the Fed acquired a number of toxic assets from their asset swaps with Bear Stearns and other financial firms, and goodness only knows how much value those toxic assets have already lost. The loss in value wasn't trivial and is nowhere to be found in the published data.

Government guarantees of all the mortgage liabilities of Fannie Mae, Ginnie Mae, and Freddie Mac were also huge. Today Fannie Mae and Freddie Mac guarantee somewhere around $5.0 to

$5.5 trillion worth of mortgages in the United States. The equivalent amount of transfers representing the unfunded liabilities from defaults of these guaranteed mortgages I put at about $550 billion. I obviously really can't be sure of that number, which I've estimated to be a little over 10 percent of the total guarantees in expected defaults. The unfunded liabilities number could be substantially larger than $550 billion.

Figure 7-1 **Federal Government Expenditures and Receipts as a % of GDP.**

(quarterly through 1Q2009)

Source: Bureau of Economic Analysis, National Income and Product Accounts.

After the Fannie Mae and Freddie Mac guarantees, along came the Paulson plan, the bailout plan, which was a $700 billion program on top of the earlier stimulus spending. The next stimulus package was $787 billion, which came in under President Barack Obama. In the meantime there were numerous bank bailouts, auto company takeovers, direct intervention in investment banks, taxpayer-funded acquisitions of insurance companies, guarantees of loans by banks via the FDIC, and a threatened total control of the health-care and health-insurance industries, not to mention more than thirty official policy czars tasked with micromanaging various sectors of the economy. These numbers, in the words of the incredible linguist Bill Safire of the *New York Times*, are MEGO numbers, which stands for "My Eyes Glaze Over!"

Figure 7-2 **Federal Deficit(–)/Surplus(+), and as a % of GDP.**

(annual through 2009[e])

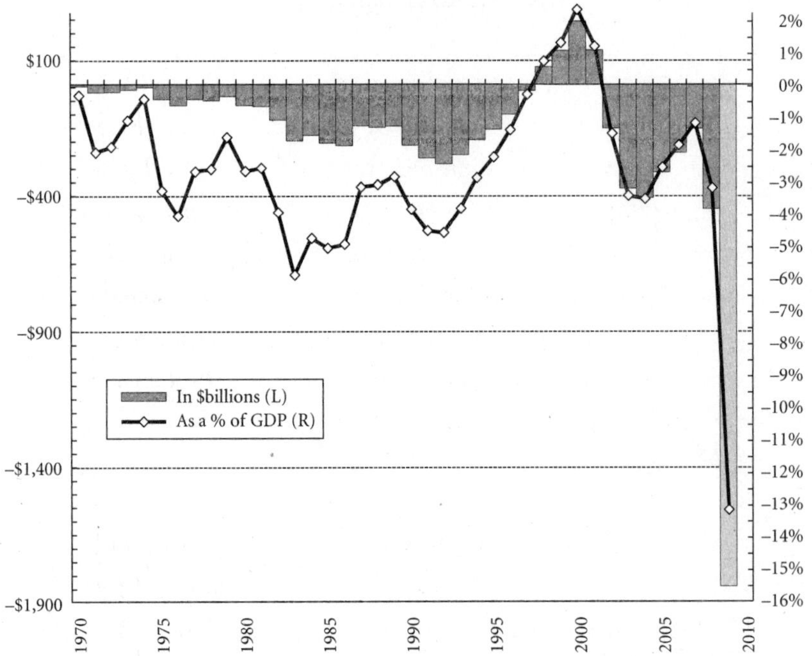

Source: Bureau of Economic Analysis, National Income and Product Accounts.

Altogether, including the projected federal budget deficit for fiscal year 2009 of about $1.8 trillion shown in Figure 7-2, I estimate the total amount of stimulus spending to be somewhere in the neighborhood of $3.6 trillion, net.

Back at the end of 2001, the federal net national debt was 35.3 percent of GDP. Today, that figure is reported to be 59.0 percent of GDP in 2009 and is estimated to be 69.3 percent in 2010.[1] Over the past eight years there has been a huge increase in the net national debt as a share of GDP, as officially measured. But these numbers don't take into account the net losses or unfunded liabilities from the federal government's asset swaps. My guess, if you looked at the unfunded liabilities of Fannie Mae, Freddie Mac, AIG, and all these other government transfers, is that the grand total of federal net debt would be about 100 percent of GDP instead of 59.0 percent of GDP.

And the truly scary part is that President Obama does not want to change course. Martin Feldstein agrees with my assessment in a recent *Wall Street Journal* editorial:

> The deficits projected for the next decade and beyond are unprecedented. . . . The CBO's deficit projections are based on the optimistic assumptions that the economy will grow at a healthy 3% pace with no recessions during the next decade; that there will be no new spending programs after this year's budget; and that the rising national debt will increase the rate of interest on government bonds by less than 1%. More realistic assumptions would imply a 2019 deficit of more than 8% of GDP and a government debt of more than 100% of GDP.[2]

To get a flavor of what the 100 percent of GDP number by itself means, imagine a constant long-term government bond rate of interest of 4 percent. At the end of 2001, a national debt of 35 percent of GDP with a 4 percent rate of interest on that debt would mean that annual interest payments would be 1.4 percent of GDP.

---

1.   As defined by the OECD, "All financial liabilities of general government, typically mainly in the form of government bills and bonds, minus all financial assets of general government." Due to reporting differences, primarily with employee pension plans, country data may not be directly comparable. Source: OECD.

2.   Martin Feldstein, "Obama Care's Crippling Deficits: The higher taxes, debt payments and interest rates needed to pay for health reform mean lower living standards," *Wall Street Journal*, September 8, 2009.

Now in 2001, because we had such a strong economy and also because the tax codes are so highly progressive, federal tax receipts were 22 percent of GDP (please see Figure 7-1). Therefore, a little less than 6.5 percent of total tax receipts had to be dedicated to paying interest on the national debt. Today total debt is around 100 percent of GDP. With a 4 percent rate of interest on that debt, total annual interest payments will be 4 percent of GDP just to keep the official debt where it is.

Because of all these truly ill-conceived public policies under Presidents Bush and Obama, the economy is reaching new lows. Not only has GDP fallen dramatically, but also tax receipts as a share of GDP have fallen dramatically, again because of the very progressive nature of U.S. federal taxes (Figure 7-1). Today, federal tax receipts are 16 percent of GDP. To pay 4 percent of GDP in interest on the national debt, and yet collect only 16 percent of GDP in the form of taxes, means that 25 percent of total federal tax receipts has to go to pay annual interest on the national debt. Yikes!

In a mere eight years from 2001 to today, the United States has gone from a little under 6.5 percent of total tax receipts going to paying interest on the national debt to about 25 percent. This is a disastrous trend with no end in sight. Not only is it impossible for a poor person to spend himself into prosperity, it's also impossible for a country to borrow itself into prosperity.

The spending spree of 2008 and 2009 and the subsequent economic collapse has worsened an already insurmountable problem facing the United States—total unfunded liabilities of the U.S. federal government. Unfunded liabilities are promises for future payment that the federal government has made to individuals without having either the current resources or future taxes in place to pay for these promises. Unfunded liabilities include:

Unfunded Liability	Obligation ($ in trillions)
The actual federal debt as of 2009	7.6
Future Social Security payments	18.7

Future Medicare hospital insurance payments	14.5
Future Medicare Supplementary (Part B) payments	13.5
Future Medicare Prescription Drug Benefit payments	5.2
Disabled veterans' compensation	1.5
Pensions for military personnel	1.2
Pensions for other civilian government employees	1.5
Health benefits for military personnel	0.8
Health benefits for other civilian government employees	0.3
Railroad retirement fund	0.08
Expected Pension Benefit Guaranty Corporation costs	0.06
Expected costs to the FDIC	0.01
Other federal civilian employees benefits	0.05
Loan guarantees	0.07
Other military/veteran benefits	0.03
Other insurance	0.03
National flood insurance	0.005
TOTAL	**65.135**

These unfunded liabilities, when totaled, increased by $8.1 trillion in 2008 to $65.1 trillion. Put another way, every household in the United States today owes $557,745 due to the current federal unfunded liabilities! And these don't even include the potential unfunded liabilities that could arise due to the government's explicit backing of Fannie Mae's, Freddie Mac's, and Ginnie Mae's mortgage portfolios or the potential costs to the Federal Reserve's balance sheet due to all the risky assets they have purchased.[3] Truly these numbers are astronomical.

When considered in the context of current U.S. GDP and federal tax receipts, the numbers surrounding unfunded liabilities

---

3.   It is also true that the government owns many assets whose value is very large. The point here is that the numbers are moving in the wrong direction.

are mind-numbing. At the end of 2008 total federal government unfunded liabilities were somewhere between four and five times U.S. annual GDP. The increase in these unfunded liabilities in 2008 alone was more than half of one year's GDP.

In terms of total federal tax revenues, total unfunded liabilities represent twenty-six-plus years of all taxes, including every tax now collected by the U.S. federal government. The increase in last year's unfunded liabilities represented more than three years' worth of federal tax receipts. These numbers swamp any official deficit numbers, and they don't even include the unfunded liabilities of state and local governments. The economy is like a train heading toward a granite wall at one hundred miles per hour. It will stop! The only question is how.

It astounds me how much damage a few people can cause when they take control of government. Their policies reflect a basic ignorance of Econ 1. If government taxes people who work, and pays people who don't work, it should come as no surprise if a lot of people stop working. It's just common sense.

If after all the tragedy that has befallen the U.S. economy since Secretary Paulson and Congress squealed like five-year-olds in a scary movie, you still believe that something should have been done, then I'll show you a far better way to solve the economy's problems. Imagine what would have happened if Presidents Bush or Obama had used the supply-side solution.

Total federal tax receipts are currently projected to be about $2.2 trillion on an annual basis. According to my estimates, the Bush and Obama administrations have used in total about $3.6 trillion in spending to stimulate the economy, which happens to be one and a half years' worth of total federal tax receipts. Imagine what the U.S. economy would look like today if instead of spending $3.6 trillion, we had instead had a federal tax holiday for a full one and one half years.

Total federal tax receipts today amount to $2.2 trillion. I'm not talking just about the income tax, either. The personal federal income tax is currently projected to raise almost $1 trillion in fiscal year 2009. The corporate income tax will raise $175 billion, and the federal payroll tax, both employer and employee contributions, should amount to $800 billion. And all federal excise taxes, including gas taxes, amount to about $66 billion. The inheritance tax will raise $26 billion. If you look at all federal taxes combined, you come up with a total number for all taxes of $2.2 trillion. Total federal taxes for a year and a half add up to $3.3 trillion, which is almost exactly what the Bush and Obama administrations spent to supposedly stimulate the economy.

Imagine what the unemployment rate would be today if President Obama had proposed a federal tax holiday for a year and a half. The unemployment rate today, instead of being about 10 percent, would be 3 percent. And people would not have dropped out of the labor force because there were no jobs. Average full-time hours would be way up, as would participation rates. High-paying jobs would be rapidly outpacing low-paying jobs and the number of part-time workers would be declining relative to full-time workers.

Not only would the unemployment rate have gone way down, but output, employment, and production would have soared, and the deficit consequences would have been no worse than they have been for all the misguided spending programs that President Obama, President Bush, and Congress have foisted on us.

That's what should have been done if anything should have been done at all. If only politicians understood Econ 1. If taxes on workers and producers are reduced there will be more workers and producers. Is that so hard to understand?

If more production and employment is what is wanted, then reduce taxes on employment and reduce taxes on production. That's how to create prosperity. Bingo.

Never again should our federal government be allowed to deliberately run a budget deficit larger than 5 percent of GDP including increases in unfunded liabilities of federal government programs. All federal programs, to the extent possible, should be based on defined-contribution characteristics, not defined-benefit characteristics.[4] Government accounting should be subjected to the same accounting standards private industry is currently required to adhere to, with similar penalties for malfeasance.

---

4.   In defined-contribution plans, the employer's contribution to an employee's retirement plan is defined, but the future benefit is determined by contributions and investment returns. IRAs and 401(k) plans are common defined-contribution plans in the United States.

8

IS THE STIMULUS WORKING?

But as they say in the trade, the proof of the pudding is in the eating. No matter how good or bad the theory is, if the policy works, it works. But if the policy doesn't work, every proponent of the policy will look anywhere but at themselves to affix blame. Successes have many parents; failures are orphans.

As a final point on stimulus packages and all the other spending programs of this administration, I'd like once again to refer the reader to the research paper by Jared Bernstein and Christina Romer.[1] In this paper these two economists gave their best estimate of what would happen to the unemployment rate for the U.S. economy if the stimulus package were adopted (which it was) and what would happen if it weren't.

I know Jared Bernstein well and I think very highly of him. He's a fine, honest, diligent hard worker who cares very much about America. I don't personally know Christina Romer, but I do know her research, and her research is exceptional. She has worked extensively on taxes and their effects on the economy. Her work shows that tax-rate reductions really do stimulate output, employment, and production; and that tax increases reduce output, employment, and production and act as a damper on the economy whenever and

---

1.   Christina Romer and Jared Bernstein, "The Job Impact of the American Recovery and Reinvestment Plan," January 10, 2009, http://otrans.3cdn.net/45593e8ecbd339d074_l3m6bt1te.pdf (August 10, 2009).

wherever they are imposed. As an academic she is a good econo-mist, pure and simple.

Recent research by Christina Romer concluded that "tax in-creases appear to have a very large, sustained, and highly significant negative impact on output," while "tax cuts have very large and per-sistent positive output effects."[2]

The Bernstein/Romer chart, reproduced as Figure 8-1, shows the authors' estimate of what the unemployment rate for the economy would have been had nothing been done by the government—that is, if there had been no stimulus. The authors then have another line that shows their estimate of what the unemployment rate would be with the stimulus packages. Their analysis, which was uncritically based on assumed multipliers, concluded that the unemployment rate would be much lower and would fall much faster with the stim-ulus package than without the stimulus package.

Since the early January 2009 publication of their paper sufficient time has elapsed that we now know how the economy has actually performed with Obama's stimulus package and his other policies. At the time of this writing, the economy is far, far worse than Romer and Bernstein thought it would have been had there not been a stimulus package at all. Judging from their work, the stimulus pack-age has been empirically tested and has been shown not only not to have helped the economy, but to have failed (see Figure 8-1). What I hope Bernsetin and Romer don't do is justify their forecast ex-post. After all, there is always the argument that no matter how bad things are, they would have been worse without the stimulus package.

My opinion agrees fully with the data that these activist poli-cies have been shown to have made the economy worse, not better, and at the same time have increased our national debt enormously as a burden for generations to come. This is a perfect example of

---

2.   Christina and David Romer (2007), "The Macroeconomic Effects of Tax Changes: Estimates Based on A New Measure of Fiscal Policy," working paper: http://elsa.berkelev.edu/~dromer/papers/RomerandRomer.pdf, *American Economic Review*, forthcoming.

the key point I'm making, about governments that make panicked decisions.

Figure 8-1 Unemployment Rate With and Without Recovery Plan vs. Actual With Laffer Q309 Forecast

(quarterly, percent, actual through Q2–09, estimate through Q3–09)

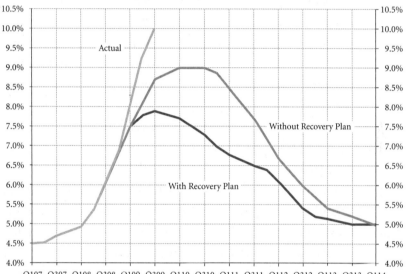

Source: Christina Romer and Jared Bernstein, "The Job Impact of the American Recovery and Reinvestment Plan," January 10, 2009, http://otrans.3cdn.net/45593e8ecbd339d074_13m6bt1te.pdf (August 10, 2009).

The Bernstein/Romer paper is exactly the type of high-quality honest work that needs to be ubiquitous in government. Standards should be set so that results can be directly compared with the outcome that was expected. Only in this way can we advance science and our honest understanding of what does and does not work.

9

CASH FOR CLUNKERS

A sure sign that the people who run government don't understand basic economics is when they take employment data as an actual measure of prosperity rather than as a proxy for prosperity. In normal times the consumption and production of goods and services move closely with measures of total employment, and therefore, using one or the other as a prosperity metric is not a huge leap of faith. But when government enacts policies to increase employment or capacity utilization without increasing the production and consumption of goods and services, or worse yet, tries to increase employment at the expense of people's well-being and consumption, then economic thinking has been derailed. In fact, I can think of no example worse as an indicator of an impending economic train wreck than the "Cash for Clunkers" program. It's sparkle-headed.

In economics, employment, work, and the use of capital are always costs, not benefits. Working is the price society has to pay in order to be able to consume the goods and services society wants. The Cash for Clunkers program destroys perfectly good cars in order to artificially stimulate the demand for and production of new cars. This Cash for Clunkers program increases the production of cars and employment in the auto industry by lowering people's consumption of car services and future demand for cars.

In normal markets a customer can always pay more than the market price for something, but rarely does the customer pay less than the market price. Something for nothing has always been an elusive dream and is the reason we all seek productivity gains.

Increases in productivity are instances where we actually *do* get more production and consumption for the same or less input—literally "something for nothing." We measure increases in productivity as the change in the number of man-hours it takes to produce one unit of output. Output per man-hour is a key metric of economic development, and increases in productivity are an unmitigated good. Figure 9-1 compares output per hour across several developed and less-developed countries. Clearly wealthy economies such as that of the United States are more productive than those of less wealthy countries such as Turkey and Mexico.

Figure 9-1 **Output per Hour in Selected Countries as a Percentage of U.S. Output per Hour**

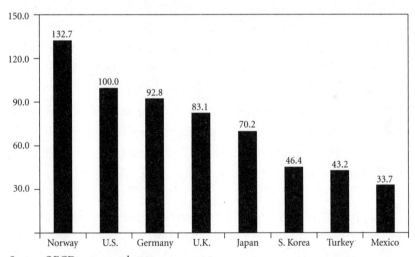

Source: OECD, www.oecd.stat.

When consumption and employment are confused by politicians, all sorts of mischievous consequences result. In the 1930s, the confusion of consumption and employment led to government works projects where people were actually paid to dig ditches and then fill them up again. These works projects, when all was said and done, created a whole lot of make-work employment and resulted in no additional net production of goods and services or consumption. What a waste. Make-work projects were ubiquitous in the 1930s. Employers were also encouraged to pay workers higher wages than markets would dictate because those workers would then buy more and stimulate the economy. Sound familiar?

In short, if someone is willing to trade in an old car that meets certain requirements (i.e., a clunker), the government will give that person up to $4,500 toward the purchase of a new car. The clunkers that are traded in for the new cars are subsequently destroyed. Thus the name Cash for Clunkers.

The primary logic underlying the Cash for Clunkers program is that by getting these older cars off the roads one will increase the demand for new cars—especially given that a person actually has to buy a new car to get the Cash for Clunkers check. Increased demand for new cars saves U.S. Auto Works (alias G.M. and Chrysler) and bails out Michigan (the worst-administered state in our nation) and the United Auto Workers and their hugely underfunded pensions and super-high uncompetitive wages. It's obviously a winner for everyone (just kidding).

The Cash for Clunkers program is similar to an example of the confusion of employment with production and consumption that I used in the macroeconomics class I taught when I was on the faculty of the University of Chicago. The story went something like this.

Imagine that Charlie Manson, the creepy mass murderer currently held in prison in California who sports a self-carved swastika on his forehead, escapes from prison. During his short period of chaotic freedom he goes to a railroad yard and finds several boxcars full of Ohio Blue Tip matches and proceeds to burn 99 percent of all the houses in the United States to the ground. He doesn't kill anyone but he leaves a trail of ashes and embers where people's homes used to be.

The government, with its incredible sleuthing talent, finally catches Charlie Manson. He is sentenced to death and is shot on the steps of the Capitol building in Washington, D.C., for all the nation to see. Everyone knows he's dead and that there never will be a recurrence of the national home burning that occurred when he escaped prison.

The question I posed to my class: What would happen to new housing starts and employment in the construction industry? The answer is obvious: If 99 percent of all existing homes are destroyed, new housing starts will soar and home construction activity will boom. But on the other side of the ledger, people will have to sleep outside in the snow in the winter or with mosquitoes in the summer. The consumption of housing services will be way, way down and we'll all be far worse off, even though the number of jobs has increased. Jobs per se are not good and not all projects that create jobs are good, either.

Getting back to the Cash for Clunkers program, my question is, Why stop at $4,500 for old cars? Let's authorize enough money to remove all cars from the roads that are over three months old. Heck, we could hype auto production to heights never before seen. Detroit would boom, and meanwhile people would be forced to walk back and forth to work without any cars.

Oh, by the way, don't forget how much we'd save on energy costs and carbon emissions.

Seriously, have you ever heard of a dumber program in your life? And yet our government has not only put it into effect, but was so pleased with Cash for Clunkers that the program was expanded manifold.

The Cash for Clunkers program is only one of a number of such programs being implemented today by the Obama administration, Congress, and the Fed. The Fed, along with Fannie Mae, Ginnie Mae, and Freddie Mac, have purchased a huge number of home mortgages at taxpayer expense, which has pushed down mortgage rates and artificially buoyed home prices. By subsidizing home prices, government has extended the length of and deepened the decline in home building by encouraging suppliers not to withdraw supplies and enticing demanders to overpurchase homes.

Government should not be in the business of supporting any one specific industry, whether that industry be housing, autos, insurance, or anything else. Where government programs make sense is in the areas where people *do* need help, not businesses. Even with products such as health care and food, extreme caution should be used whenever government provides minimum consumption magnitudes. This is not to say that there aren't instances where people really can't make good decisions for themselves, because there are. But, in general, it would be far better if government provided income supplements and let the consumers choose what they want.

10

TAX THE RICH TO PAY FOR GOVERNMENT

When my class graduated from Yale in 1962 President John F. Kennedy gave the commencement address. After several delightful quips about Yalies—he being a Harvard man himself—he launched into his main thesis. Kennedy said:

> We must move on from the reassuring repetition of stale phrases to a new, difficult, but essential confrontation with reality.
>
> For the great enemy of truth is very often not the lie—deliberate, contrived, and dishonest—but the myth—persistent, persuasive, and unrealistic. Too often we hold fast to the clichés of our forebears. We subject all facts to a prefabricated set of interpretations. We enjoy the comfort of opinion without the discomfort of thought.
>
> Mythology distracts us everywhere—in government as in business, in politics as in economics, in foreign affairs as in domestic affairs. But today I want to particularly consider the myth and reality in our national economy.

Sometimes what seems to be an obviously correct answer upon careful consideration turns out to be egregiously in error. And when these "surprise" errors have massive consequences, the economic fate of a nation can hang in the balance. I can think of no example that fits the above description better than the idea that increased government spending or tax cuts for low- and middle-income earners can be financed by taxing the rich at higher income-tax rates.

President Kennedy, in fact, cut tax rates on the rich, cut the corporate income-tax rate, cut the capital-gains tax rate, cut tax rates on dividends, cut tax rates on traded products, increased defense spending, and balanced the federal budget. And he did this as often as not facing strong opposition from a wall of Republicans led by Arizona Senator Barry Goldwater. Go figure!

Over the period 1980 to the present the United States has cut tax rates every which way (see Figure 10-1). We've not only cut tax rates on the rich, but we've cut the lowest tax rates, and those in the middle as well. We've cut tax rates on traded products (see Figure 1-1) and on inheritances, capital gains, and dividends. We've reduced effective tax rates on the elderly who work and on people who jump, fly, swim, crawl, run, and dig as well as those who just sit on their couches and watch TV. The last quarter century has been twenty-five-plus years of tax cuts.

Tax data are also probably the best data government produces. Government really cares how much it collects, which is how much you pay in taxes, and the government therefore keeps immaculate records on tax collections. They know who owes how much and where the taxpayers live, how much they earn, what they're worth, and what they do. One of the earliest books ever written in the British Isles was called the *Domesday Book;* it was compiled in A.D. 1086. The *Domesday Book* was an incredibly comprehensive accounting of tax records. According to Wikipedia, "The *Domesday Book* is the record of the great survey of England completed in 1086, executed for William I of England, or William the Conqueror. While spending the Christmas of 1086 in Gloucester, William 'had deep speech with his counselors and sent men all over England to each shire to find out what or how much each landholder had in land and livestock, and what it was worth' (*Anglo-Saxon Chronicle*)."

Figure 10-1 Highest Marginal Tax Rates on Personal Income, Corporate Income, Capital Gains, and Inheritance, 1955–Present

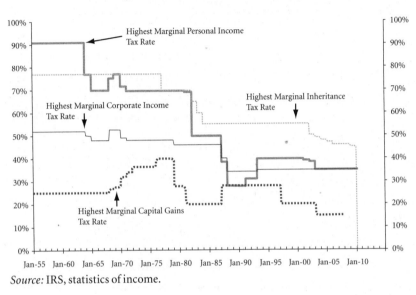

Source: IRS, statistics of income.

Virtually every country's government has a department of revenue with detailed records concerning the government's sources of revenues. Some of these records go back centuries, as witnessed by the *Domesday Book*. These accounts have turned out to be unbelievably accurate and a rich source of economic information, and the Internal Revenue Service of the United States and its publication *The Statistics of Income* is no exception. We in the United States have detailed data on tax returns that can be sliced and diced any which way a person would choose. We literally have the ability to corroborate or disprove any hypothesis a creative politician can put forward. And President Obama's idea of raising taxes on the rich to pay for spending programs and tax cuts for those making $250,000 or less is one idea that is easy to assess using the rich trove of tax data.

In Figure 10-2 I have plotted the percentage of total income taxes paid by the top 1 percent of all income earners (the rich) and the bottom 95 percent of all income earners (the nonrich) for each year from 1980 through 2007.

Figure 10-2 **Income Taxes Paid as a % of Total Income Taxes**

(annual, through 2007)

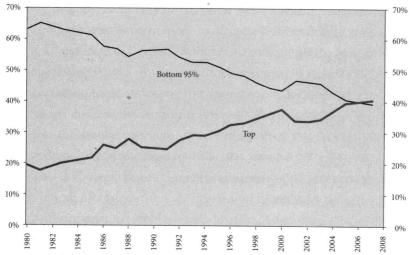

Source: US BEA, Table 1.1.5; The Tax Foundation, Summary of Latest Federal Individual Income Tax Data, Table 4 http://www.taxfoundation.org/publications/show250.html; http://www.bea.gov/national/nipaweb/TableView.asp?SelectedTable=5&Freq=Qtr& FirstYear=2007&LastYear=2009.

What jumps off the page at the reader is the incredible upward march in the share of all income taxes collected from the top 1 percent of income earners and the decline in the share of all income taxes collected from the bottom 95 percent of all income earners. It's amazing. Here is a prolonged period in U.S. history where tax rates on the rich have been cut time and again and yet total taxes collected from the rich as a share of all income taxes have done nothing but increase. The top 1 percent of income earners paid less than 20 percent of all income taxes in the early 1980s when tax rates were much, much higher than they are today. As tax rates fell, the share of taxes collected from the rich rose dramatically. By 2007 the top 1 percent paid over 40 percent of all income taxes in the United States.

Now, these numbers relating to the percentage of total income taxes paid by various income groups are accurate and great for cocktail party conversations and thirty-second sound bites on TV. But percentages of total taxes collected by income category are not numbers that are well suited for fiscal policy and budget analyses. For fiscal policy and budget purposes a more appropriate measure of the impact of tax cuts would be each category's total income taxes paid divided by GDP, i.e., the share of GDP that is paid by the rich and the nonrich in income taxes during an era of falling tax rates. The obvious approach when assessing what has happened is to use those results to figure out what will happen.

In Figure 10-3 I have plotted income-tax receipts by the top 1 percent of income earners as a share of GDP and income tax receipts of the bottom 95 percent of income earners as a share of GDP, both plotted annually over the full period from 1980 through 2007.

Figure 10-3 Income Taxes Paid as a % of GDP

(annual, through 2007)

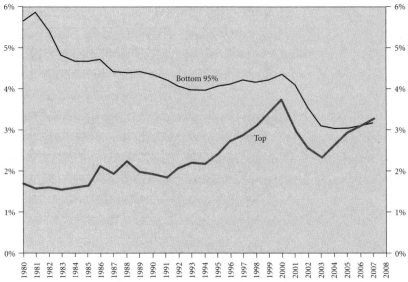

Source: The Tax Foundation, Summary of Latest Federal Individual Income Tax Data, Table 5, http://www.taxfoundation.org/publications/show/250.html.

What again jumps off the page is the fact that total income taxes paid by the top 1 percent of income earners as a share of GDP has doubled since the early 1980s. Total income taxes paid by the bottom 95 percent as a share of GDP have not only *not* increased, they have fallen sharply. If we break these data out into more detailed income groupings the answers wouldn't change. The top 1 percent are the only income earners over the period 1980 through 2007 who have increased their payments of income taxes as a share of GDP. All other groupings have either stayed flat (the 2 percent to 5 percent group) or have fallen. In point of fact, the bottom 20 percent of income earners have gone from paying taxes in the early 1980s to actually collecting money from the IRS now as a result of the Earned Income Tax Credit (EITC).[1]

These results are wholly consistent with what we find when the data for the 1920s and 1960s are examined. During the administrations of Presidents Harding and Coolidge in the 1920s and John F. Kennedy in the 1960s, tax rates were also cut drastically and tax collections from the highest income earners rose sharply. Likewise, during periods in history when tax rates were raised, tax collections from the rich fell as a share of GDP. It's really straightforward and simple.

None of this should come as a surprise to anyone with even a casual knowledge of the practical side of taxes. The rich can avail themselves of many schemes to lower their tax bill if tax rates get too high. The rich really hate paying taxes, probably even more than everyone else, and they are more able than others to control the amount of taxes they actually do pay.

Rich people can change the timing of their incomes. They can

---

1.   The Earned Income Tax Credit (EITC) was instituted on a small scale in 1975. In 1986, 1990, 1993, and 2001, Congress expanded the coverage of the EITC for low-income tax filers. To be eligible to receive the refundable EITC, a tax return must be filed. From 1983 to 2005, there has been a big surge in the percentage of tax returns filed with zero tax liability. This is clearly evidenced in the official tax return data, which show that in 1983, 19 percent of returns had zero tax liability, a figure that climbed steadily and reached 33 percent in 2005.

use Individual Retirement Accounts (IRAs), Keoghs, and 401(k) plans where contributions out of income today are not taxed and can be deferred to some future time when supposedly tax rates for the individual will be lower. In the very highest tax brackets customized income-deferral plans are readily available. Lower-income individuals have much less access to such tax-deferred-income schemes, and also, because they are taxed at lower rates, they find tax-deferred-income schemes less attractive.

The top 1 percent of income earners can also change the location of their income far more easily than can low-income earners. Corporations readily use state tax rates as a factor in determining where income and expenses are realized. High-income individuals in choosing where to be domiciled are also sensitive to state and local tax rates. Mobility from state to state is not the only avenue possible to juxtapose locations and taxes. Offshore corporations and other exotic schemes are easily accessible to the rich but are not as accessible to other income earners.

High-income earners can also alter the composition of their income as no other income-earning group can. Different forms of income, as well as different volumes of income, are taxed at different rates. High-income earners often have the ability to change the forms in which they receive their income, and therefore can take advantage of differing tax rates. Income forms are fungible and high-income individuals can exploit tax differentials. Lower-income individuals have far less flexibility than do high-income individuals.

The rich can change the volume of their income to reduce tax liabilities. The most efficient tax shelter of all is to report no income. To summarize, the rich can control, to some extent at least, the timing, location, composition, and volume of their income to compensate for variations in taxes. Lower- and middle-income people are far less able to control their income for tax purposes.

Finally, rich people can more readily afford lawyers, accountants, and deferred-income specialists than can the less wealthy. Rich people also have far more pull with politicians than do lower- and middle-income earners.

From the standpoint of pure logic, rich people should be more sensitive to tax rates than are poorer people, which is consistent with the data above. If President Obama proceeds to raise taxes on the rich and lower taxes on middle- and lower-income earners, don't be surprised to see tax collections from both groups drop. To believe otherwise is to be oblivious to basic economics.

President Obama and this Congress should immediately make permanent all of Bush's tax cuts that are set to expire in 2011. The Alternative Minimum Tax should also be eliminated if possible, or, at a bare minimum, indexed for inflation. The rest of the tax changes that I am going to recommend are going to be in the next section of this book.

11

President Obama and Health Care

As I write this book I'm unsure what the specific structure of President Obama's health-care legislation will actually be. But what the president would like his health-care legislation to be is crystal clear. The differences between what President Obama would like and what will actually happen reflect near-term politics. But the president has made no bones about the fact that he would not only like a "government option," i.e., a federal government insurance plan for one and all as a competitor for private insurance, he would prefer a government single-payer plan where the government is the only primary insurer.

There are many other aspects of health-care legislation that are up in the air, but the general theme is obvious. This administration wants universal health-care coverage. In order to pay for this universal coverage the president's and Congress' preferred options include an add-on tax on all those who earn more than $250,000, up to 5.4 percent for those with incomes over $1 million. In addition to this add-on tax for high-income earners there could also be a tax on private insurance contracts and a hefty payroll tax add-on for all employers who do not provide comprehensive health-care insurance for their employees.

Not only is there quite a bit of uncertainty about what the total percentage of the population covered by the president's version of health care will be, but there is also uncertainty about the type and magnitude of additional taxes that will be needed to help finance health care. There is also a considerable degree of uncertainty about what services actually constitute the government's portion of health care for those who are covered.

All this uncertainty about the specifics of President Obama's health-care wishes notwithstanding, the economics are straightforward.

From the standpoint of Econ 1, a market keeps check on prices and costs through a dynamic interchange between suppliers of products and demanders of products. When a person walks into a store, he has a vast array of wants and needs and a budget. Whenever a product is a little too pricey the consumer either buys less of the product or abstains from buying any of it at all. Suppliers seeing their sales fall either lower their prices or withdraw some supply from the marketplace.

It's a no-brainer. Consumers of any product keep suppliers in check and control prices. Health-care services are no different from any other product. But when health-care expenditures are covered by private insurance or public funds, individual consumers care less about price and thus exercise less control over unwarranted price increases. Consumers also tend to consume larger quantities of the higher-priced products than they would if they had to pay for those products out of their own pocket. It's really as simple as that. It would be bad for my waistline if I were to eat at a smorgasbord where there's one fixed price that allows me to eat all I want. Consumers who don't have to pay the full price for each additional unit they buy will consume too much. That's Econ 1.

The huge increase in health-care costs over the past half century, in my opinion, has been greatly exacerbated by the sharp decline in the percentage of health-care costs paid for by individuals out of their own pockets and the ever-increasing role played by the government and private insurance. Tax deductibility only makes matters worse.

Having health-care purchases tax-deductible and/or privately insured or funded by the government increases demand for these services beyond what would be warranted in a free, unfettered market and removes the discipline of the marketplace for pricing.

In Figure 11-1, I've plotted the shares of health-care expenditures paid for by individuals, government, and private insurance.

Figure 11-1 **Share of Health-Care Spending Paid by, 1960–2007**

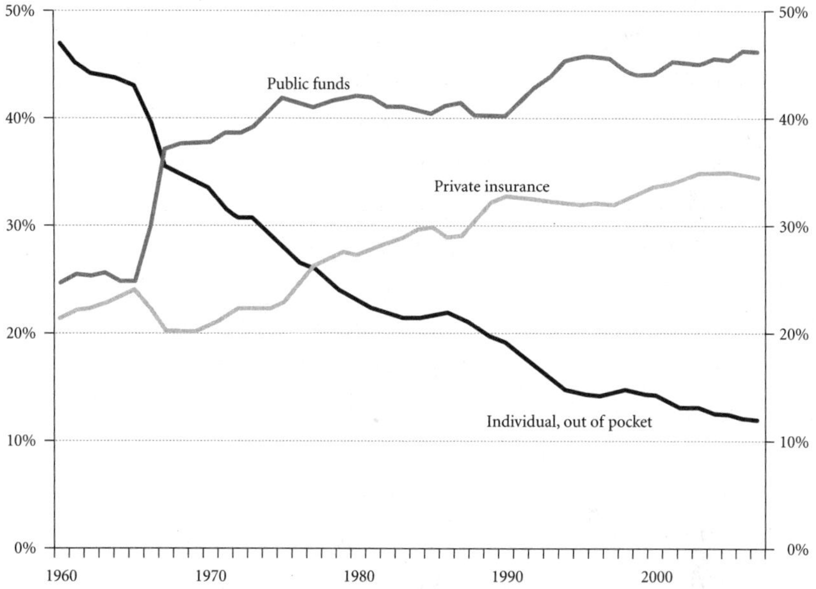

Source: Centers for Medicare and Medicaid Services, National Health Expenditures by type of service and source of funds, http://www.cms.hhs.gov/NationalHealthExpend Data/02_NationalHealthAccountsHistorical.asp.

President Obama and his team's lack of understanding of basic economics is starkly illustrated by the fact that he is proposing more government and more insurance. By raising tax rates, as will automatically happen in 2011, they ensure that the benefits of health-care insurance tax deductibility will greatly increase. The end result will be much higher costs, budgetary crises, and ultimately government control of access and quality.

• • •

Plans for health-care reform as currently outlined in legislation in the House and Senate should be abandoned. Further changes in health care should include a national catastrophic health-insurance plan for all citizens. For the rest of health-care needs, health-care services should be treated like any other product where purchases are not subsidized through the tax code. Income supplements (i.e., vouchers for low-income individuals to purchase health insurance) are a far more preferable method for helping people who can't help themselves to providing government health services at below market costs.

In certain cases, such as polio vaccines, where there are clear positive externalities, or health-care centers where the competence of the patient is not sufficient to warrant income supplements, the government role should be extensive.

12

Minimum Wage Laws and Unions Create Unemployment

As of July 24, 2009, the federal minimum wage is $7.25, the third and final stage increase in the minimum wage that began July 24, 2007. Since July 23, 2007, the federal minimum wage has increased 41 percent, from $5.15 to $7.25.[1] Individual states may set a higher minimum wage and in fact a number of states actually have minimum wages higher than $7.25 an hour. Accordingly, the minimum wage is effectively rising in thirty-two states across the country.[2]

This increase, put into place during the second term of George W. Bush's presidency, is but another example of government failing Econ 1. While the ill-advised polices started under President Bush, the current administration has only expanded upon them. Unfortunately, they will soon come to realize that their policies are most detrimental to those they profess to want to help the most. And they do the most damage when the overall economy is in the worst shape, as it is now.

Unfortunately, the current political sentiment is for increasing

---

1.   The minimum wage increase was coupled with targeted tax breaks for small businesses to win bipartisan support in the Senate and then included in H.R. 2206, a supplemental spending bill regarding the Iraq War and Hurricane Katrina relief, which passed the House of Representatives on a near party-line vote (ten Democrats against, two Republicans for) and the Senate by voice vote (no voting records kept). President George W. Bush signed the bill into law on May 25, 2007.

2.   There will also still be thirteen states with a minimum wage set above the federal minimum wage, http://www.dol.gov/esa/minwage/america.htm.

the minimum wage even further. Such sentiment emanates from a mistaken belief in the benefits of make-work projects. Today the argument for a higher minimum wage is couched in terms of a "living wage," but seriously, isn't some wage better than no wage? The unemployment rate today is 9.5 percent, and that doesn't take into account lower average hours, lower labor force participation rates, and more part-time workers.

Figure 12-1 **Real Minimum Wage vs. Percentage of Hourly Paid Workers Paid at or Below Prevailing Federal Minimum Wage**

(real minimum wage: monthly, May 2009 $, through May-09; percent of workers: yearly, through 2008)

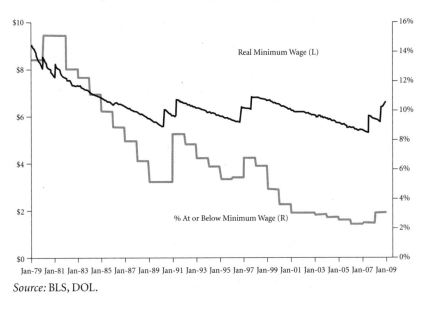

Source: BLS, DOL.

Starting with the supply-side policies put in place by President Reagan, for the last quarter century the U.S. government has paid less and less attention to the minimum wage. Instead, the government has focused on policies that would encourage production, thereby increasing employment. The Reagan/Clinton view has always been the famous President Kennedy statement that the best form of welfare is still a good high-paying job. This progrowth focus caused the percentage of the labor force paid the minimum wage and the ratio of the federal minimum wage to the average wage to fall dramatically. Yet the recent change in the direction of policy and the economy has caused each of those trends to reverse direction (see Figures 12-1 and 12-2).

While increasing the minimum wage is a seductive populist agenda item, it is incredibly harmful to the economy. All an increase in the minimum wage succeeds in doing is pricing people out of the job market, and particularly those people who have no ability to defend themselves, such as the poor, minorities, and the disenfranchised. The people who need entry-level jobs in order to gain the requisite skills to earn above the minimum wage are precluded from ever getting jobs in the first place if the minimum wage is too high.

Figure 12-2 Ratio of the Federal Minimum Wage to the Average Wage*

(wage per hour, monthly, through Jun-09)

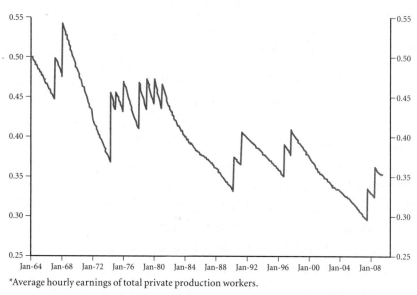

*Average hourly earnings of total private production workers.

Source: BLS.

When times are good, as they were during the Reagan and Clinton eras, the minimum wage is not a large concern. In economic parlance, the equilibrium price for unskilled labor is above the price floor set by the minimum wage. When the economy turns south, as it has during the Bush and Obama eras, a high minimum wage is often above the market-clearing wage for unskilled labor, meaning there is a surplus of labor, which shows up as higher unemployment among the least-qualified workers. And that certainly seems to be the case today. Teenage unemployment has surged from 15.1 percent in July 2007 to 24.0 percent in June 2009. Meanwhile, black teenage unemployment has risen from 26.4 percent in July 2007 to 37.9 percent in June 2009.

Even though teenagers represent a relatively small portion of the labor force, they are a valuable and useful proxy for the least employable demographic. Already, the threat or reality of a variety of negative policy changes has driven up the cost of labor in terms of output, leading to higher unemployment. To add in another minimum wage increase on top of the already high cost of labor will truly price many people out of the market.

Unions have a similarly negative impact on the economy. Excessive union influence appears to have been one of the pivotal factors that turned an economic downturn in 1929 into the Great Depression. According to a 2009 study by Lee Ohanian, an economics professor at UCLA and economist with the Federal Reserve Bank of Minneapolis, union influence caused companies to strike a deal that effectively, but artificially, increased real wages for manufacturer workers in the midst of a recession.[3] The result is precisely what economics would predict: "By September 1931, manufacturing hours worked had declined more than 40 percent, and the average workweek in manufacturing had declined by about 20 percent."[4] On the other hand, output and hours worked in the agricultural sector, which did not face the same union pressures, increased by 4 percent

---

3.   Lee Ohanian, "Who—or What—Started the Great Depression?" Preprint submitted to *Journal of Economic Theory*, July 29, 2009.
4.   Ibid.

and 1.5 percent, respectively.[5] The lesson for the U.S. economy is clear: Rising union influence has a strong and negative impact on the health of the U.S. economy.

In what has been a very positive trend for the U.S. economy, the total percentage of U.S. workers who are union members has been in a steady and sharp decline for about thirty years. However, this trend reversed in 2008 (see Figure 12-3). Judging by the policies and priorities of the Obama administration, this reversal may persist for many years.

Figure 12-3 **Union Membership as a % of Total U.S. Workforce**

(annual through 2008)

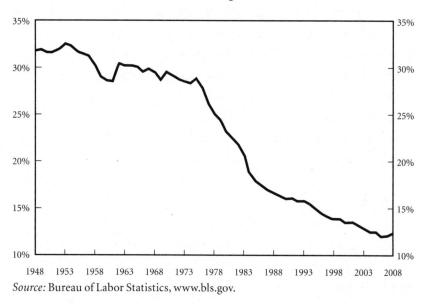

Source: Bureau of Labor Statistics, www.bls.gov.

In my view, the explanation for the decline in union strength for the previous thirty years in all areas except government is simple enough: Unions place firms at a competitive disadvantage and they do little to benefit the workers directly. As the forces of globalization make business more and more competitive, American firms

---

5.   Ibid.

cannot survive if they are hobbled by inefficient labor arrangements demanded by union leaders. Also, many union members vehemently disagree with the way union leaders use their union dues for political purposes.

So long as a labor market is competitive, workers generally get paid their marginal product. This isn't because of the employer's sense of benevolence or fair play. But if a particular worker annually adds $50,000 to the firm's bottom line, while his total cost to the firm is only $45,000, there's in essence $5,000 lying on the street, waiting for a rival firm to bend over and pick it up.

Unions for sure don't change these fundamental facts for the better. Although they might serve to reduce transactions costs when negotiating arrangements between employers and huge pools of workers, unions typically achieve deals (through threats of strikes or worse) that force a firm to pay more total compensation (in the form of wages, health insurance, and so on) than is justified by the employee's marginal product. Unions tend to negotiate counterproductive or excessive work rules, vacation time, sick leave, health benefits, pension benefits, and so on. They also tend to become very political, enforcing their ends via political means.

All these excessive costs above a worker's actual value erode the firm's profits and leave it vulnerable to other firms. A nonunion firm, presumably operating at a point where its real wage is equal to the marginal product of labor, can easily undercut the unionized firm and steal away its customers, its business, and its profits. In a competitive industry, unionization has a devastating effect on a firm's profits. In the long run, unionized firms are forced to shut down because nonunion firms seize the business by selling a similar good at a lower cost. When a firm shuts down, the union worker is out of luck and out of work. This outcome doesn't help the workers in the unionized firm.

The recent experience of GM, Chrysler, and Ford should remove any doubts concerning the devastating impact unions can have on the future viability of a company or industry. And it is not just private industry, either. The unions dominate state government in California, more so now than in 1990, and that power is growing every day. It's downright scary. California's pension systems are far, far worse today than they were in 1990. Pensions of state teachers, state employees, and those in cities, counties, and local districts are considerably underfunded. The public unions are literally bankrupting the state. And that's precisely why unions were fading away as global competition intensified.

It is for these reasons that unions find government jobs their only refuge. Competition and quality products are not union attributes. Just check the Post Office, the Department of Motor Vehicles, public schools, or public prisons if you don't believe me.

Now enter the Obama administration. Following up on the minimum-wage increase signed by President Bush, the Obama administration is not tilting government policies in order to revive unions at the expense of the American taxpayer. Joe Biden, in a speech to the AFL-CIO Executive Committee, laid out this vision:

> Look at what he [President Obama] did. The first bill to pass [was the] Lilly Ledbetter Fair Pay Act [This act changed the statute of limitations on pay discrimination cases from 180 days from the date the pay contract was agreed upon to 180 days from the last paycheck received].
>
> What happened then? . . . We named a Secretary of Labor who is a daughter of union members, not the darling of union busters. A little change over the first executive orders, first version in the past eight years, and making it clear we want to see a project labor agreement on federal construction projects. (Applause.) Second order: making sure that taxpayer dollars go to something other than union-busting activities. (Applause.)
>
> And where has been the focus on our recovery package, the one the President now calls me the sheriff of? (Laughter.) Man. (Laughter.) Well, I guess it's easier to watch and help

spend out $788 billion than trying to raise it, you know? But, look, guys, and ladies, look at the focus—what's been the focus? The focus of this administration the first month has been to rebuild American roads, bridges, waterways—jobs for the building trades union.[6]

Commenting at the same meeting, President Obama said, "I do not view the labor movement as part of the problem. To me, and to my administration, labor unions are a big part of the solution."[7] He wants to have stronger union activity, and unfortunately that is a problem for the economy.

Speaking of the stimulus package, the prevailing wage provision in legislation such as the Obama stimulus packages mandates that government expenditures on labor be at or above the highest union wage prevailing at the time and where the spending occurs. Specifically, the ARRA requires that "all laborers and mechanics employed by contractors and subcontractors on projects funded directly by or assisted in whole or in part by and through the Federal Government pursuant to this Act . . . shall be paid [prevailing wages]."[8] This is a perfect example of the abject failure of our current government to understand what is a cost and what is a benefit. They just don't get it. With their logic we should pay the janitor $1 billion or more per hour. Wouldn't that help the economy now?

At certain times in the past, productivity gains were seen as a problem, not as a solution. The original movement of saboteurs was composed of workers who threw their wooden shoes (sabots) into productivity-enhancing machines to stop progress and to keep their jobs.[9] Unfortunately, this is a major focus of some unions to-

---

6.   The White House, Office of the Vice President, "Remarks by the Vice President to the AFL-CIO Executive Council at their Annual Conference," March 5, 2009, http://www.whitehouse.gov/the_press_office/Transcript-of-Remarks-by-the-Vice-President-to-the-AFL-CIO-Executive-Council-in-Mi/.

7.   S. A. Miller, "Unions benefit from Obama decisions," *Washington Times,* May 5, 2009.

8.   H.R., "American Recovery and Reinvestment Act of 2009."

9.   "Sabotage," *Wikipedia,* http://en.wikipedia.org/wiki/Sabotage (August 10, 2009).

day as well. Through threats of output-crippling strikes, unions try to force employers to pay higher wages than their work would naturally receive in a freely competitive environment.

Unions today, like their predecessors the saboteurs and Luddites before them, bargain for all sorts of featherbedding rules to reduce productivity. We can expect a lot more of this confusion between consumption and output and employment.

The Obama administration and this Congress are pushing other union-enhancing legislation as well, such as card check (the Employee Free Choice Act). The Employee Free Choice Act would get rid of secret ballots in union elections. Instead, a union would be automatically formed so long as more than 50 percent of workers sign a petition. In this case, the last thing anyone wants to do is defend getting rid of secret ballots in elections. Essentially the bill comes down to the fact that its proponents believe unions need more power; to get more power they need more members and more money; and the way to achieve that is to change the rules.

Labor leaders are also expanding their role in other areas. For instance, Denis Hughes, president of the New York state branch of the AFL-CIO, has been chosen by the Federal Reserve as the chairman of the Federal Reserve Board of New York's private-sector board of directors. He succeeded a former Goldman Sachs executive.

The explicit policy of the Obama administration has been to skew economic policies in favor of unions as opposed to the health of the economy. These policies need to be repealed. U.S. economic policy should neither encourage nor discourage the formation of unions. Government contracts should be neutral with respect to a firm's allowable costs. In a competitive bidding process, the firm that can provide the best product with the lowest costs should be awarded the contract—regardless of its policy toward unions. Right-to-work laws should apply to all states.

Government unions—such as schoolteachers, police and fire,

nurses, and prison guards—should not be allowed to strike and should be subjected to antitrust supervision. By their very nature government unions should also be nonpartisan and uninvolved as unions in the political process.

Similarly, ideally, the minimum-wage law should be repealed in its entirety. If complete repeal of the minimum wage is not possible, then the second-best policy would be to exempt teenagers and lock in the current nominal dollar value of the minimum wage.

Part Two

FISCAL POLICY

13

GETTING TAX POLICIES RIGHT

The Costs of Our Current Tax Code

When it comes to reversing our current economic slide, it's not enough to just undo the damage done by the Bush and Obama administrations and the current Congress led by Speaker of the House Nancy Pelosi (D-CA) and Majority Leader of the Senate Harry Reid (D-NV). We really have to implement positive tax reforms and, even more to the point, we should start with the whole structure of taxation rather than just the dollar amount collected. Our current tax structure is hopelessly flawed. The solution is to throw out the current tax code and implement in its stead a true flat-rate tax.

The dollar amount collected in taxes is a good way to gauge the economic problems of the current tax system. Combined, federal, state, and local governments collect about 30 percent of our nation's GDP in taxes (see Figure 7-1). When you stop and think about it, that's a lot of money, somewhere to the north of $4 trillion—$4,000,000,000,000—and that's every year.

From the taxpayers' perspective, however, the actual cost is considerably greater than $4 trillion. Taxpayers not only have to pay the $4 trillion governments collect; taxpayers also have to pay for all their own costs in filling out tax returns. And these costs are not trivial; after all, as Albert Einstein once said, "The hardest thing to understand in the world is the income tax."[1] Our current tax code

---

1.   See www.brainyquote.com.

91

is currently nearly five times the size of the King James Bible.[2] According to the National Taxpayer Advocate of the Internal Revenue Service:

> *The Code has grown so long that it has become challenging even to figure out how long it is. A search of the Code conducted in the course of preparing this report turned up 3.7 million words. A 2001 study published by the Joint Committee on Taxation put the number of words in the Code at that time at 1,395,000. A 2005 report by a tax research organization put the number of words at 2.1 million, and notably, found that the number of words in the Code has more than tripled since 1975.*[3]

Not only is our current tax code enormous, it is constantly changing. The last major tax simplification occurred in 1986. Congress has re-created numerous complications since then. As of 2006, Congress had passed "14,400 amendments to the tax code. That's an average of 2.9 changes for every single working day in the year for 19 years."[4]

With tax rules at all levels of government as confusing and complicated as they are today, few people actually prepare their own tax returns. Specialists abound in a flourishing tax-preparation industry all focused on specific areas where they supposedly have expertise with respect to tax rules. All these costs are paid by taxpayers, to be sure, but they are not collected by government. In 2006 there were ninety thousand firms dedicated to preparing taxes with a total cost of $65 billion.[5]

---

2. The precise word count of the Bible varies, but generally ranges from 770,000 to 790,000 words.
3. National Taxpayer Advocate: 2008 Annual Report to Congress, Volume One, Internal Revenue Service, December 31, 2008.
4. Charles O. Rossotti, Testimony Before the US Senate Finance Committee September 20, 2006.
5. "Accounting Services—Industry Profile," *Market Research Reports*, April 2006. http://www.researchandmarkets.com/reports/c36297.

Because of the tax code's complexity, even hiring a professional does not guarantee that your tax returns will be filled out correctly. Way back in the 1990s, when the tax code was less complex than it is today, *Money* magazine used to do an annual survey of professional tax preparers. In the 1996 survey, the magazine asked forty-five different professionals to prepare a tax return for the same hypothetical family. The financials for this hypothetical family were not simple—for instance, the husband received both self-employment income and retirement income during the year—but not necessarily uncommon for many families. The details on the hypothetical family were:

> *[Curt Baker, the husband, made] . . . $30,831 in 1996. He also received a $60,000 lump-sum payout from his 401(k) when he retired. Ann, a lawyer, switched from one corporate job to another in '96. Her income for the year: $80,900. She also inherited $30,500 from her uncle. The Bakers' investments include a mix of stocks, bonds and mutual funds that threw off $21,298 in interest, dividends and capital gains. The couple, whose joint income put them in the 36% tax bracket, own their own home, which they refinanced in February 1996.*[6]

The forty-five different professional tax preparers estimated forty-five different tax liabilities that this hypothetical family would owe that ranged from $36,000 to $94,000. This was the largest range in the seven years of the survey.

In case you think that tax professionals now have reached consensus, *USA Today* did a smaller survey in 2007 of only five tax professionals, asking them to calculate a hypothetical family's tax bill.

---

6.   Teresa Tritch, "Why Your Tax Return Could Cost You A Bundle: We Asked 45 Tax Preparers to Fill Out One Hypothetical Family's Tax Return—And We Got 45 Different Answers. Here's What You Can Learn from the Pros' Many Mistakes," *CNN Money.com*, March 1, 1997, http://money.cnn.com/magazines/moneymag/moneymag_archive/1997/03/01/222962/Index.htm.

Consistent with the *Money* magazine survey of the 1990s, the five tax professionals provided five different tax liabilities for the same family. *USA Today*'s commentary from its experiment says it all: "As the Tax Code turns ever more unwieldy, deciphering it has become more art than science, tax experts say."[7]

The $65 billion tax-preparation cost is only part of the actual costs paid by taxpayers in terms of time spent and personal costs that have not been outsourced. Beyond the total dollars directly spent, taxpayers dedicate hours upon hours to filing their taxes.

To be precise, the IRS Taxpayer Advocate calculates that individuals and businesses spend 7.6 billion hours a year complying with the U.S. tax code, "[a]nd that figure does not even include the millions of additional hours that taxpayers must spend when they are required to respond to an IRS notice or an audit. . . . If tax compliance were an industry, it would be one of the largest in the United States. To consume 7.6 billion hours, the 'tax industry' requires the equivalent of 3.8 million full-time workers."[8]

David Keating, of the National Taxpayers Union, provides a nice perspective on the hours we dedicate to complying with the U.S. tax code. As of 2009, the tax industry employs "more workers than are employed at the five biggest employers among Fortune 500 companies—more than all the workers at Wal-Mart Stores, United Parcel Service, McDonald's, International Business Machines, and Citigroup combined."[9]

As we all know, time is money. Estimates of the dollar value of all these hours vary by researcher depending upon the estimated hourly rate. The Taxpayer Advocate Service estimates that based on the average hourly cost of a civilian employee, "the costs of complying with the individual and corporate income tax requirements in

---

7.   Sandra Block, "A taxing challenge: Even experts can't agree when preparing a sample tax return," *USA Today*, March 25, 2007, http://www.usatoday.com/money/perfi/taxes/2007–03–25-tax-preparers-hypothetical_N.htm.

8.   National Taxpayer Advocate, *2008 Annual Report to Congress*, December 31, 2008.

9.   David Keating, "A Taxing Trend: The Rise in Complexity, Forms, and Paperwork Burdens," *NTU Policy Paper 126*, April 15, 2008.

2006 amounted to $193 billion—or a staggering 14 percent of aggregate income tax receipts."[10]

Other groups believe that the IRS's estimate of the value of the time spent is too low. According to the Tax Foundation, "In 2005 individuals, businesses and nonprofits will spend an estimated 6 billion hours complying with the federal income tax code, with an estimated compliance cost of over $265.1 billion. This amounts to imposing a 22-cent tax compliance surcharge for every dollar the income tax system collects. Projections show that by 2015 the compliance cost will grow to $482.7 billion."[11]

The additional costs taxpayers pay as described above relate only to the income tax. When all taxes are considered, we have massive costs paid by taxpayers here and abroad, large and small, public and private. These costs are huge.

But a full measure of the tax code's enormous burden is far more than what is quantifiable. In addition to payments made by taxpayers but never collected by the government, there are a whole host of decisions made by taxpayers directed solely to the taxpayers' understandable desire to avoid paying taxes.

Approximately one hundred thousand people work directly for the IRS, yet despite their best efforts, the Government Accountability Office (GAO) estimates that the "Tax Gap" (a measure of the amount of tax revenues the government estimates it should have received compared to what it did receive) was $345 billion in 2001 (the latest estimate available).[12]

Another example of people paying more than the government collects that is not part of the $345 billion mentioned above as the "tax gap" involves state and local tax-exempt bonds. The interest earned on state and local tax-exempt bonds is, as the name would

10.   National Taxpayer Advocate, *2008 Annual Report to Congress*, December 31, 2008.

11.   J. Scott Moody, Wendy P. Warcholik, and Hodge A. Scott, "The Rising Cost of Complying with the Federal Income Tax," *Tax Foundation Special Report*, No. 138, December 2005.

12.   Government Accountability Office, "Letter to The Honorable Max Baucus and Charles E. Grassley: Using Data from the Internal Revenue Service's Research Program to Identify Potential Opportunities to Reduce the Tax Gap," March 15, 2007.

suggest, not taxable at the federal level, but is also not taxable at the state and local levels if the owner of the bond is a resident for tax purposes of the state that issued the bond.

Because the yields on these municipal bonds are tax-exempt, they are more valuable to the owner than are taxable bonds, especially the high-tax-bracket owner. As a result, yields on tax-exempt bonds are considerably lower than are yields on taxable bonds of comparable risk. Municipal bonds, in large part because of their special tax status, yield somewhere between 100 and 150 basis points less than equivalent-maturity corporate AAA bonds.[13] The simple point I'm trying to make here is that while the federal government doesn't collect any taxes on the income from tax-exempt bonds, the owners of those bonds earn considerably less than they would have earned had they been invested in taxable bonds. Once again, the taxpayer in effect pays taxes that the government never collects.

To provide some perspective on just how important municipal bonds are, in 2008 alone almost $400 billion worth of these bonds were issued.[14] With my tax proposal, all interest on future state and local bonds will be fully taxable. Previously issued bonds will have their interest payments grandfathered and therefore not be taxed.

People often change the decisions they make as a result of tax codes. And these decisions can have insidious consequences, which also drive a wedge between taxes governments collect and the costs taxpayers actually incur. The point here is simply that the time path of actual taxable income changes when tax codes change. As we'll see later, people and businesses can change the volume of their income and do so in response to taxes. With my tax proposal, idiosyncrasies in the tax code that contribute to taxpayers' gaming the system will be reduced to a minimum.

---

13. Data compiled from Bloomberg.
14. Securities Industry and Financial Markets Association (SIMFA). Research and Statistics, http://www.sifma.org/uploadedFiles/Research/Statistics/SIFMA_USMunicipalissuance_Coupon .pdf.

It should come as no surprise to anyone that if government increases taxes on people who work and pays more to people who don't work, there will be less work. It's a no-brainer. For those jobs that are lost as a consequence of higher taxes, the government doesn't collect taxes and is usually obligated to pay welfare to the unemployed. And yet those who are unemployed pay the ultimate price of no income. Being unemployed entails a lot more pain than simply not having the income from a job. People lose their self-esteem, families come under stress, and the collateral damage in terms of human welfare can be substantial. This is the classic example where the dollar amount of taxes collected by government grossly understates the costs paid by those who are taxed. My flat tax will be as progrowth as possible, thereby holding collateral damage to the economy way down.

People and businesses can also change the timing of their income as a result of the intricacies and complications of tax codes. We've all heard of IRAs (Individual Retirement Accounts), Keoghs, and 401(k)s, programs that have been deliberately set up by the government to allow income earners to defer the taxation of their income to some later date when the taxpayers hope tax rates will be lower. Businesses have also set up defined-contribution and defined-benefit pension plans, and governments at all levels have their own pension plans. Pension plans again are nothing more than a way income taxation can be deferred to some later date. Within these tax-deferred accounts income can be earned tax-free even on the deferred taxes. In addition to these well-known tax-deferral plans there are simply mountains of other ways people can defer taxes on income, thereby driving a wedge between taxes paid by taxpayers and taxes actually collected by government. As of the end of 2007 it is estimated that taxpayers had deferred slightly less than $18 trillion (yes, that's right, trillion).[15] If implemented,

---

15. "The U.S. Retirement Market, Third Quarter 2008," Investment Company Institute, http://www.ici.org/stats/mf/Index.html#Retirement%20Market%20Statistics.

my tax plan will not provide specific tax advantages for income deferral.

Because tax rates and tax structures differ by location, businesses and people will often opt to change the location where they report and earn taxable income in order to reduce tax liabilities. Several years ago I chose to leave California, where the state's highest marginal personal income-tax rate was 10.3 percent, and moved to Tennessee, which does not have a state personal income tax. (Tennessee does have an income tax on "unearned" income called the Hall Tax but does not tax earned income or most capital gains.) Now, the gains to me on strictly a tax basis were not as great as the 10.3 percent and 0 percent would suggest, because California income-tax payments can usually be deducted on a person's federal income tax return. To oversimplify, but to make my point, the highest federal income-tax rate when I moved was 35 percent, and I was able to keep sixty-five cents out of every marginal dollar I earned as a resident of Tennessee, whereas I would have kept only a little over fifty-eight cents out of every marginal dollar earned had I remained in California. Depending on how much one earns, the difference between California and Tennessee can add up to a whole lot of money. In my proposal for tax reform, state and local taxes will no longer be deductible on federal tax returns. This will have the additional benefit of states' having to bear the full cost of their taxes, which just might make them rethink how much they should tax and spend.

To make matters worse for high-income California taxpayers, the federal government has something called the Alternative Minimum Tax (AMT). If a person's tax liability as a percentage of gross income, excluding deductions for "preferred" items, is below a certain number, the taxpayer is required to pay a minimum percentage of his or her gross income irrespective of the deductions. State and local income-tax payments are a "preferred" deduction and therefore many California taxpayers don't get the full benefit of deducting state income-tax payments against their taxable income for federal tax purposes. Again, with my flat-tax proposal there will be no Alternative Minimum Tax, just one tax rate for every dollar of income for everyone and every business.

Now, the move itself from California to Tennessee not only cost me in out-of-pocket dollars but also entailed a lot of other costs. Just imagine what it's like being sixty-five years old and moving your reluctant family and business to a place you've never been before, which is what I did. In retrospect it was one of my best decisions ever. And people and businesses do it all the time, not only from state to state but also from country to country. Migration patterns make it crystal clear that people move to avoid taxes. Here again what the tax codes cost taxpayers is massively more than the actual taxes the governments collect.

Without being overly pedantic, in Table 13-1 I've listed state-to-state migrations over the decade from 1997 through 2007 for the nine states that have no income tax and the nine states with the highest maximum personal income-tax rates. People move for taxes and job opportunities created by tax differentials. My proposal will not directly affect state and local taxes, but to the extent competition among the states escalates, I would expect state taxes and tax differences to fall.

As a final direct effect of how people's behavior drives a wedge between the sums paid by taxpayers and the monies received by government, people and businesses can and do change the form in which they receive their income. Different forms of income currently are taxed at wildly different rates, and these rates change a lot over time depending upon the political whims and fancies of those who occupy public office. Capital gains have historically been taxed at a different rate than, say, "unearned" income, such as dividends. Partnerships are taxed at different rates than corporations. And at different levels of income there can be very different tax rates even when the source of income is the same. And believe me when I write that clever businessmen and even the not-so-clever ones can shift their income into tax-preferred categories. My flat tax will not differentiate among the various forms of income. They will all be taxed at the same rate.

Table 13-1 The Nine States with the Lowest and the Highest Marginal Personal Income Tax (PIT) Rates

Ten-Year Economic Performance
(performance between 1997 and 2007 unless otherwise noted)

	Top PIT Rate*	Population Growth	Net Domestic In-Migration as a % of Population
Alaska	0.00%	11.5%	−1.9%
Florida	0.00%	20.2%	8.7%
Nevada	0.00%	45.4%	18.8%
New Hampshire	0.00%	10.6%	4.5%
South Dakota	0.00%	7.0%	−0.6%
Tennessee	0.00%	12.0%	4.5%
Texas	0.00%	21.1%	3.1%
Washington	0.00%	14.0%	3.2%
Wyoming	0.00%	6.8%	0.3%
9 States with no PIT**	**0.00%**	**16.51%**	**4.50%**
9 States with Highest Marginal Pit Rate**	**9.12%**	**6.55%**	**−2.03%**
Kentucky	8.20%	7.3%	1.9%
Hawaii	8.25%	5.9%	−5.0%
Maine	8.50%	5.0%	2.9%
Ohio	8.89%	1.7%	−3.5%
New Jersey	8.97%	5.7%	−5.4%
Oregon	9.00%	13.4%	4.6%
Vermont	9.50%	4.0%	0.1%
California	10.30%	12.5%	−3.9%
New York	10.50%	3.4%	−10.0%

*Highest marginal state and local personal income tax rate imposed as of 1/1/07 using the tax rate of each state's largest city as a proxy for the local tax. The effect of the deductibility of federal taxes from state tax liability is included where applicable. Deductibility of federal taxes from state tax liability is included where applicable. New Hampshire and Tennessee tax dividend and interest income only.
**Equal-weighted averages.

Source: "Rich States, Poor States: ALEC-Laffer State Economic Competitiveness Index," 2nd ed., 2008.

In 2008 Warren Buffett was listed by *Forbes* magazine as the wealthiest man in the world.[16] He was reputed to be worth $62 billion—a little more than the entire GDP of Vietnam and the combined total GDPs of the forty-two poorest countries in the world.[17] The neatest thing about Warren Buffett's wealth is that he has paid almost nothing in income taxes, and yet he is the wealthiest man in the world. Warren Buffett's wealth is predominantly in the form of unrealized capital gains on the stock of a company named Berkshire Hathaway. Buffett received Berkshire Hathaway stock a long time ago when it was worth almost nothing. As a result of his diligent stewardship, Berkshire Hathaway's stock has appreciated enormously, leaving Warren Buffet with a huge increase in wealth, mostly in the form of unrealized capital gains. And the tax rate on unrealized capital gains is? You guessed it: zero.

When Warren Buffett says he pays less in taxes than his secretary, he's not exaggerating. And if, when he dies, he gives his estate to the Bill and Melinda Gates Foundation, which he has said he will do, it's just possible that all that income will never see a tax either, and yet Warren Buffett lives like a king.

Unrealized capital gains should be a full component of the tax base, with the future tax basis raised by all past reported unrealized gains.

Now, the purpose of my telling this story is not to cast aspersions on Warren Buffett, because he's doing nothing more than legally pursue his own self-interest. My purpose is to show the reader a real-life example of how careful legal manipulations of the tax codes can radically change the tax revenues collected by government.

The above examples where people and businesses change the amount of taxes they pay by changing the volume of their income, the timing of their income, the locations where their income is taxed, and the composition of their income are all legal and aboveboard.

---

16. "The World's Billionaires," *Forbes*, March 5, 2006, http://www.forbes.com/2008/03/05/richest-people-billionaires-billionaires06-cx_lk_0305billie_land.html.
17. Organisation for Economic Co-operation and Development (OECD).

Unfortunately, people and businesses sometimes turn to the dark side, where their behavior is, as the British would say, "dodgy." Illegal activities are not taxable, because those who engage in illegal activities deliberately evade taxes. Whether the evasion of taxes is an indirect consequence of the fact that those people are involved in illegal activities, such as drugs or prostitution or the illegality is solely a consequence of the evasion of taxes, these numbers can be huge. And these unpaid taxes can build up over time. Tax evasion is a major source of the difference between the sums governments collect and the monies people pay in taxes. The federal government believes that if everyone paid the federal taxes they actually owe, the IRS would collect $345 billion more than it does now.[18]

My complete flat tax contains a transitional tax amnesty plan within its structure that will greatly reduce tax evasion resulting from a desire solely to evade taxes. The amnesty plan itself will raise huge amounts of revenue as it unlocks years' worth of unreported income. It also will increase annual revenues because more people and businesses will be reporting income they otherwise would not have reported. With lower overall tax evasion the resources to monitor tax scofflaws will be more focused.

In broad strokes, then, what government collects is a great deal less than what people pay. Just how great these differences are I can't be sure, but they are huge. When I write that taxes are about 30 percent of GDP, or $4 trillion, that's a lowball number from the perspective of what taxpayers pay. In truth taxes are an enormous component of the U.S. economy and they are getting larger by the minute. What amazes me is that of the developed world we in the United States are at the low end of the official tax spectrum.

In Table 13-2 I've listed all the G-7 countries including the United States and the percentages of GDP they collected in taxes in 2006.[19]

---

18. "Random Tax Audits Return to the IRS," National Public Radio. October 9, 2007, http://www.npr.org/templates/story/story/php?storyid=15111003.

19. Organisation for Economic Co-operation and Development (OECD).

Table 13-2

G-7 Nations

Tax Collections as a % of GDP, 2006

Japan	27.90%
United States	28.00%
Canada	33.33%
Germany	35.58%
United Kingdom	37.12%
Italy	42.15%
France	44.17%

But all the above numbers and logic hide the most important characteristics tax codes should have. Tax codes should encourage income growth, promote income stability, be simple to calculate, and encourage a fair distribution of income. People do like to make more money rather than less; they like to have stable income streams rather than feasts and famines; they like computational simplicity in their taxes, so they know what's going on and don't have to pay exorbitant sums to tax preparers; and they also like to have a society where fewer people are poor, and for those who are poor, they are not as poor. Tax structures do affect the growth of national income, the stability of that income, computational simplicity, and the distribution of income.

What we have today in the United States is an economic policy, and most specifically a tax policy, that has gone far off course. Our tax codes are unambiguously antigrowth. We tax success and reward failure at every bend in the road. There's hardly a tax around, or a spending program, for that matter, that doesn't punish people and businesses who are successful, all in the name of helping the poor. These programs of supposed redistribution exist at every level of the pyramid, and they cascade down throughout the economy from the highest levels of the federal income tax codes to the lowest levels of city-subsidized transportation for the poor.

No one has any clue what the aggregate impact of these policies has been or will be on income growth, income stability, or income distribution. Goodness knows these policies make dealing with government insanely complex. My guess is that our plethora of current tax codes has made us as a nation grow a lot more slowly than we should have, has increased the volatility of our economic cycles dramatically, and has made the poor a whole lot poorer than they should be.

The points I'm making here really aren't partisan points. President Obama had a hard time finding high-level staffers who didn't have tax problems. And the tax problems these high-level staffers had were, in my opinion, not indicative of personal character flaws of the individuals concerned, but instead truly highlight the rotten core of our entire tax structure. Because of the complexity of the law, people strive to do only what's legal, whether they believe it to be right or wrong. They don't even think about right or wrong; they just ask their tax preparer. For example:

- Rahm Emanuel, the White House chief of staff, faced tax problems due to his decision to live rent-free at a colleague's home in Washington, D.C. The free rent would constitute taxable income for Rahm Emanuel or, under House ethics rules, the free rent gift required a written waiver from the Standards Committee.[20]
- Tim Geithner's nomination for treasury secretary was nearly derailed due to his failure to pay self-employment taxes for money he earned from 2001 to 2004 while working for the International Monetary Fund, and he employed an immi-

20.   "Tax troubles for president's chief of staff Emanuel's rent-free Washington residence draws questioning," *WorldNetDaily*, February 17, 2009, http://www.wnd.com/Index.php?fs=PAGE.view& pageid=89242.

grant housekeeper who lacked proper work papers for a short period of time.[21]

• Tom Daschle withdrew his nomination to be health and human services secretary due to unpaid taxes for a car and driver service that had been provided to him gratis.[22]

• Nancy Killefer withdrew her nomination to become deputy director of management at the Office of Management and Budget due to unspecified Washington, D.C., tax problems.[23]

• Hilda L. Solis, Obama's labor secretary, ran into trouble due to her husband's failure to pay thousands of dollars in outstanding tax liens to Los Angeles County.[24]

• Kathleen Sebelius, the health and human services secretary, had to pay back taxes of $7,000 plus interest due to errors on her tax returns for the years 2005–2007 related to charitable contributions, business expenses, and the sale of a home.[25]

• Former Dallas mayor Ron Kirk was President Obama's choice to be U.S. trade representative until problems concerning back taxes derailed his nomination.[26]

Not to just pick on the executive branch, Charlie Rangel, chairman of the House Ways and Means Committee—the committee in the House of Representatives responsible for tax policy in the United States—is having tax problems due to $75,000 in rental income from a beachfront villa he owns in the Dominican Republic. He's also had problems on his four rent-controlled apartments in

21.   Tom Raum, "Geithner tax and housekeeper problems jolt Obama," *The Examiner,* January 14, 2009, http://www.sfexaminer.com/local/Geithner_tax_and_housekeeper_problems_jolt_Obama.html.

22.   Ed Henry, "Tax issues prompt Obama nominee to withdraw," CNN.com, 2009, http://www.cnn.com/2009/POLITICS/02/03/performance.nominee.withdraw.

23.   Ibid.

24.   Matt Kelley, "Tax Snafus Add Up for Obama Team," *USA Today* Feburay 5, 2009, http://www.usatoday.com/news/washington/2009–02–05-solis-husband-taxes_N.htm.

25.   Brian Montopoli, "Another Obama Nominee Has Tax Issues," CBSNews.com, March 31, 2009, http://www.cbsnews.com/blogs/2009/03/31/politics/politicalhotsheet/entry4908247.shtml.

26.   "Another Obama Nominee Has Tax Issues," BET.com, March 3, 2009, http://www.bet.com/News/Decision08/beheard_news_ObamaNomineeRonKirkHasTaxissues.htm.

New York, which are for primary residence only; and a residence in Washington, D.C., for which he took a homeowner's credit that is available only to persons whose primary residence is in Washington; D.C., even though he officially resides in New York.[27]

Believe me when I write that all these people were not tax cheats. In fact, I would be surprised if even one was a true tax cheat. What happened was simply that good people were caught in an incomprehensibly bad tax code. They probably didn't even know they had a tax problem until their confirmation hearings.

Let's go through the six most desirable characteristics of the tax code individually, for it is our adherence to strict accountability that will allow us to create a tax code that serves rather than undermines our nation. The ideal tax code:

1. Fosters economic growth.
2. Reduces income volatility.
3. Is simple and efficient with low compliance costs.
4. Increases fairness.
5. Provides the requisite tax revenue at low cost.
6. Is flexible and can adjust to changing needs.

As the discussion above illustrates, our current tax system contains none of the six essential characteristics and is drifting further and further away from these ideals every day. A necessary step for reversing our current economic malaise is replacing the current tax code with one that more closely resembles the ideal.

Before detailing a tax reform that will achieve these goals, it is helpful to review some of the most egregious aspects of our current tax code and the classic Econ 1 mistakes that policymakers are currently committing that will make things worse, not better.

---

27. Sheela Kolhatkar, "Charles Rangel: The Lion of Harlem," *Time*, Thursday, August 6, 2009, http://www.time.com/time/politics/article/0.8599.1914697.00.html.

Capital-Gains Taxes

Time and time again history shows an inverse relationship in the United States between the level of the top tax rate on capital gains and tax receipts from realized capital gains. The relationship is fascinating and important, but is not the be-all and end-all with respect to the issue of whether to tax capital gains and, if so, at what rate.

It is hard to understand why anyone would ever wish to tax capital gains at tax rates that exceed those tax rates where revenues are maximized. It seems that if lowering capital-gains tax rates would actually increase capital-gains tax revenues, then we should lower those tax rates until at least capital-gains tax revenues stopped rising. Everyone would be better off—both taxpayers, who would pay less, and those who receive benefits from the government, who would receive more.

Even if a capital-gains tax-rate cut did not yield more direct capital-gains tax revenues, there may still be compelling, unambiguous reasons to cut the capital-gains tax rate. A capital-gains tax-rate cut will increase investment, employment, profits, sales, and so on, in addition to yielding more realized capital gains. Each of these, and all these together, will increase tax receipts from other sources, such as income taxes, payroll taxes, and sales taxes. From the standpoint of U.S. government tax revenues, it is appropriate to look at the total increase (or decrease) in U.S. tax receipts from a capital-gains tax-rate cut (or any other tax-rate cut), not just those receipts from the capital-gains tax alone. Here again, it's a no-brainer to cut the capital-gains tax rate if total federal tax receipts rose as a result of a capital-gains tax-rate reduction. Again, everyone would be better off—taxpayers and government spending beneficiaries.

A capital-gains tax-rate cut will expand output, employment, and productivity, which in turn will reduce federal expenditures—especially those expenditures predicated upon needs tests, means tests, and incomes tests. Quite simply, a capital-gains tax-rate cut will reduce the number of people in need and therefore federal expenditures. Lower expenditures, if sufficiently large to offset a potential shortfall in total federal tax revenues, will still make a capital-gains tax-rate cut an unambiguous win-win situation. There are still no arguments against cutting capital-gains tax rates under these circumstances.

Going even further, if federal tax receipts fall by more than federal expenditures decline, state and local fiscal conditions are also a serious consideration. If the increase in the federal debt were to be offset by a decline in state and local debt, then it is still very hard to see why a cut in the federal capital-gains tax rate wouldn't be warranted for virtually all constituencies. Such a tax-rate cut should not be controversial. If total government debt resulting from a capital-gains tax-rate cut were not to increase, there are really no arguments against cutting the capital-gains tax rate.

Even the above points aren't enough to contain the issue. When considering whether a cut in the capital-gains tax rate increases or lowers total government debt, there needs to be an effective time frame. In general, the longer the time frame, the more likely it will be that revenue feedback effects and spending reduction effects will materialize. Conceptually, what would be ideal is to take the discounted present value of all the net debt effects resulting from a cut in the capital-gains tax rate, and if that present-value calculation reveals a reduction in net debt, to cut the federal capital-gains tax rate under any and all circumstances. This truly is what the prohibitive range of the Laffer Curve is all about.[28]

However, the Laffer Curve is not—I repeat not—the whole consideration for deciding whether to tax capital gains and, if so, at what rate. Total government revenue, expenditure, and debt feedbacks are only three considerations, albeit big ones. The role of government is to improve the lot of all Americans. The special

---

28. For a complete description of the history of the Laffer Curve, see Appendix.

role of taxes is to provide government with the requisite revenues to achieve our national objectives. All taxes—save sin taxes—are bad because they have the effect of reducing the taxed activity. Therefore, the role of the state should be to collect the requisite revenues while doing the least damage. Any tax rate at or above that tax's maximum revenue point hurts total economic activity with no revenue offset. How dumb is that? But tax rates should be significantly below the maximum revenue tax. The purpose of government is to make people better off, *not* to maximize revenues.

Unfair Features of the Capital-Gains Tax

There are many unfair features deeply embedded in the current tax treatment of capital gains: Capital gains are not indexed for inflation; the capital-gains tax represents double taxation on capital income; and the tax treatment of capital gains introduces a bias against risk-taking due to the annual limit on the deduction of capital losses. Our tax reform will index capital gains for inflation.

Taxing Illusory Gains: Capital gains are not indexed for inflation; the seller thus pays tax not only on the real gain in purchasing power from the sale of an asset but also on the illusory gain attributable to inflation. This leads to an effective tax rate (the top line in Figure 13-1) higher than the statutory rate (the bottom line in Figure 13-1)—dramatically higher in inflationary periods. In fact, Princeton economist Alan Blinder, a former vice chairman of the Federal Reserve Board, noted in 1980 that, up until that time, "most capital gains were not gains of real purchasing power at all, but simply represented the maintenance of principal in an inflationary world."[29] The inflation penalty is one reason why capital gains have historically been taxed at lower rates than ordinary income.

---

29. Alan S. Blinder, "The Level and Distribution of Economic Well-Being," in *The American Economy in Transition*, ed. Martin Feldstein (Chicago: University of Chicago Press, 1980), p. 48.

Figure 13-1 **The Capital-Gains Tax Rate: Statutory and Effective**
A Look at the Effect of Inflation on the Effective Rate*

(through 2007, maximum long-term rate used, federal taxes only)

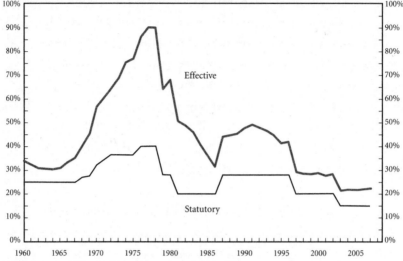

*Assumes annual 5% real yield on investments held for five years.
Source: Laffer Associates Chartbook (from U.S. tax code/BLS).

The nonpartisan Tax Foundation reports that failure to index for inflation can have major distortion effects on what an individual pays in capital-gains taxes and can—indeed, often does—lead to circumstances in which investors "pay effective tax rates that substantially exceed 100 percent of their gain."[30]

The Tax Foundation has found that about $50 billion a year in the past decade, or about 20 to 25 percent of total gains, has been a tax based purely on inflationary gains. It found that in some years in the late 1970s and early 1980s, 100 percent of the gain was due to inflation. The lower tax rate on capital gains relative to ordinary income does offset some, but usually not all, of the phantom gains due to inflation, but that is an exceptionally inefficient way to compensate for inflation.

---

30.   Arthur P. Hall, "Issues in the indexation of Capital Gains," Tax Foundation Special Report, April 1995.

Then–Federal Reserve Board governor Wayne Angell calculated in 1993 that the average real tax rate on investments in NASDAQ stocks from 1972 to 1992 had been 68 percent; the average real tax rate on investments in the Standard & Poor's Composite Index over the same time period was 101 percent; the average real tax on a portfolio of New York Stock Exchange stocks was 123 percent; and the average real tax on the Dow Jones Industrial Average was an astounding 233 percent.[31] In other words, according to three of the four indexes, investors paid average capital-gains taxes on investments that actually lost them money after adjusting for inflation—and thus the tax simply diminished the principal. Angell concluded:

> *If we are to reduce the damaging effects that we know are caused by all capital taxation, it makes sense to eliminate the worst aspect of the most damaging tax on capital—the tax on phantom gains. The tax on real capital gains is a middle-of-the-road bad tax. But the tax on nominal capital gains without regard to whether the gain is real or only the effect of inflation is truly the worst tax.[32]*

Double Taxation on Capital Income: The capital gains tax represents an unfair double taxation on capital income. A government can choose to tax either the value of an asset or its yield, but it should not tax both. Capital gains are literally the appreciation in the value of an existing asset, and the value of an asset is the discounted present value of that asset's after-tax earnings. Any appreciation in the value of an existing asset therefore reflects the discounted present value of the increase in that asset's after-tax rate of return. The taxes implicit in the asset's after-tax future earnings are already fully reflected in the change in the asset's price; therefore, any additional tax is strictly double taxation.

---

31.   Wayne Angell, Governor, Federal Reserve Board, Statement before the Republican members of the Joint Economic Committee, June 22, 1993.
32.   Ibid.

The problem here, however, is that many items that are reported as capital gains are really not capital gains as described above; they are income items reported as capital gains. This is the Warren Buffett example. Therefore our proposal will tax capital gains until a better reporting system comes along.

Limit on Deductibility of Losses: Another unfair feature of the capital-gains tax as it stands is that individuals are permitted to deduct only a portion of capital losses while paying taxes on all the gains. This tax asymmetry introduces a bias in the tax code against risk-taking: When taxpayers undertake risky investments, the government taxes any gain fully if the investment has a positive return but allows only partial tax deduction (up to $3,000 per year) if the venture goes sour and results in a loss.[33] Our tax proposal will allow for all losses as deductions against gains.

Table 13-3 States with the Highest Capital-Gains Tax Rates*

(includes top federal rate of 15%)

Rate After Deductibility	Combined Federal + State Rate	Federal
California	25.30%	21.70%
Iowa	23.98%	20.83%
New Jersey	23.97%	20.83%
District of Columbia	23.70%	20.66%
Hawaii	23.25%	20.36%
Minnesota	22.85%	20.10%

Note: Nine states—Alaska, Florida, Nevada, New Hampshire, South Dakota, Tennessee, Texas, Washington, and Wyoming—do not impose a state capital-gains tax; therefore, the highest marginal tax rate in these states is 15%.

*Castle United, "Capital Gains State Tax Rates," 1031 exchange URL: http://www.1031x.com/capital-gains-state-tax-rate.cfm.

In May 2003, the highest capital-gains tax rate was lowered from 20 percent to 15 percent, but only until 2010. In addition to the

---

33. Congressional Budget Office, "Indexing Capital Gains," August 1990.

15 percent (soon to be 20 percent, if not higher) federal tax levy on capital gains, many states impose their own add-on capital-gains tax (Table 13-3). In states such as California, Iowa, and New Jersey, the combined federal-state capital-gains tax rate, when the state deductibility of federal capital-gains taxes paid is factored in, can reach 21 percent or even a bit higher. Unfortunately, with the Alternative Minimum Tax (AMT), many taxpayers will find that they won't be able to deduct state and local taxes, raising their capital-gains tax rate even further.

Beginning in 2010 the tax rate is scheduled to increase back up to 20 percent and President Obama and Congress are eager to let this tax increase become effective. This tax increase will be another blow to an already weakened economic foundation. Putting the U.S. economy back on the road to prosperity necessitates further reforms of the capital-gains tax that lessens its burden, *not* policies that increase the burden. A quick review of the history of the capital-gains tax clearly shows that another negative economic shock is waiting for the U.S. economy in 2010.

Trends in Capital Gains Tax Rates and Receipts

Over the past thirty years, a consistent pattern has emerged: When the capital-gains tax rate has been cut, capital-gains tax revenues have risen, both in absolute terms and as a share of GDP; when the capital-gains tax rate has been raised, capital-gains tax revenues have fallen, both in absolute terms and as a share of GDP. Here are some prominent examples:[34]

In 1968, real capital-gains tax receipts were $34 billion (as measured in 2006 dollars) at a 27 percent tax rate. Over the next eight years the tax rate was raised to 36.5 percent, yet real capital-gains

---

34. In almost every instance, tax rate increases and reductions on capital gains reflected overall tax policy. This was not true in the 1986 Tax Reform Act. In 1986, capital-gains tax rates moved in the opposite direction from personal-income-tax rates.

tax revenues in 1977 were only $27 billion—21 percent below the 1968 level.

In 1978, when the top marginal tax rate on capital gains was 39.8 percent, $28 billion of capital-gains tax revenue (2006 dollars) was collected. By 1984, after the maximum tax rate had been slashed all the way down to 20 percent, inflation-adjusted revenues were $42 billion—50 percent above their 1978 level.

In 1986, the tax rate increased from 20 percent to 28 percent (a 40 percent increase in the rate). Did tax revenues climb by 40 percent? In fact, just the opposite occurred. Tax revenues did spike ahead of the tax increase, as we'd expect, but they then fell sharply. In 1990, the federal government took in 13 percent less revenue at the 28 percent rate than it did in 1985 at the 20 percent rate.

In 1997, the tax-rate cut on capital gains from 28 percent to 20 percent did not lead to any of the revenue losses that many expected. The dramatic results described below proved the critics of the capital-gains tax cut wrong; investment, new business creation, economic growth, and job creation soared to record levels, and the United States enjoyed historic prosperity.

In 1995 and 1996, the last two years with the 28 percent tax rate, the government collected $59 billion and $85 billion, respectively, in capital-gains tax receipts (2006 dollars). Four years later, capital-gains tax revenues had almost doubled to $149 billion in 2006 dollars.[35]

In 1996, the year before the capital-gains tax-rate cut from 28 percent to 20 percent, the total amount of net capital gains on assets sold was $261 billion. A year later, total realized capital gains had mysteriously jumped to $365 billion. (The capital-gains tax cut was retroactive to May 1997). In 1998, realized capital gains climbed to $455 billion, and by 1999, to $552 billion.

A similar scenario unfolded with the 2003 reduction in the max-

---

35.   But even this way, way, way underestimates the full revenue and deficit effects of a capital-gains tax-rate cut, as we have explained.

114

imum tax rate of capital gains from 20 percent to 15 percent. Real-izations were $269 billion in 2002 and are estimated by the CBO to have reached $729 billion in 2006. Taxes paid on capital gains over this period increased from $49 billion to an estimated $110 billion. Also, after the 2003 capital-gains tax-rate cut, total federal revenues increased in four years by $745 billion. The budget deficit fell from 3.6 percent of GDP in 2004 to 2.1 percent of GDP in 2007 on a National Income and Product Account basis.

Of course, a big part of this surge in realized capital gains in the late 1990s and then again in the 2003–07 period was a result of healthy stock-market gains. But a cut to the capital-gains tax rate means that the after-tax rate of return on stocks rises, so the value of the stock market should rise because its value is inversely related to the rate of tax on capital gains. Indeed, the two events—a higher stock market and the lowering of the capital-gains tax—are not in-dependent. It's all part of a dynamic incentive-based economy and the Laffer Curve.

Slashing income-tax rates (corporate and personal) and capital-gains tax rates in 1981 helped launch what we now appreciate as the greatest and longest period of wealth creation in world history. Once the Reagan tax cut was fully phased in, the stock market just took off. From July 1982 through August 2000, the S&P 500 returned 16.1 percent per year in nominal terms and 12.5 percent per year in real terms. Now, that's a bull market!

The Lock-In Effect

To understand why capital-gains tax cuts create such large revenue increases (and why capital-gains tax increases miss revenue projections by such wide margins), it is important to understand the "lock-in effect." Capital gains are a special component of income because their realization is more voluntary and therefore more easily controlled to avoid taxation. When the tax rate is high, investors simply delay selling their assets (the "lock-in" effect) to keep the tax collector away from their door.[36] When the capital-gains tax rate is cut, asset holders are inspired to sell. Moreover, a lower capital-gains tax rate substantially lowers the cost of capital, increases asset values, and causes the economy to grow faster, thus raising all government receipts. So the torrent of new revenues into the government coffers should really be no mystery at all. It's common sense. Our proposal of including unrealized capital gains in the overall tax base will for all practical purposes eliminate the lock-in effect.

The Congressional Budget Office stated, "There is strong evidence that realizations of capital gains decline when tax rates on gains are increased."[37] Even opponents of a capital-gains tax rate cut generally concede that there is a lock-in effect. Alan Reynolds, chief economist with the Cato Institute, explains the consistently misguided forecasts:

> All of the many studies of the revenue effect of the capital gains tax simply assume that there is no effect at all on the price of stocks and bonds, and also no effect on business investment or real GNP. That is, the revenue estimators ignore the most important effect.[38]

If the government revenue forecasters were to incorporate even modest economic growth responses into their static models and appropriately estimate the lock-in effect, the computers would spew out substantially different conclusions. That was the finding of a recent analysis on the sensitivity of government models to changes

---

36.   See Martin Feldstein, Joel Siemrod, and Shiomo Yitzhaki, "The Effects of Taxation on the Selling of Corporate Stock and the Realization of Capital Gains," *Quarterly Journal of Economics*, June 1980.

37.   Congressional Budget Office, "How Capital Gains Tax Rates Affect Revenues: The Historical Evidence," 1988, p. xi.

38.   Alan Reynolds, "Time to Cut the Capital Gains Tax," *Supply Side Analytics*, Polyconomics Inc., 1989.

in economic growth by economist Martin Feldstein of the National Bureau of Economic Research. Feldstein concludes that if

> ... the improved incentives for saving, investment, and en-
> trepreneurship were to increase the annual growth rate of
> GNP [over five years] by even a microscopically small 4 one-
> hundredths of one percent—for example, from the CBO's es-
> timate of an average 2.44 percent real GNP growth per year
> to 2.48 percent—the additional tax revenue would be about
> $5 billion a year and would turn CBO's estimated revenue
> loss into a revenue gain. In short, the potential economic
> gains from a capital gains [tax] reduction are substantial
> and the potential revenue loss is doubtful at best. . . . The
> slightest improvement in economic performance would be
> enough to turn [CBO's] revenue loss into a revenue gain.[39]

In sum, if one accepts the notion that a capital-gains tax cut promotes economic growth—as the evidence suggests is the case—then the revenue losses from lower capital-gains taxes will be much lower than anticipated. Lower capital-gains tax rates, in fact, appear to generate more tax revenues.

In theory, we would expect lower capital-gains tax rates to inspire a chain reaction of greater investment spending and higher asset values. When Congress chops the capital-gains tax rate, it increases the after-tax rate of return on real assets (such as plant, equipment, and technology), and thus stocks rise. This is exactly what happened following the most recent capital-gains tax cut in 2003. After falling again at the beginning of the decade, investment saw a sharp increase following the 2003 tax-rate cut. Remember, a capital-gains tax is merely a punitive second layer of tax: The value of a capital asset is no more or less than the discounted present value

---

39. Quoted by American Council for Capital Formation, Martin Feldstein, James R. Hines, Jr., and R. Glenn Hubbard, "The Effects of Taxation on Multinational Corporations," National Bureau of Economic Research Project Report.

of the after-tax earnings stream that capital asset produces. Under a rational tax system, we would tax the income stream or the asset value, but not both.

Are Capital-Gains Tax Cuts "Fair"?

For nearly three decades, the so-called tax fairness issue has dominated the capital-gains tax debate. Who are the winners and who are the losers from a capital-gains tax cut? Every new analysis seems to provide a different answer to that question.

For example, when President Bush proposed the reduction in the capital-gains tax rate in 2003, his critics argued that about 60 percent of the tax break would go to the richest 1 percent of Americans. But if we start by looking at the impact of the investment tax cut as a whole, we find that the share of taxes paid by the richest 1 percent and 5 percent of Americans actually increased after the tax cuts were enacted. In 2005, the percentage of income taxes (which includes dividends and capital gains) paid by the richest 1 percent hit an all-time high of 39 percent. The top 5 percent paid nearly 60 percent of the income tax, close to an all-time record. The richest 1 percent and 5 percent of Americans didn't pay less taxes on their capital-gains realizations, they paid more. One heckuva break, if you ask me.

Capital gains are not reported just by wealthy individuals. If we examine just the taxes on capital gains, we find that although the wealthy pay the most in capital-gains taxes, millions of middle-income Americans claim capital gains on their tax returns as well. In fact, 2005 Internal Revenue Service data indicate that 47 percent of all returns reporting capital gains were from households with incomes below $50,000, and 79 percent of all returns reporting capital gains were households with incomes below $100,000. Moreover, these tax-return data overstate the income status of those with capital gains because capital gains are themselves included in income and, in addition, reflect the sales of assets that are highly irregu-lar or even a once-in-a-lifetime event. For example, when someone sells a home or ranch, the income from the sale may be $1 million, but the seller may have never earned more than $50,000 annually in his working life. He appears "rich" in the income statistics that year because of the cash from the one-time sale.

The Capital-Gains Tax and U.S. Global Competitiveness

One indication of which nations will prosper and which will fall be-hind is the flow of international capital. Money flows to where the action is. In the 1980s, after marginal income-tax rates were reduced by more than one-third, the United States attracted more than one-half trillion dollars of net foreign capital. That is, foreigners invested $520 billion more in the United States than U.S. citizens and compa-nies invested abroad. In recent years, nations around the world have dramatically cut capital-gains and income-tax rates to become more competitive. The average income-tax rate abroad is twenty percent-age points lower today than in 1985 and the average corporate tax rate is almost twenty-five percentage points lower.

Today, the United States, even with the 2003 rate cut, still has a higher capital-gains tax rate than many industrial nations.[40] Figure 13-2 shows that many of America's principal trading partners have lower tax rates on capital gains than does the United States. In fact, many of our major international competitors—including Germany and Switzerland—impose no tax whatsoever on long-term capital gains. Australia and the United Kingdom have higher capital-gains tax rates, but because both of those nations allow for indexing for inflation of the tax basis, the effective tax rate may still be lower than the U.S. effective tax rate.

---

40. As a matter of fact, capital-gains tax laws both here in the United States and in the numerous jurisdictions abroad are very complicated, complex, and arcane. For the purposes of this book, we use the maximum federal, state, and local statutory tax rate as the measure of capital-gains taxation.

Figure 13-2 Long-Term Capital-Gains Tax Rates Around the World, 2005–2006

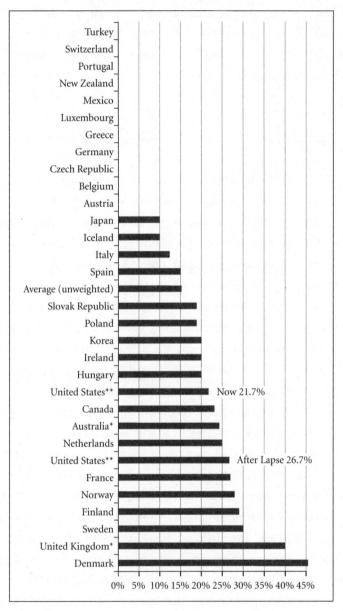

*Indexed for inflation.

**Includes federal, state, and city taxes based on California

Source: Australian Treasury, "International Comparison of Australia's Taxes." April 2008, p. 208.

What is of even greater concern is that if the United States were to repeal the Bush tax cuts, the U.S. capital-gains tax rate would be even further above the international average, according to data from the American Council for Capital Formation. And that would be bad news for the U.S. economy. Figure 13-2 shows that returning to the 20 percent capital-gains rate might repel foreign direct investment in the United States by increasing the cost of investing in the United States.

Estate Taxes: Spend It in Vegas, or Die Paying Taxes

In most cases, people who inherit wealth are lucky by an accident of birth and really don't deserve their inheritance any more than people who don't inherit wealth. After all, few of us get to choose our parents. It's also arguable that inherited wealth sometimes induces slothfulness and overindulgence. But the facts that beneficiaries of inheritances are just lucky and that the actual inheritance may make beneficiaries less productive don't justify having an estate tax.

These same observations about serendipitous birth can be made for intelligence, education, attractiveness, health, size, sex, disposition, race, and so on. And yet no one would suggest that the government should remove any portion of these attributes from people simply because they came from their parents. Surely we have not moved into Kurt Vonnegut's world of Harrison Bergeron.[41]

As of this writing, President Barack Obama intends to prolong the federal estate tax rather than ending it in 2010, as is scheduled under current law. The president's plan would extend this year's $3.5 million exemption level and the 45 percent top rate. But will this really help America recover from recession and reduce our growing deficits? In order to assess the pros and cons of the estate

---

41. Kurt Vonnegut, "Harrison Bergeron," *Magazine of Fantasy and Science Fiction*, October 1961. An online version of Harrison Bergeron can be found at: http://Instruct.westvalley.edu/lafave/hb.html.

tax, we should focus on its impact on those who bequeath wealth, not on the impact on those who receive wealth.

Advocates of the estate tax argue that such a tax will reduce the concentrations of wealth in a few families, but there is little evidence to suggest that the estate tax has much, if any, impact on the distribution of wealth. To see the silliness of using the estate tax as a tool to redistribute wealth, realize that those who die and leave estates would be taxed just as much if they bequeathed their money to poor people as they would if they left their money to rich people. If the objective were to redistribute, surely an inheritance tax (a tax on the recipients) would make far more sense than an estate tax.

Indeed, from a societal standpoint, inheritance is an unmitigated good. Passing on to successive generations greater health, wealth, and wisdom is what society in general, and America specifically, is all about. Imagine what America would look like today if our forefathers had been selfish and had left us nothing. We have all benefited greatly from a history of intergenerational American generosity. But just being an American is as much an accident of birth as being the child of wealthy parents. If you are an American, it's likely because ancestors of yours chose to become Americans and also chose to have children.

In its most basic form, it's about as silly an idea as can be imagined that America in the aggregate can increase the standard of living of future generations by taxing individual Americans for passing on a higher standard of living to future generations of Americans of their choice. Clearly, taxing estates at death will induce people who wish to leave estates to future generations to leave smaller estates and to find ways to avoid estate taxes. On a conceptual level, it makes no sense to tax estates at death.

Study after study finds that the estate tax significantly reduces the size of estates and, as an added consequence, reduces the nation's capital stock and income. This commonsense finding is documented ad nauseam in the 2006 U.S. Joint Economic Committee Report on the Costs and Consequences of the Federal Estate Tax.

The Joint Economic Committee estimates that the estate tax has reduced the capital stock by approximately $850 billion because it reduces incentives to save and invest, has excessively high compliance costs, and results in significant economic inefficiencies.[42]

Today in America you can take your after-tax income and go to Las Vegas and carouse, gamble, drink, and smoke, and as far as our government is concerned that's just fine. But if you take that same after-tax income and leave it to your children and grandchildren, the government will tax that after-tax income one additional time at rates of up to 55 percent. I especially like an oft-quoted line from Joseph Stiglitz and David L. Bevan, who wrote in the *Greek Economic Review*, "Of course, prohibitively high inheritance tax rates generate no revenue; they simply force the individual to consume his income during his lifetime."[43] Hurray for Vegas!

If you're rich enough, however, you can hire professionals who can, for a price, show you how to avoid estate taxes. Many of the very largest estates are so tax-sheltered that the inheritances go to their beneficiaries having paid little or no taxes at all. And all the costs associated with these tax shelters and tax-avoidance schemes are pure waste for the country as a whole and exist solely to circumvent the estate tax. The estate tax in and of itself causes people to waste resources.

Again, a number of studies suggest that the costs of sheltering estates from the taxman actually are about as high as the total tax revenues collected from the estate tax. And these estimates don't even take into account lost output, employment, and production resulting from perverse incentives. This makes the estate tax one of the least efficient taxes. And yet for all the hardship and expense associated with the estate tax, the total monies collected in any one year account for only about 1 percent of federal tax receipts.

---

42. "Costs and Consequences of the Federal Estate Tax," *Report of the Joint Economic Committee of the United States*, 109th Cong., 2nd Sess., Report 109–726, p. 19.

43. David L. Bevan and Joseph E. Stiglitz. "International Transfers and Inequality." *Greek Economic Review* 1, no. 1 (August 1979): 8–26.

It is important to realize that less than half of the estates that must go through the burden of complying with the paperwork and reporting requirements of the tax actually pay even a nickel of the tax. And the largest estates that actually do pay taxes generally pay lower marginal tax rates than smaller estates because of tax shelters. The inmates are really running the asylum.

In 1982, Californians overwhelmingly voted to eliminate the state's estate tax. It seems that even in the highest-taxed state in the nation there are some taxes voters cannot abide. It shouldn't surprise anyone that ultrawealthy liberal senator Howard Metzenbaum, supporter of the estate tax and lifetime resident of Ohio, where there is a state estate tax, chose to die as a resident of Florida, where there is no state estate tax. Differential state estate-tax rates incentivize people to move from state to state. Global estate-tax rates do the same thing, only the moves are from country to country. In 2005 the United States, at a 47 percent marginal tax rate, had the third-highest estate-tax rate of the fifty countries covered in a 2005 report by Price Waterhouse Coopers, LLP. A full twenty-six countries had no "Inheritance/Death" tax rate at all.[44]

In the summary of its 2006 report, the Joint Economic Committee wrote, "The detrimental effects of the estate tax are grossly disproportionate to the modest amount of federal revenues it raises (if it raises any net revenue at all)."[45] Even economists in favor of the estate tax concede that its current structure does not work. Henry Aaron and Alicia Munnell concluded, "In short, the estate and gift taxes in the United States have failed to achieve their intended purposes. They raise little revenue. They impose large excess burdens. They are unfair."[46]

For all these reasons, the estate tax needs to go, along with the

---

44.   "New International Survey Shows U.S. Death Tax Rates Among Highest," American Council for Capital Formation, July 2005.

45.   "Costs and Consequences of the Federal Estate Tax," *Report of the Joint Economic Committee of the United States*, 109th Cong., 2nd Sess., Report 109–726, p. 28.

46.   Henry J. Aaron and Alicia H. Munnell, "Reassessing the Role for Wealth Transfer Taxes," *National Tax Journal* 45, No. 2 (June 1992), p. 138.

step-up basis at death of capital gains (which values an asset not at the purchase price but at the price at the buyer's death). On purely a static basis, the Joint Tax Committee estimates that over the period 2011 through 2015, the static revenue losses from eliminating the estate tax would be $281 billion, while the additional capital-gains tax receipts from repeal of the step-up basis would be $293 billion.

To counter the fact that economists like me obsess about the deleterious effects of the estate tax, advocates of the estate tax note with some pride that 98 percent of Americans will never pay this tax. Let's make it 100 percent, and I'll get off my soapbox. My tax proposal totally eliminates the estate tax.

14

GROW THE PIE OR DIVIDE THE PIE

A rising tide lifts all boats

—JOHN F. KENNEDY

The election of President Obama has brought the age-old topic of income equality versus economic growth to a prominent position in our political discourse. Should U.S. economic policies be focused on expanding the economy or on reducing income inequality? That is, should we expand the income pie at a faster rate, or slice it up more evenly?

A top priority of the Obama administration is to slice up the economic pie more equitably so that we have a "shared prosperity." The mantra is: Raise tax rates on the top 5 percent of income earners and "cut taxes for the other 95 percent of Americans." Based upon the evidence and theory, such a redistribution plan will reduce income and wealth across the *entire* income distribution.

The fundamental problem with plans to redistribute income is that they don't take actual human behavior into account. If the government taxes rich people and gives the money to poor people, sooner rather than later we'll have a lot more poor people and fewer rich people. It is well known that people respond to incentives. In a low-tax environment, people work more and harder, more people work, people devote less energy to sheltering income, people get more educated, and people's entrepreneurial spirit is exceptionally strong. The dream in America has always been to make the poor rich, not to make the rich poor.

The Virtues of the Invisible Hand

When people's entrepreneurial spirit is unleashed, they make the world a better place, not because of altruistic motives or selfless intentions, but actually as a direct result of their personal motives to better their lives financially. Without industry, other parts of our society would be less productive and less wealthy. Entrepreneurial efforts motivated by self-interest make a positive difference to many others, whether intended or not. In 1776, in a book titled *An Inquiry into the Nature and Causes of the Wealth of Nations*, authored by one Adam Smith, these indirect effects of the pursuit of one's own self-interest were named "the invisible hand."[1]

Pursuing dreams of prospering benefits everyone. If you do well by doing good, the whole world benefits. It is truly a win-win relationship.

It is a badge of honor to be wealthy and financially successful if those rewards are achieved morally and legally through hard work. While many people profess to be proud of their humble origins or that they made it on their own out of poverty, these same people try their damnedest to make sure their children's lives are different from their own. To think otherwise is a mistake, but that mistaken thought is very seductive.

At every stage in life, it is hard to comprehend the wide divergence of economic results: why some people live in abject poverty with broken families and any number of other cruel afflictions, and yet other people are wealthy, happy, and have all the benefits society has to offer. In the most fundamental sense of the word, it simply isn't fair.

---

1.   Adam Smith, *An Inquiry into the Nature and Causes of the Wealth of Nations*, 1776.

To attempt to redress these inequalities through your own personal actions is what I meant by the phrase "doing well by doing good." Sometimes holding a hand out to those less affluent is the greatest reward of all. But that's when you do it for yourself. In fact, Adam Smith, in his first book, *The Theory of Moral Sentiments*, wrote:

> *How selfish soever man may be supposed, there are evidently some principles in his nature, which interest him in the fortune of others, and render their happiness necessary to him, though he derives nothing from it, except the pleasure of seeing it.*[2]

Altruism is part of being a human being.

To attempt to redress the obvious inequalities of life, however, by forcing others to give up their wealth is what I mean by mistaken actions. Using the powers of the state to redistribute income or wealth will have massive unintended consequences and often will actually hurt those whom the policies were intended to help.

Good economics should always make common sense. It is as basic as it is right that if government taxes people who work and pays people who don't work there will be few people working and more people out of work as a consequence. Similarly, if government taxes rich people and gives the money to poor people, society will end up with lots of poor people and few rich people. People respond to incentives. It's a simple fact of life, neither good nor bad, but simply what is. But feeling compassion for the poor is what makes each and every one of us human.

I have six children, and I want each of my children to succeed equally. When one child has special needs, I divert resources from the other five to provide more resources for the one with greater needs. If one child is exceptionally successful, I'll withdraw re-

---

2.   Adam Smith, *The Theory of Moral Sentiments*, 1759, p 1.

sources from that child. In a very basic and simple sense, I do my very best to redistribute the resources of our family to achieve equal success for one and all.

And to carry the family analogy further, I would personally like nothing more than to see every American be equally successful. If I were the omnipotent ruler of our wonderful country and there were no supply-side responses, I would tax everyone who made more than the average wage 100 percent of the excess, and I would subsidize everyone who earns less than the average wage up to the average wage. I would do this, if I may repeat, only if there were no supply-side responses. Their existence makes all the difference in the world.

If I actually implemented a policy of taxing everyone who makes above the average wage 100 percent of the excess and subsidizing everyone who earns less than the wage up to the average wage, I can assure you beyond a shadow of a doubt that the disparities in income will be greatly reduced. Everyone will earn the same—and it will be zero.[3] I can imagine no worse result.

The example I described above may be extreme, but it illustrates the point. Any attempt to force a redistribution of income from successful to unsuccessful will make all less successful. The more successful one person is, the more successful everyone will be.

The Rising Tide Lifted All Boats

The story of the United States since President Reagan lowered taxes in the early 1980s and created an economic environment conducive to economic growth and prosperity is one of increasing wealth and incomes for all families over time. How different people can look at

---

3.   While this result is not always obvious at first, it is certain. Such a system removes all incentive to supply work effort.

some of the same data and come to a much grimmer conclusion is fascinating.

As an example, according to my friend Jared Bernstein, CNBC contributor, former senior economist at the Economic Policy Institute, and current chief economist for Vice President Joe Biden, "You know what does happen when you cut rich people's taxes? They get richer. In this way, Bush managed to amplify the historically extreme wealth inequality that the market itself was generating over the 2000s, as did Reagan in the 1980s."[4]

Yet that logic is flawed. In this section I will walk through the proper logic as I unveil some of the most pertinent income and wealth data for the United States. The objective is to present the facts on income growth and income distribution over the past twenty-five years or so.

Let's start right out of the gate with the most recent report on the state of economic affairs for American workers. The Census Bureau released its "Income, Poverty, and Health Insurance Coverage in the United States: 2007" in August 2008.[5]

Here are a few of the main facts:

- Real median household income increased between 2006 and 2007. Median income in 2007 was $50,233, a 1.2 percent or $600 increase from 2006—nothing to sneeze at.
- Real median incomes of both black and non-Hispanic white households rose between 2006 and 2007.
- Both the number and the percentage of people without health insurance coverage decreased between 2006 and 2007.
- The percentage of Americans who are *chronically* in poverty (thirty-six months or more) is low, just 2.5 percent.

---

4.   Jared Bernstein, "Ideology Takes a Breather, Maybe," *Huffington Post*, October 19, 2008, http://www.hufflingtonpost.com/jared-bernstein/ideology-takes-a-breather_b_135929.html.
5.   U.S. Census Bureau, "Income, Poverty, and Health Insurance Coverage: 2001, http://www.census.gov/prod/2006pubs/p60–235.pdf.

- The reported poverty rate of 12 percent is in fact closer to 5 percent when government benefits are taken into account.
- The distribution of income became more equal in 2007. The percentage of income that went to the bottom 95 percent of income earners rose from 77 percent to 78 percent.

Income Evolution across the Income Distribution

It's true that the richest 1 percent and 5 percent of tax filers have corralled a larger share of income during the last roughly three decades. In 1980 the wealthiest 1 percent and 5 percent of Americans earned 8 percent and 20 percent of the nation's total income respectively as adduced by income tax returns. By 2006 those percentages had jumped to 22 percent and 37 percent.[6] It is also true that over the past quarter century the share of income that has gone to the lowest income group for tax filers—the bottom 20 percent—has fallen from 5.3 percent to 4.1 percent.[7]

So by this measure it appears that "economic fairness" has declined in America, and many pundits end the story here. Yet the U.S. economy has been growing about 3.5 percent in real terms annually during this period, so the above numbers hide the fact that the entire income distribution has shifted up. Imagine that the U.S. economic pie were equal to 100 units in 1980 and equal to 250 in 2006. This means that the top 1 percent of income earners received 8 units in income in 1980 and 55 units in 2006. The bottom 20 percent of income earners had an income equal to 5.3 units in 1980 and 10.3 units in 2006. Thus, both ends of the income distribution experienced economic prosperity.

Table 14-1 presents the exact income numbers and shows that the gains to the rich have been the greatest, but also that the entire

---

6. Internal Revenue Service, Statistics of Income, Table 1.
7. U.S. Census Bureau, Table F-2, http://www.census.gov/hhes/www/income/histinct/102AR .html.

income distribution has been lifted up. The idea that the incomes of all income groups have increased is the untold story. Once you correct for income mobility, household size, and the number of zero-tax filers, the story is even more impressive.

- People move from the bottom of the income distribution to the middle or higher as they get educated and gain experience. Many of the people who today make up the bottom part of the income distribution will be in the top part within a generation.
- The average number of people per household (and per tax return) has been declining over the last three decades. This is especially true for households and filers in the lower-income classes. So household income numbers as we've reported above understate the true gains in per-capita income.
- The number of tax filers with zero income-tax liability has increased over time because of expanded credits and deductions in the tax code.

Table 14-1 **After-Tax Real Comprehensive Household Income**

Year*	Lowest Quintile	Second Quintile	Middle Quintile	Fourth Quintile	Highest Quintile	All Quintiles
1983	12,500	26,200	38,600	52,700	99,800	45,900
1993	14,000	28,800	42,500	58,500	117,300	52,200
2005	15,300	33,700	50,200	70,300	172,200	67,400
% Change						
1983–1993	12.00%	9.92%	10.10%	11.01%	17.54%	13.73%
1993–2005	9.29%	17.01%	18.12%	20.17%	46.80%	29.12%

*I chose to look at these time periods, as they represent complete business cycles.
Source: CBO, "Historical Effective Federal Tax Rates: 1979 to 2005."

An interesting point springs from the data provided in Table 14-1. During the Reagan years of 1983–93, all incomes grew at roughly the same pace, but during the 1993–2005 period, the top quintile grew at more than twice the pace of the rest of the income distribution. This differential in income disparity between the Reagan years and the Clinton/Bush years is hard to reconcile with the argument that Reagan's tax cuts were the primary cause for increased disparity.

Figure 14-1 Middle-Class Income Limits

(annual, through 2007)

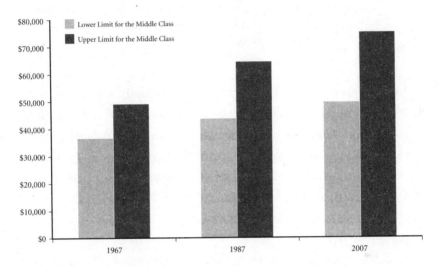

The Middle Class

Far from disappearing, the middle class has been getting steadily richer over time. Figure 14-1 shows the income range of what is traditionally classified as the middle class for selected years. In 1967 average real (inflation-adjusted) income for the middle class (families with incomes between the fortieth and sixtieth percentiles of the income distribution) was about $43,000; in 2007 it was more than $61,000.[8] This increase does not include the increased generosity

---

8.   U.S. Census Bureau, Historical Income Tables—Families, Table F-3, http://www.census.gov/hhes/www/income/histinc/f03AR.html.

of nonwage and nonsalary benefits such as health care, pensions, flexible workweeks, more family leave, more vacation, and holidays.

In 1967 the real income range for the middle class ran from $36,600 to $49,000. But now, in 2007, the income range for the middle class runs from $49,500 to $75,000. Finally, in 1967 one in twenty families had a real income of $100,000 or more. In 2005 one in six families did. This is a clear demonstration of progress for the middle class.

The Poor

A number of Americans are struggling financially, especially in today's weak economy. But the long-term trend for the poor is rising. Consider, for example, Figure 14-2, from Michael Cox at the Dallas Fed. He shows that the poor in America can afford more goods and services today than the middle class could afford thirty years ago. It's an amazing story of the wonders of technological advance. In this technology age, new inventions are quickly becoming affordable.

My favorite example is the cell phone. In 1987 a cell phone cost about $4,600 for lousy service and the clumsy gadget was the size of a brick. Now a cell phone costs about $46 and comes with cameras, internet service, calendars, calculators, clocks, and so on.

Things fifty years ago were not of the same quality as are those things today. This suggests that we've been dramatically overstating inflation and understating living-standard gains by not taking into account improvements in the quality of the things we buy today versus in the past.[9]

Don Boudreaux, an economist at George Mason University, compared prices in the Sears catalog thirty years ago versus today and then adjusted those prices for wages. Table 14-2 shows the re-

---

9.   Don Boudreaux, http://cafehayek.typepad.com/hayek/2006/01/working_for_sea. html.

sults of his study.[10] Notice how much less people have to work to afford similar goods today.

Figure 14-2 Consumption of Goods by Type of Good and Household

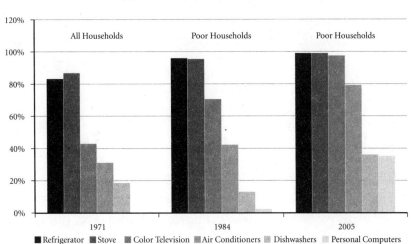

Table 14-2 Sears' Catalog Prices 1975 and 2006

Sears' lowest-priced 10-inch table saw: 52.35 hours of work required in 1975; 7.34 hours of work required in 2006.

Sears' lowest-priced gasoline-powered lawn mower: 13.14 hours of work required in 1975 (to buy a lawn mower that cuts a 20-inch swathe); 8.56 hours of work required in 2006 (to buy a lawn mower that cuts a 22-inch swathe; Sears no longer sells a power mower that cuts a swathe smaller than 22 inches).

Sears' Best freezer: 79 hours of work required in 1975 (to buy a freezer with 22.3 cubic feet of storage capacity); 39.77 hours of work required in 2006 (to buy a freezer with 24.9 cubic feet

---

10. Don Boudreaux, http://cafehayek.typepad.com/hayek/2006/01/working_for_sea. html.

of storage capacity; this size freezer is the closest size available today to that of Sears' Best in 1975).

Sears' Best side-by-side fridge-freezer: 139.62 hours of work required in 1975 (to buy a fridge with 22.1 cubic feet of storage capacity); 79.56 hours of work required in 2006 (to buy a comparable fridge with 22.0 cubic feet of storage capacity).

Sears' lowest-priced answering machine: 20.43 hours of work required in 1975; 1.1 hours of work required in 2006.

A ½-horsepower garbage disposer: 20.52 hours of work required in 1975; 4.59 hours of work required in 2006.

Sears' lowest-priced garage-door opener: 20.1 hours of work required in 1975 (to buy a ¼-horsepower opener); 8.57 hours of work required in 2006 (to buy a ½-horsepower opener; Sears no longer sells garage-door openers with less than ½-horsepower).

Sears' highest-priced work boots: 11.49 hours of work required in 1975; 8.26 hours of work required in 2006.

One gallon of Sears' Best interior latex paint: 2.4 hours of work required in 1975; 1.84 hours of work required in 2006. (Actually, Sears sells no paint online, so the price I got for a premium gallon of interior latex paint is from Restoration Hardware.)

Sears' Best automobile tire (with specs 165/13, and a tread life warranty of 40,000 miles): 8.37 hours of work required in 1975: 2.92 hours of work required in 2006—although the price here is of a Bridgestone tire that I found at another online merchant. Judging from its website, Sears no longer sells tires with specs 165/13 and a 40,000-mile warranty.

White Heads of Households' Income

Jared Bernstein argues that real wages for white male workers haven't increased in more than twenty years. Their living standards are flat, according to Bernstein.

Wage and salary income isn't the only way people get compensated today. More and more worker compensation today is in benefits that didn't even exist thirty years ago: adoption assistance, mental-health coverage, paid parental leave, tuition assistance, more vacation days and holidays, and so on.

Figure 14-3 is instructive. It shows that median real salaries and wages are up 26 percent since 1980. But when benefits are accounted for, the compensation to workers is up 34 percent. Furthermore, per-capita income is up over 50 percent.[11]

Figure 14-3 Worker Well-Being
(annual, 1980 = 100, through 2007)

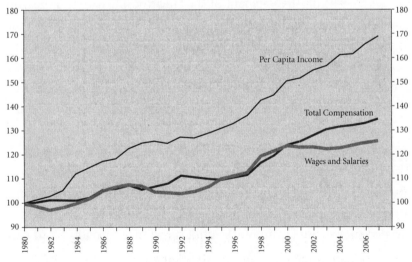

A 2007 study by the Treasury Department tapped into IRS data to track family incomes over two periods, 1987–96 and 1996–

---

11.   Bureau of Labor Statistics.

2005.[12] Over both periods, the findings were nearly identical: The poorer a household was at the start of the period, the more rapid that family's subsequent income gain. This result is obvious once you think about it but is frequently overlooked. The gains for the poorest households more than doubled from 1996 to 2005. All income groups gained over the period, except for the super-rich, or the top 1 percent. Again, this result is obvious because these people have nowhere to go but down. And yet the point is almost always overlooked.

A typical poor family with a real income of, say, $15,000 in 1996 had a real income of roughly $31,000 by 2005. In wealthy neighborhoods with millionaire households, incomes actually fell. Many of the super-rich in America are people whose high incomes are fleeting.

The Federal Reserve Bank of Dallas looked at the same income data over a slightly longer period, from 1975 to 1991. It found that an incredible 98 percent of poor households in 1975 were not poor by 1991.[13] Seventy-five percent of the "near poor," which is the bottom 20 percent to 40 percent in family income, climbed into the middle class or higher over this period. One explanation for this rapid mobility is that age has a lot to do with one's income status. Those in the bottom quintile tend to be younger people with little education and experience. Many are in school with scant income because they do little work for pay.

Figure 14-4 shows that with each passing year in the labor force, income, on average, rises up to about age fifty. The Congressional Budget Office, which came to a very similar conclusion on income mobility, finds that the landmark welfare reform bill of 1996 succeeded in moving families off public assistance into jobs, and that

---

12.   United States Department of the Treasury, *Income Mobility in the U.S. from 1996 to 2005*, November 13, 2007, http://www.ustreas.gov/offices/tax-policy/library/incomemobilitystudy03–06 revise.pdf.
13.   Federal Reserve Bank of Dallas, *By Our Own Bootstraps*, Annual Report, 1995, http://www .dallasfed.org/fed/annual/1999p/ar95.pdf.

those families then saw impressive income gains over the next decade.[14]

When a poor person moves into the middle or upper class (income mobility), that person no longer is classified as poor. If someone who was earning $20,000 a year saw his or her income move to, say, $50,000, then that 150 percent gain in income for a poor person isn't reported as such because we no longer classify that person as poor. But every penny of income gain by a rich person is counted because there is no higher-income class the richest can move into.

Furthermore, about 1 million to 1.5 million new immigrants enter the United States every year.[15] A fairly high percentage of these immigrants start at the bottom of the income ladder. America is constantly replenishing the people who are at the bottom rungs of the economic ladder. Immigration helps create the statistical mirage that poor people do not make progress in the American labor force.

Figure 14-4 Median Household Incomes by Age, 2006

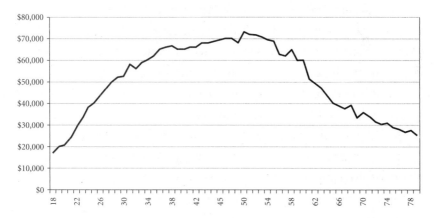

14. Congressional Budget Office, *Changes in the Economic Resources of Low-Income Households with Children*, May 2007, http://www.cbo.gov/ftpdoc/81xx/doc8113/05–16-Low-Income.pdf.
15. U.S. Census Bureau, Foreign-Born Profiles, http://www.census.gov/population/www/socdemo/foreign/datatbls.html.

Intergenerational Poverty

The latest study on income mobility, funded by the Pew Charitable Trusts, compares the economic status of parents in 1967–71 with the income level of their children in 2000–2002.[16] This study confirms that children from wealthy families have a head start in life, but it's not an insurmountable lead. Of those children who grow up in poor households, more than half are not poor as adults.[17] One serious obstacle to children in poor families growing up to be rich is the miserable state of inner-city schools and of public schools in general.

But even with this severe handicap that poor children face, in most cases they are able to break out of the poverty cycle. The Pew study finds that 66 percent of children coming from the bottom income quintile grow up to exceed their parents' range.[18] It's also noteworthy that about one-third of children growing up in wealthy households ended up poorer than their parents. Parentage does matter, but individual initiative matters more.

The latest Forbes 400 list of the richest people confirms that America remains an opportunity society and that it's not easy to stay on the top perch of the wealth ladder for long. Of the four hundred wealthiest people, only thirty-two were there when the list began in 1982.[19] Only 18 percent inherited their whole fortune, while about 70 percent—people like Jeff Bezos, Michael Dell, Sergy Brin, and Steven Spielberg—amassed fortunes by giving the rest of us products we want.

---

16. Julia B. Isaacs, *Economic Mobility of Black and White Families*, Pew Charitable Trust, http://www.pewtrusts.org/uploadedFiles/wwwpewtrustsorg/Reports/Economic_Mobility/EMP%20Black%20and%20White%20Families%20ES+Chapter.pdf.

17. Ibid.

18. Bhashkar Mazumder, *Upward Intergenerational Economic Mobility in the United States*, Pew Charitable Trust, p. 12, http://www.pewtrusts.org/uploadedFiles/wwwpewtrustsorg/Reports/Economic_Mobility/PEW_Upward%20EM%2014.pdf.

19. John Tamny, "The Forbes 400 as a Lesson in Economics," *Real Clear Politics*, September 28, 2007, http://www.realclearpolitics.com/articles/2007/09/the_forbes_400_as_a_lesson_in.html.

Conspicuous Consumption?[20]

According to calculations by former Labor Department economist Diana Furchtgott-Roth, who has analyzed Census Bureau data on household spending patterns in 2006, the wealthiest fifth of Americans consume $28,272 a year per person compared to $15,639 for the middle class and $11,247 of spending for the poor.[21] Virginia senator Jim Webb may be right that corporate CEOs now earn one hundred times more than their employees, but they don't consume anywhere near one hundred times more.

It's a sign of the growing affluence of the poor that the single largest increase in expenditures for low-income households over the past twenty years was for audio and visual entertainment systems, which was up 120 percent.[22] The poor actually spend less money now than twenty years ago on such necessities as food and clothing, meaning they have more disposable income for other purchases— call it the Wal-Mart effect.

A new study by Christian Broda and John Romalis at the University of Chicago finds that we have been statistically understating income gains of lower-income Americans because they buy a different basket of goods than do the wealthy.[23] The poor spend a big percentage of their income on food, clothing, and other basic consumer items that have been stable or even falling in price. And that means we understate the income gains of the poor fairly systematically.

20.　Thorstein Veblen, in *The Theory of the Leisure Class*, coined the phrase "conspicuous consumption."

21.　Diana Furchtgott-Roth, *Economic Security for Working Families*, Testimony before the House Committee on Education and Labor, January 31, 2007, http://edlabor.house.gov/testimony/013107 DianaFurchtgottRothtestimony.pdf.

22.　Ibid.

23.　Christian Broda and John Romalis, *Inequality and Prices: Does China Benefit the Poor in America?* March 26, 2008, http://faculty.chicagogsb.edu/christian.broda/website/research/unrestricted/ Broda_Tradeinequality.pdf.

Additional Biases in the Data

One reason high-income families have higher earnings than low-income families is that there are more workers in high-income families than in low-income families. The average household in the lowest income quintile has only half a person working (see Table 14-3). It's hard to have much of an income if no one in the family works. The average high-income family has two people working—usually husband and wife. So it should not be too surprising that wealthy families have more income, since they have four workers for every worker in the lowest-income group.

Table 14-3 Workers per Quintile

Quintile	Average Number of Workers
Bottom Quintile	0.48
Second Quintile	1.1
Middle Quintile	1.45
Fourth Quintile	1.8
Top Quintile	2.1

The average poor household consists on average of about 1.5 people. This means that at a minimum half of low-income households consist of a single person living alone. By contrast, the average high-income household has about three people. So when we adjust for the number of people in the household and the number of workers in the household, we find that at least two-thirds of the income gap disappears.

Actual income gains by the lower-income groups get undercounted because the number of people living in low-income households has been shrinking during the last three decades, as a result of family break-up, fewer children in these homes, and a larger percentage of poor "households" that constitute a single person living alone.

On a per-capita basis, the income gains for poor households were 20.3 percent from 1983 to 1993 and 12.2 percent from 1993 to 2005.

Figure 14-5 **U.S. Distribution of Income in 2002: Conventional Census Bureau Figures**

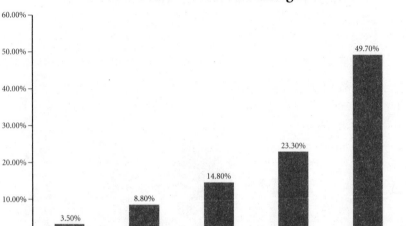

Robert Rector of the Heritage Foundation recently looked at the income distribution data (Figure 14-5) and corrected for many of these problems, and others, with the official data. He found that when you correct for family size, number of workers, government benefits, capital gains, and taxes, the income distribution looks much more equal (Figure 14-6).[24]

Income Gaps, Race, and Sex

Figure 14-7 shows the income gains by sex and race from 1980 to 2007. Since 1980 women have seen larger percentage income gains than men, and blacks have greater income gains than whites. In

---

24.   Robert Rector and Rea Hederman, Jr., *Two Americas: One Rich, One Poor? Understanding Income Inequality in the United States*, Heritage Foundation, Backgrounder #1791, August 24, 2004, http://www.heritage.org/Research/Taxes/bg1791.cfm.

other words, gaps based on the color of one's skin or one's sex are rapidly disappearing in America.

Figure 14-6 **U.S. Distribution of Income in 2002: Distribution of Income with Equal Numbers of Persons in Each Quintile**

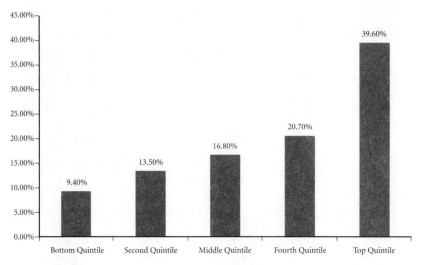

Since 1980 black females have made the fastest income gains of any group. White males still earn the most, but the gap is narrowing. The gaps in income are widening within groups and narrowing between groups, which is consistent with the theme here that divisions in wages and salaries are based on talent and productivity, not subjective measures such as skin color. We are becoming more, not less, of a meritocracy in America. Since 1980, the average income of black families has risen by 44 percent, for Hispanic households by 28 percent, and for white households by 38 percent.[25]

---

25.   Census Bureau.

Big Return on Education

What is the biggest determinant of whether someone will be rich or poor as an adult? Well, one of the biggest determinants is the education that a child receives. Incomes are highly dependent on years of education. Heads of households with a high-school education have average earnings that are $40,456, compared to $77,605 for those with a bachelor's degree and $90,660 for those with a master's degree (Figure 14-8).[26]

Figure 14-7 Real Income Gains 1980 to 2007

(annual, percent, through 2007)

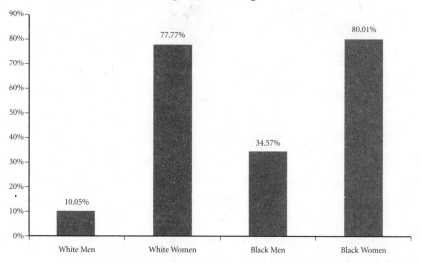

Not everyone has to go to college to earn a lot. But a high-school diploma is essential and unless something is done to fix America's dreadful inner-city schools, poor children face a hefty disadvantage in the workplace. One thing almost everyone agrees on—those on both left and right—is that in a global economy, returns to education are larger today than ever before.

---

26.   Census Bureau.

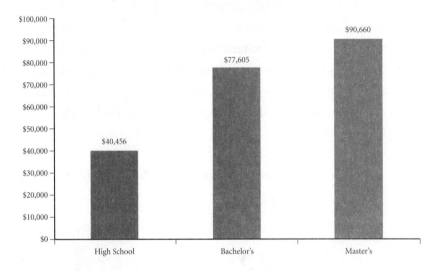

Figure 14-8 Average Household Income
by Educational Attainment, 2007

(annual, head of household, through 2007)

How to Lift All Boats

High tax rates on the rich are not a good way to redistribute income.

History teaches us that high tax rates don't redistribute income to the poor and the middle class. I recently reviewed IRS tax-return data by income group going back to 1972. The results are jaw-dropping. In 1972, when the highest tax rate on the rich was 70 percent and the top capital-gains tax rate was 35 percent, the richest 1 percent of Americans paid 17 percent of the income-tax burden. Today, with a top income-tax rate of 35 percent and capital gains at 15 percent, they pay over 40 percent.[27]

With higher income-tax rates the rich shelter more of their income through tax carve-outs, they invest less here in the United States and more abroad, and they work less. The government's Robin Hood strategy has almost always failed because it means less,

---

27. Internal Revenue Service, Statistics of Income, Table 1.

not more income to take from the rich and give to the poor. President Obama should already have discovered that when you put "tax fairness" ahead of economic growth, you produce neither.

Low tax rates also lead to more rich people—which, in my opinion, should be the goal of good tax policy. Bush's investment tax cuts have had a stunning effect in this regard. Figure 14-9 shows what has happened to the number of Americans who declare more than $1 million in income on their tax returns. In just three years, a blink of an eye, there were almost twice as many millionaires. The tax payments more than doubled.[28]

Figure 14-9 Tax Returns Reporting $1 Million or More

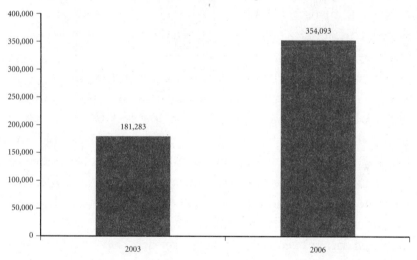

Why? Two reasons. First, lower tax rates expanded the economy and helped move more people up the income ladder into a category that was once considered super-duper-rich. Before this past economic collapse, millionaires were everywhere in America. Second, lower tax rates incentivized people to work more and to declare more taxable income.

There was a huge surge in dividend income after the tax cuts.

28.   Internal Revenue Service.

Capital-gains income, which can be sheltered by not selling an asset, more than doubled from 2003 to 2006.[29] And the rich simply invested less in tax shelters and more in higher-return taxable ventures. That is to say, there was a Laffer Curve effect at the top of the income scale from the lower tax rates on investment and income.

Americans are not made poorer because Bill Gates, Warren Buffett, Tiger Woods, and the members of the Walton family have gotten fabulously wealthy. In fact, each of these people in their own way have not just gotten rich themselves, they have created jobs and higher incomes for many others.

It is estimated that Bill Gates alone, whose personal wealth is estimated at $50 billion, is responsible for making ten thousand people millionaires, including former Microsoft secretaries.[30] The same is true of the people who got in on the ground floor of Google and eBay.

These entrepreneurs not only carry other people with them as investors in their journey to super wealth, they also provide meaningful jobs and high-quality products at low cost. Consumers and workers benefit above and beyond where they otherwise would have been. These entrepreneurs bring new "disruptive" technologies to the market that reorganize the entire concept of product and production. Josef Schumpeter, the great Austrian economist, called this process "creative destruction."[31]

When entrepreneurs and investors get rich, they tend to make a lot of other people rich with them. This will occur on a substantially reduced scale in a high-tax environment.

There are those who say that there have been almost no gains in living standards since the 1950s in America. So try this thought experiment. What if you had your choice between working in the

---

29.   Stephen Moore and Tyler Grimm, "The Bush Capital Gains Tax Cut after Four Years: More Growth, More Investment, More Revenues," National Center for Policy Analysis, NCPA Policy Report No. 307, January 2008, http://www.ncpa.org/pub/st/st307/st307.pdf.

30.   Brad Lockwood, *Bill Gates: Profile of a Digital Entrepreneur,* Rosen Publishing Group, 2007, p. 60.

31.   In *Capitalism, Socialism and Democracy.*

1950s and working today? Would it have been easier to raise a family? To buy things that you and your loved ones want? To get good health care if you got cancer or had a heart attack? To send your kids to college?

The answer to each of these questions is obviously, heck no!

For those who got that answer wrong, try living for a week or two without a personal computer, a cell phone, a color TV (much less cable or satellite or HD), the internet, air-conditioning, modern medicines, Wal-Mart, a washing machine, cheap air travel, and so on. For most of us, our kids are our most prized assets, and fifty years ago the death rate for children was twice as high as it is today.[32]

In sum, the typical middle-class family today has a higher living standard than a rich person in the 1950s when accounting for all the things they can afford to buy now that even the rich couldn't get fifty years ago. Your chances of surviving cancer or heart disease are multiples higher today than in the 1950s. What is that worth? For anyone who is black or for women, the gains have been extraordinary. In the 1950s most women were still confined to the drudgery of housework. Now women have career options that our grandmothers never would have dreamed of.

One last point. I started this analysis by asking: Should we divide the pie or grow it? The U.S. model for the past twenty-five years has been to grow the pie so that everyone gets a bigger piece—even if some people get way more than others. The Western European model—until very recent reforms—has been oriented toward fairness and equity, and making sure everyone gets pretty much an equal slice.

What has been the result? The United States has created 40 million jobs, while Europe, with more people, has created less than half that number. Average purchasing power in the United States today is much higher than that in almost all European nations. On

---

32. Statistical Abstract of the United States, 2008.

average the U.S. family earns about a dollar for every seventy-five cents earned by the French, Italians, and Germans.

When fairness is put ahead of economic growth, societies get less of both. And this is why the optimistic story of the past twenty-five years may be ending.

15

ECONOMIC FICTION IS
DRIVING FISCAL POLICIES

President Obama's tax priorities are attempting to reverse those policies that have focused on growing the pie for the benefit of all. The threat of creating higher tax rates for the so-called rich and using the proceeds to lower tax rates on middle- and lower-income earners or creating vast increases in new government programs for the benefit of middle- and lower-income earners looms. The taxes to be raised are the highest rates on the personal income tax, capital-gains tax, dividend tax, corporate income tax, and inheritance tax. In its simplest form, President Obama intends to allow President Bush's tax cuts to expire, thereby pushing the highest tax rates back up to where they were before Bush's tax cuts.[1]

The lessons from history show that progrowth policies raise economic growth, increase welfare for the rich and poor alike, and lead to growing tax revenues for the government. President Obama's policies that focus on the division of the pie rarely meet revenue expectations. As collateral damage, he will cause the poor to become poorer right along with the rich becoming poorer. Policies that focus on a more even distribution of income will bring

---

1. Under the sunset provisions of the Economic Growth and Tax Relief Reconciliation Act of 2001, the Jobs and Growth Tax Relief Reconciliation Act of 2003, and Tax Increase Prevention and Reconciliation Act of 2005, on January 1, 2011, the top marginal income-tax rate will increase from 35 percent to 39.6 percent, the top tax rate on dividends will rise from 15 percent to match tax rates on standard income, the top tax rate on capital gains will increase from 15 percent to 20 percent, and the top tax rate on inheritance will increase from 45 percent (and 0 percent in 2010) to 55 percent.

with it lower incomes for all.[2] We have reviewed the positive outcomes on the upside. This chapter reviews the negative outcomes on
the downside and then presents the evidence.

The Logic

Just as with our earlier discussion about capital-gains taxes, save
for sin taxes, where one of the benefits of a tax increase is an actual
diminution of the activity itself, there is no logic to raising a tax
rate if the actual revenues collected decline. If the tax rate is raised,
those people who engage in the activity are unambiguously worse
off and at the same time beneficiaries of government programs are
also worse off as a result of diminished tax revenues. No one with
good intentions would ever advocate such a tax increase if the facts
are as I described them.

All income earners in the highest income-tax bracket face the
highest income-tax rate as their marginal tax rate. It is this highest
marginal tax rate that influences the very highest-income earners'
decision whether to work more, invest more, move to a preferable
location, or engage the services of tax lawyers, accountants, and so
on. In some cases it could be this rate that pushes someone into illegal activities. In fact, back in the 1970s, the world-renowned liberal
Swedish economist and Nobel laureate Gunnar Myrdal bemoaned
the fact that the progressive income tax in his country had created such strong incentives as to turn normally law-abiding, rule-
following Swedes—especially those with high incomes—into tax
avoiders and, in some cases, even outright tax evaders, without redistributing income as was promised.[3]

---

2.   For a conceptual and empirical framework on this issue, see Arthur B. Laffer, "The Onslaught
from the Left, Part I: Fact vs. Fiction," Laffer Associates, October 31, 2007.
3.   See "Tax Policy in the Real World," ed. Joel Siemrod, Cambridge: University of Cambridge,
1999, p. 332. See also Gunnar Myrdal, "Time for a New Tax System," in *Ekonomisk Debatt* 6, November 1978, pp. 493–506.

Whatever the actual consequences, it is important to understand that people make their decisions based on their highest marginal tax rate, *not* their average or lowest tax rate. In the highest income-tax bracket everyone—100 percent of all income earners—faces the same marginal tax rate, which is the highest rate.

But the highest-income earners also pay the lowest bracket's and middle brackets' tax rates in addition to the highest tax rate. If you go back to your income tax return (Form 1040), you can see that for the first category of income your tax liability is based on the lowest tax rate, and then incrementally you add the tax liability from the second-lowest category of income and its tax rate, and so on until you come to the highest tax category, which is unbounded. For this last category, you take all your additional income above the sum of the incomes in all the lower categories and calculate your additional tax liability using the highest tax rate. If the lower tax rates are increased, higher-income earners will unambiguously pay more taxes, and if the lower tax rates are reduced, higher-income earners will for sure pay less. It's as simple as that.

The important point here is that while all people in the highest income category base their decisions on the highest tax rate, they too pay taxes in each and every lower-income category. For those people in the highest tax bracket, the tax rates applicable to the lower income-tax categories are what we economists call inframarginal tax rates and do not affect behavior. For high-income earners, changes in the tax rates applicable to lower income-tax brackets will have revenue consequences but no behavioral consequences.

From this it should be easy to see that as we go from the highest income category to the lowest income category, more and more people pay the lower category's marginal tax rate and yet their behavior is not influenced by this tax rate (Table 15-1). As a result, cutting lower income categories' tax rates will create greater and greater deadweight revenue losses for the government and yet will influence fewer and fewer people's decisions to increase the amount of taxable income through output responses.

Table 15-1 2005 Tax Filers by Tax Bracket

Highest Tax Rate	Number of Tax Returns	Percentage of All Filers Paying This Rate	Percentage of Filers Paying This Rate for Whom It Is the Marginal Rate
5%	1,186,478	100.00%	1.14%
8%	651	98.86%	0.00%
10%	25,508,822	98.86%	24.73%
15%	49,321,395	74.41%	63.54%
20%	2,960	27.13%	0.01%
25%	21,996,816	27.13%	77.72%
28%	3,730,002	6.04%	59.17%
33%	1,479,592	2.47%	57.48%
35%*	1,094,617	1.05%	100.00%

*This category also includes 141,612 tax returns of people who use Form 8615, which includes the Alternative Minimum Tax and the associated tax returns of people eighteen and under who pay tax rates in their parents' bracket.

Source: IRS, Statistics of Income.

Lowering the lowest bracket's tax rates, because there are no supply-side effects from people who are in higher tax brackets yet pay taxes at the lower rates, will unambiguously lower these people's tax payments and thus will reduce this portion of the tax receipts to the federal government. Cutting tax rates in ever-lower tax brackets will increasingly result in revenue losses without corresponding output responses, whereas raising tax rates in the highest tax bracket will result in universal negative taxable income responses.

People don't work to pay taxes; people work to earn what they can after tax. It's this very personal and private incentive that motivates people to give up leisure in order to work, change jobs, get more education, invest their capital, take risk, and so on. Likewise, people don't save to go bankrupt; they save to make an after-tax rate of return on their savings. It's the after-tax incentive that is instrumental in determining America's capital stock and the composition of our capital stock. With respect to the location of our capital stock, it is also true that businesses don't locate their plant facilities as a matter of social conscience. Businesses locate their plant facilities to make an after-tax rate of return for their shareholders.[4]

Again, in all these instances it's the marginal after-tax rate of return that determines people's behavior, not tax rates. Now, clearly marginal tax rates influence after-tax rates of return, but marginal tax rates are not the same as the after-tax rates of return. To illustrate what I'm driving at, I'll use an example of a time sufficiently far in the distant past that, while people will remember the events, the political passion has long since subsided.

When John F. Kennedy took office as president of the United States in January 1961, the highest federal marginal personal income-tax rate was 91 percent and the lowest federal marginal personal income-tax rate was 20 percent. As president, he proposed, among other things, to cut the highest tax rate from 91 percent to 70 percent and the lowest tax rate from 20 percent to 14 percent (see Figure 9-1). He succeeded. But seeing how these tax-rate cuts differentially affected after-tax incentives is crucial to understanding how taxes work today.

Cutting the highest tax rate from 91 percent to 70 percent represents a 23 percent cut in tax rates (21/91). If there were no supply-side responses, that is, if everyone earned the same after the tax cut as they had earned before the tax cut, this would have resulted in 23 percent less tax revenue to the government from the highest tax bracket.

Using the same logic, the cut in the lowest tax rate from 20 percent to 14 percent would have reduced tax receipts in that tax bracket by 30 percent (6/20) if there had been no supply-side responses. But of course, the whole purpose of cutting tax rates is to trigger supply-side responses.

In the highest tax bracket, the key to the supply-side response

---

4.   Arthur B. Laffer and Stephen Moore, *Rich States, Poor States: ALEC-Laffer State Economic Competitive Index*, The American Legislative Exchange Council, 2007, www.alec.org.

rests on after-tax incentives. If before Kennedy's tax cut a person in the highest tax bracket earned one additional dollar before tax, then he would have 91 cents in additional taxes and would be allowed to keep 9 cents. This 9 cents was the person's incentive for earning the additional dollar.

After Kennedy's tax cuts, however, if the same person earned the same additional dollar, instead of paying 91 cents in taxes, he would have to pay only 70 cents in taxes and would be allowed to keep 30 cents after tax instead of 9 cents. The person's incentive for earning that same additional dollar would have risen from 9 cents to 30 cents, or a 233 percent increase in incentives (21/9) for a 23 percent tax-rate reduction. This represents a 10:1 benefit-cost ratio (233/23) in the highest tax bracket.

In the lowest tax brackets, the incentive effects are very, very different than they are in the highest tax bracket. Not only are far fewer people working on the margin in the lowest tax bracket, but even for those who are on the margin, the incentive increases emanating from a tax-rate cut are a lot less than are the incentive increases in the highest tax bracket.

If a worker on the margin in the lowest tax bracket were to earn an additional dollar pretax, the additional tax liability would be 20 cents before Kennedy's tax cut and 14 cents after Kennedy's tax cut. The worker would have been able to keep 80 cents as an incentive before the tax cut and 86 cents after the tax cut. This represents a 7.5 percent increase in incentives (6/80) for a 30 percent cut in tax rates, even if we assume everyone in the lowest tax bracket were working on the margin—which they aren't. This is a 1:4 benefit-cost ratio (7.5/30).

When you compare the 10:1 benefit-cost ratio of a tax cut in the highest tax bracket to the 1:4 benefit-cost ratio in the lowest tax bracket, it elevates the supply-side incentive effect to its stark reality. Using these figures, there was a fortyfold increase in incentives in the highest tax bracket versus the lowest tax bracket per dollar of static revenue loss when Kennedy cut tax rates.

Clearly, using just federal personal income-tax rates today, the extreme results of the example used above for President Kennedy's tax cut would be greatly weakened. But don't delude yourself into thinking the differences are negligible today just because they may not be as large as they were in the early 1960s. The principle is still the same: the lower tax rates are, the less will be the incentive effect for any given tax rate change.

As we will see later, the actual taxes paid by the highest-tax-bracket filers are rarely held hostage to the highest tax rate (see Figure 15-2). The highest-bracket tax filers have deductions, exemptions, exclusions, and all sorts of other methods available to them to pay far lower rates on average. Yet in spite of all these loopholes, the rich still paid a lot more taxes after Kennedy's tax cut, and they pay more now as well.

Today in our tax codes we have lots and lots of other impediments in addition to income taxes that affect the benefit-cost ratios for cutting tax rates in the various tax brackets. Compared to the Kennedy era, we have very different payroll taxes, state and local taxes, sales taxes, earned-income tax credits, and so on. It is still true that for every dollar of static revenue change there is a much larger incentive effect in the highest tax bracket than in the lowest tax bracket. Again you can see why on a conceptual level I question the fiscal wisdom of cutting tax rates in the lower income categories while raising tax rates on higher income categories. The supply-side responses in the higher income categories should be far greater than the responses in the lower income categories. The result would be a huge decrease in tax revenues and huge increase in the budget deficit. For output, employment, and production purposes—as well as for helping the poor—the answer is a true flat tax.

The U.S. Income-Tax-Return Data—Taxing the Rich

Over the past quarter century, we have witnessed enormous shifts in the composition and volume of income-tax payments by the highest-income earners. In the year Ronald Reagan took office (1981) the top 1 percent of income earners as reflected by the Adjusted Gross Income of all tax filers paid 17.58 percent of all federal income taxes.[5] Twenty-five years later, in 2005, the top 1 percent paid 39.38 percent of all income taxes, representing a more than doubling of the share of tax payments made by this group.

But even more to the point, from 1981 to 2005 the income taxes paid by the top 1 percent rose from 1.59 percent of GDP to 2.96 percent of GDP (see Figure 15-1). In addition to the huge rise in the percentage of GDP paid in income taxes by the top 1 percent of income earners and the more than doubling of the share of taxes paid by this group there was the huge absolute increase in real taxes (2005 dollars using the GDP price deflator) from 1981 through 2005. In 1981, total tax payments from the richest 1 percent were $94.84 billion, while in 2005 the top 1 percent paid $368.13 billion in income taxes; that's a 288 percent increase in twenty-five years. In rough numbers, that means that each of the richest 1 percent of filers in 1981 paid a little over $100,000 in 2005 dollars, while in 2005 each filer on average paid over $288,000. And remember, that's inflation-adjusted dollars.

In the year 2000 this teeny, tiny group of only 1 percent of all taxpayers actually paid income taxes equal to 3.75 percent of GDP, which is why President Clinton had a budget surplus. Much of this huge surge in tax payments by the top 1 percent of tax filers resulted from the huge increase in capital gains resulting from President Clinton's reducing the federal capital-gains tax rate from 28 percent to 20 percent in 1997 (see Figure 15-2). He also effectively elimi-

---

5.   Tax Foundation Tables 1–7, IRS, Statistics of Income.

nated the capital-gains tax on owner-occupied homes. But more on this later.

Let's take a look at the bottom 75 percent of taxpayers over this same time period. This has to be the group which the current Democrats refer to as middle- and lower-income earners. From 1981 through 2005, the bottom 75 percent of all income earners as reported on the individual income-tax returns went from 27.71 percent of all income taxes paid to 14.01 percent in 2005. Yes, that's 75 percent of all taxpayers save the top 25 percent. As a share of GDP, total taxes paid by the bottom 75 percent of all taxpayers fell from 2.50 percent of GDP in 1981 to 1.05 percent of GDP in 2005. The bottom 75 percent of all taxpayers today pay less than 35 percent of all the taxes paid by the top 1 percent of all income earners. This is the very group the Democrats are targeting for tax cuts. Over the last twenty-five years, the bottom 75 percent of all taxpayers' tax payments fell and their tax rates fell. Guess what will happen if they lower these tax rates further?

Figure 15-1 **Income Taxes Paid as a Percentage of GDP:**
Top 1%, Top 2–5%, Top 6–25%, Bottom 75%

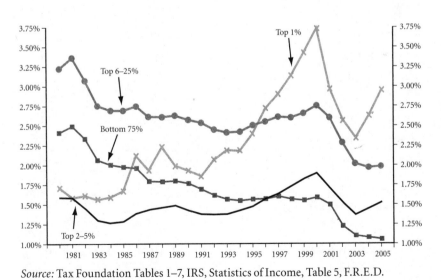

Source: Tax Foundation Tables 1–7, IRS, Statistics of Income, Table 5, F.R.E.D.

159

The important point here is that over the last twenty-five-plus years the only group that experienced an increase in income taxes paid as a share of GDP was the top 1 percent of income earners. Even the top 2 to 5 percent of income earners saw a decline in the GDP share of their income taxes paid. It is amazing. But this is only the beginning of the story.

The second part of this story is juicy. Since 1980, statutory marginal personal income-tax rates have fallen dramatically. The highest marginal income-tax rate has fallen from 70 percent in 1980 to 35 percent today, with a low of 28 percent resulting from the 1986 tax reform act. This 28 percent highest tax rate lasted until Presidents Bush Sr. and Clinton raised it in 1991 and then again in 1993. In Figure 15-2 I have plotted the highest federal marginal income-tax rate from 1980 through 2005.

Figure 15-2 Top Marginal, Average, and Effective Individual Income Tax Rates for the Top 1%, 1980–2005

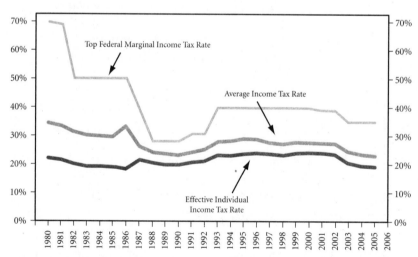

Source: Tax Foundation Table 1-7. IRS Statistics of Income Table 5, Table A. CBO, "Historical Effective Tax Rates 1979–2005," Table 1A.

To show the actual tax impact from cutting marginal income-tax rates, I have also plotted the average income-tax rate for the top

1 percent of income earners, which consists of total taxes paid by the top 1 percent of income earners divided by their total adjusted gross income as reported on their income-tax returns. There is a significant drop in this average tax rate from 1979 until about 1987 and then the average tax rate of the richest 1 percent of taxpayers levels off, rising slightly in the 1991–93 period and falling back again in the 2001–5 period.

While it would be tempting to attribute the sharp fall in the average tax rate of that top 1 percent of taxpayers to the enormous drop in the highest marginal statutory tax rate, in truth much of the answer is really a lot simpler: The definition of adjusted gross income changed over this period. To quote from the Treasury Department:

> The most significant revisions came in the Tax Reform Act of 1986 (TRA86). Among these were the full inclusion of long-term capital gains (previously, 40% was included in the AGI, and before 1979, 50% had been included). TRA86 also imposed limits on "passive losses" that would be allowed in calculating AGI. It changed moving expenses and unreimbursed employee business expenses from income "adjustments" to itemized deductions. (Starting in 1994, moving expenses were again allowed as an adjustment to income instead of as an itemized deduction.) It eliminated the adjustment to income for a married couple with a second earner and the exemption for the first $400 of dividends received. Working to narrow the definition of AGI, it allowed self-employed individuals a deduction for up to 25 percent of their health insurance premiums.[6]

But now we get to the secret sauce and the essence of what really happens in the realm of tax rates, incomes, and tax payments by

---

6.   Susan C. Nelson, "Adjusted Gross Income," Department of the Treasury, http://www.urban .org/UploadedPDF/1000514.pdf.

the rich. The Congressional Budget Office calculates "effective individual income-tax rates" by dividing the total tax payments by the comprehensive household incomes of the top 1 percent of tax filers. Because this concept is so important and is also so correct, we quote directly from the CBO:

> *Comprehensive household income equals pretax cash income plus income from other sources. Pretax cash income is the sum of wages, salaries, self-employment income, rents, taxable and nontaxable interest, dividends, realized capital gains, cash transfer payments, and retirement benefits plus taxes paid by businesses (corporate income taxes and the employer's share of Social Security, Medicare, and federal unemployment insurance payroll taxes) and employee contributions to 401 (k) retirement plans. Other sources of income include all in-kind benefits (Medicare, Medicaid, employer-paid health insurance premiums, food stamps, school lunches and breakfasts, housing assistance and energy assistance).[7]*

Now, we have accurate data on both total taxes paid by the top 1 percent of income earners and their comprehensive household income. From these two data series we can calculate the effective individual income-tax rate for the top 1 percent of all income earners (see Figure 15-3).

Surprise, surprise, the effective individual income-tax rate for the top 1 percent of income earners barely wiggles as Congress changes the tax codes repeatedly and the economy goes from boom to bust and back again. The question is, how can that effective individual income-tax rate be so stable? The answer is simply that the very highest-income earners are and have always been able to vary

---

7.   "Historical Effective Federal Tax Rates: 1979 to 2005," Congressional Budget Office, http://www.cbo.gov/ftpdoc.cfm?index=8885&TYPE=2.

their reported income and thus control the amount of taxes they pay. Whether through tax shelters, deferrals, gifts, write-offs, cross-income mobility, or any of a number of other measures, the effective individual income-tax rate barely budges. But this group's total tax payments are incredibly volatile.

Figure 15-3 Change in Comprehensive Household Income vs. Change in the Effective Individual Income Tax Rate for the Top 1% of Income Earners

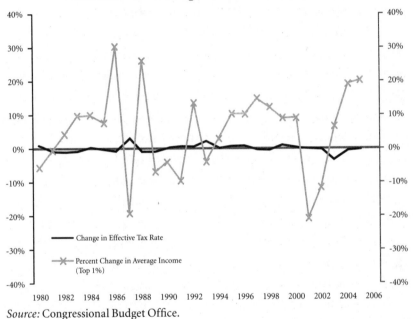

Source: Congressional Budget Office.

The only conclusion one can come to is that if statutory tax rates on the rich are raised, as proposed by President Obama, the effective individual income tax rate won't change, but the comprehensive household income earned by this group will fall, thus resulting in a sharp decline in tax receipts from the very highest-income earners. If you want to get more tax revenues from the rich, you've got to make the rich richer, and to make the rich richer, you've got to lower tax rates.

Now let's take a look at the bottom 75 percent of income earners.

Using the same measures as we did for the top 1 percent of income earners, we quickly learn that the rich are not at all like the rest of us. As we saw in Figure 15-1, the share of total taxes paid by the bottom 75 percent of income earners fell from 2.5 percent of GDP in 1981 to slightly over 1 percent of GDP in 2005.

As a share of total tax payments, the bottom 75 percent went from 27.71 percent of all income taxes paid in 1981 to 14.01 percent in 2005. But if you look at legislated statutory tax rates on the middle- and lower-income earners, they, too, have been reduced quite dramatically over the past quarter century.

In Figure 15-4, I use both the bottom 75 percent and the bottom 80 percent as our measure of the middle- and lower-class income earners. The reason for this switch is that the Congressional Budget Office uses quintiles whereas the Statistics of Income of the IRS uses quartiles. In this illustration I plot the effective individual income-tax rate for the bottom 80 percent all income earners. This number represents all taxes paid by the bottom 80 percent of income earners divided by their comprehensive household income as described by the Congressional Budget Office. As is apparent from these data, the effective individual income-tax rate of the bottom 80 percent of tax filers—that's the bottom 80 percent—has gone from 8.1 percent in 1981 to 2.8 percent in 2005. It's hard to get much money from these people when the effective tax rate is almost zero. As a result, the share of individual tax liabilities of this group is 13.7 percent of all income-tax liabilities in 2005, down from 36.1 percent in 1981.

Putting it all together, there is no way from here to Sunday that lowering tax rates on middle- and lower-income earners will do anything other than lose revenue. Lowering these already low tax rates will lower revenues from the lower- and middle-income tax filers and will also lower tax revenues from the highest-income earners.

Raising tax rates on the very highest-income earners will also lower tax revenue. No amount of wishing or hoping will change this. Based on tax-return data, President Obama's tax plan will lead to a fiscal catastrophe. We need a true flat tax devoid of class warfare rhetoric.

Figure 15-4 **Average Tax Rate and Effective Individual Income-Tax Rate of Middle- and Lower-Income Earners**

(annual, through 2005)

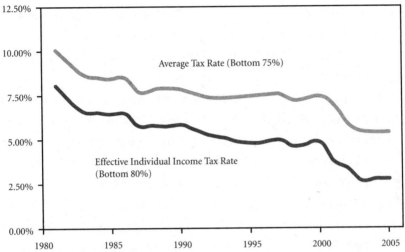

Source: Tax Foundation Table 1-7. IRS Statistics of Income Table 5, Table A. CBO, "Historical Effective Tax Rates 1979–2005," Table 1A.

The Corporate and Business Income Tax

In my view there are few taxes as counterproductive as the corporate income or profits tax. Just on a conceptual level it makes no sense whatsoever. With a personal income tax, a capital gains tax, and the gift and estate tax one can, incorrectly I believe, make the argument that the taxes are coming from those with the greatest ability to pay—the so-called rich. But when it comes to corporations, redistributing income from the rich to bail out the poor is nonsensical. Corporations and businesses aren't people. People own businesses.

It is just as likely that low-income shareholders such as pensioners own businesses with high profits that pay a lot in taxes while multi-millionaires own businesses that have losses due to deductions, tax credits, and corporate welfare. Taxing profits on a progressive basis

165

really doesn't even pretend to address income maldistribution. But it does have huge misallocation effects.

Imagine a company today that cherishes our precious natural resources by manufacturing products in an extremely cost-effective manner. This company has very tight inventory controls and purchasing standards and therefore buys only the amount of raw materials it actually needs to produce the products it sells. It has minimal waste.

The labor it uses is also kept to a bare minimum, raising the firm's productivity to the highest level possible. Employees and products are inventoried and controlled over time to have the least amount of hiring and firing and unwarranted separation and training costs or employee ill will. The firm also has the most up-to-date capital stock for the highest levels of efficiencies and it plans its shipping, distribution, and sales channels as precisely as possible. In point of fact, this is the most efficient, well-run firm imaginable.

In keeping with its focus on production efficiency, also imagine that this firm manufactures a product people really need and want. By satisfying a real need in a cost-effective manner this firm makes lots and lots of profit. Now, what does our government do? It taxes the stuffing out of this company at the highest rates allowable.

Now imagine another company that squanders our precious natural resources. It wastes people's time, has inefficient, out-of-date capital, and runs its operations sloppily with tons of waste in every operation. It markets its products poorly and distributes those products it actually sells inefficiently. And as a pièce de résistance, the product it makes really sucks. This company loses gobs and gobs of money.

What, pray tell, do you think happens to this company? Its employees get lots of unemployment and welfare benefits and the company itself not only doesn't pay taxes, it gets bailout funds and government support. I can think of no example more apropos than General Motors. This type of economics is crazy.

My flat tax will tax all companies based upon their use of our natural resources (value added) at a single flat rate from the first dollar to the last. Poorly run companies won't be helped or hindered in their life-and-death struggles with well-run companies. Adam Smith's invisible hand will be able to operate unfettered.

In addition to the obvious efficiency outlined above, businesses will finally start to collect an appropriate amount of tax receipts. While businesses don't pay taxes, they do collect taxes.[8] Over the past fifty years businesses' share of total taxes has steadily declined (see Figure 15-5).

My flat tax will bring businesses' collected taxes back up to about half of all federal tax receipts, thus allowing a major reduction in overall tax collections from individuals. Businesses are much better at collecting money than people are.

Figure 15-5 Taxes Paid by Businesses as a % of Total Tax Receipts
(annual, through 2008)

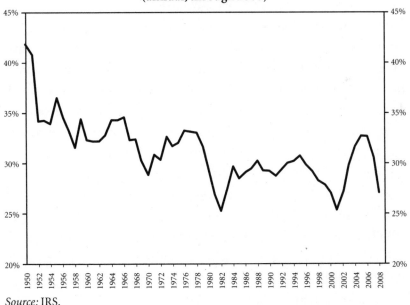

Source: IRS.

---

8.   While businesses do technically pay taxes, they are legal entities which do not bear the burden of the tax. Instead people do in the form of higher prices, lower wages, and lower returns for shareholders.

16

RIGHTING OUR ECONOMIC COURSE— THE COMPLETE FLAT TAX

During prosperous times, life is relatively easy in Washington, D.C., as high levels of economic activity result in abundant tax revenues and spending that often grows unrestrained with few consequences; it is during the bad times that flaws are exposed. Bad times expose fiscal flaws, spending flaws, and flaws in the tax codes. The current difficulty is simply another example of the challenging budget times that inevitably result from the current fiscal policy.

As discussed above, President Obama is making the classic mistake in response to our challenging budget situation. While there is truly never a good time to raise taxes, raising taxes during difficult times is especially bad. Tax increases serve only to worsen economic downturns. When taxes are raised while the economy is depressed, employers and employees face additional impediments. It makes no sense to raise taxes on the last three people working. People don't work to pay taxes, nor do businesses locate their plant facilities as a matter of social conscience. People work to earn what they can after tax—after all taxes. During tough times after-tax earnings are depressed naturally, which is why unemployment rates are so high. Piling on more taxes only exacerbates the problem.

President Obama's tax increases will cause the U.S. economy to experience slower income growth, stagnant job growth, higher rates of unemployment, and slower real tax-revenue growth for federal, state, and local governments. Additionally, there will be fewer entrepreneurial innovations—be these life-saving medical innovations or life-enhancing technologies such as DVRs and cell phones—that increase our overall quality of life.

Raising tax rates, especially during difficult times when tax increases are most frequently considered, virtually always results in forecast revenues that exceed the revenues that actually materialize. Cutting tax rates does the opposite. Static revenue estimates always assume that no one's behavior will change, and therefore a 10 percent tax increase will increase tax revenues 10 percent. In fact, this is never true. The dynamic effects of slower growth, reduced profitability, higher unemployment (and its associated costs), and tax evasion and avoidance, just to name a few, combine to ensure that actual revenues fall short of forecasted revenues.

The premise of this book is that these outcomes are not inevitable. The path to a more prosperous future begins by correcting the recent, as well as longer-standing, fiscal policy mistakes we have been committing.

My tax proposal is for the federal government to implement a true economic flat-rate tax that replaces the major federal taxes currently in effect. The flat-rate tax would eliminate the inefficiencies and perverse incentives described earlier. No longer would the choice be between spending it in Vegas and dying paying taxes—the estate tax would be gone. The proposal would end the inefficiencies of the current capital-gains taxes and the myriad other tax distortions reducing our nation's economic growth potential. The proposal would also remove economically irrational tax shelters such as unrealized capital gains, the deductibility of state and local taxes, the deductibility of interest on future municipal debt, and the income earned by tax-exempt organizations.

An example I've used to illustrate the logic of a true flat tax is that if a dog is beaten, no one knows where the dog will run, but if a dog is fed we know exactly where the dog will be—where it got the food. Negative incentives tell people what not to do, while positive incentives tell people what to do.

Taxes are negative incentives. They tell people not to report taxable income. Negative incentives don't tell people how to avoid reporting taxable income. The tax doesn't care whether people use deductions, exemptions, or exclusions, change locations, avoid or evade or even go out of business. The simple message of a tax is: Don't report taxable income.

On the other hand, government spending creates positive incentives and signals what should be done.

Therefore the best tax is one that has the lowest possible tax rate on the largest tax base. The lowest rate creates the least incentive to evade, avoid, or otherwise not report taxable income, while the broadest tax base provides the minimum number of places to which people can escape from reporting taxable income. My flat tax does exactly this.

My proposal improves our nation's tax system by broadening the tax base and significantly lowering marginal tax rates. Combining the largest possible tax base with the lowest possible tax rate provides people the smallest opportunity to avoid paying taxes and the lowest incentive to do so. Reduced incentives to avoid or evade taxes result in a reduction in the associated costs of monitoring these activities. In addition, lower tax rates go hand in hand with greater incentives to work and produce.

The proposal, however, recognizes that government should share in the rewards of this gain in efficiency. Hence, the tax rate is set so as to allow average tax rates to fall as existing depreciation and other grandfathered provisions under the existing tax law dissipate with the passage of time. This proposal, then, is a quintessential political document as well. It combines good economics with good politics, making it a forerunner of good public policy.[1]

A tax system—such as a flat single-rate tax system without deductions—that avoids excessive revenues during good times

---

1.   For those of you who remember the Democratic primary in 1992, my proposal is virtually identical to Jerry Brown's 13 percent flat-tax proposal.

will not create a temptation to build up expensive spending programs that in turn will be unaffordable during tough times. It is the volatility of spending, whereby spending actually is cut during bad times, that causes so much hardship among those most vulnerable. A flat tax with modest rainy-day provisions may well be the most moral tax structure as well as the most productive tax structure.

To summarize the strengths of this proposal, let's review the flat tax in light of the properties of the ideal tax code described earlier. These were:

1. **Fosters economic growth:** The reduction of marginal tax rates coupled with the broadening of the tax base will minimize many of the distortions that make the current tax system counterproductive. All taxes are bad, but some are worse than others. This complete flat tax chooses the least bad of the lot. The economy would undergo substantial expansion, resulting in a higher standard of living for the average American and an increase in revenues for federal, state, and local governments.

2. **Reduces income volatility:** The current progressivity of the U.S. tax code showers riches on the government during periods of prosperity, which are often spent. Then when the downturn comes, federal revenues are hit disproportionately because of the loss of high-income earners. Yet since budgets are much easier to expand than to contract, the revenue shortfalls lead to massive deficits. To close the gap, the "solution" all too often is to hike taxes even more, which serves to further discourage employment and output—and hence shrinks the tax base. Because of the dynamic effects (as illustrated by the Laffer Curve), the tax hikes don't raise as much revenue as predicted, and thus budget deficits persist. At the same time, welfare rolls and other support programs expand because of rising unemployment. The flat tax ends this excessive boom-

bust cycle—the proportion of revenues raised by the government does not rise during periods of prosperity or fall during economic contractions. From the day the flat tax is enacted, the federal government will get a more stable revenue stream from year to year.

3. **Is simple and efficient with low compliance costs:** The straightforward calculation of the tax base and the application of a single tax rate simplifies the entire tax system. By reducing the sources of revenue with a single tax rate, one ensures that everyone knows exactly what taxes are in effect. Tax returns could then be filed on a single-page form.

4. **Increases fairness:** Every taxpayer will pay the same tax rate. A single tax applies equally to all sources of income and does not change as a result of the taxpayer's volume of income. Due to the fact that payroll taxes are folded into this proposal, low- and modest-income earners will have their taxes reduced considerably.

5. **Provides the requisite tax revenue at low cost:** By eliminating the major federal taxes and replacing them with the single flat rate on the broadened tax base, one ensures revenues for the appropriate level of all federal government spending.

6. **Is flexible and can adjust to changing needs:** Almost without exception, the federal government underestimates revenues during good times and overestimates revenues during bad times. As a result of overestimating revenues during bad times, politicians believe their fiscal circumstances are not as bad as they actually are, leading to spending above and beyond revenues or delays in implementing spending cuts when they are desperately needed. Then, when deficits later appear, Congress often turns to higher taxes, which in turn result in

deeper declines in the economy, revenues again falling short of expectations, and a continuation of the spend-and-tax cycle. The simplicity of the flat tax and broad definitions of income ensure that the flat tax will end the spend-and-tax cycle and promote economic growth and revenue stability regardless of our economy's evolution.

The Theory Behind the Flat-Rate Tax

Excessive taxation is detrimental to labor and capital, poor and rich, men and women, old and young. Excessive taxation is an equal-opportunity tormentor. Businesses locate their plant facilities in order to make higher after-tax returns for their owners. In the short run, higher taxes on labor or capital lower after-tax earnings. During depressed times, businesses often are desperate to reduce costs because of a shortfall in revenues. Increased taxes in one location can be the final straw leading to businesses' relocating to more tax-friendly locations or making the ultimate decision to close down operations. In the longer run, immobile factors (such as low-wage workers and commercial and residential real estate) are left to suffer the tax burden.

The mode of taxation is as important as the amount of taxation, as noted by nineteenth-century American economist Henry George:

> *The mode of taxation is, in fact, quite as important as the amount. As a small burden badly placed may distress a horse that could carry with ease a much larger one properly adjusted, so a people may be impoverished and their power of producing wealth destroyed by taxation, which, if levied in any other way, could be borne with ease.*[2]

---

2.   Henry George, *Progress and Poverty*, 1879.

The theory of incentives provides the basis for the concept of a flat-rate tax, which is so called because a single tax applies equally to all sources of income and does not change as a result of the tax-payer's volume of income. Any exemptions, deductions, differential rates, or progressivity would, as a matter of linguistics, preclude the name flat tax. They also represent a deviation from the principles of efficient taxation. Such exemptions to the even application of a single tax narrow the tax base, lead to a higher tax rate, make for greater complexity, and increase tax avoidance.

Incentives can be either positive or negative. They are alternately described as carrots and sticks or pleasure and pain. Whatever their form, people seek positive incentives and avoid negative incentives. The principle is simple enough: If an activity should be shunned, a negative incentive is appropriate and vice versa.

In the realm of economics, taxes are negative incentives and government spending entails positive incentives, subject to all the subtleties and intricacies of the general theory of incentives. People attempt to avoid taxed activities—the higher the tax, the greater their attempt to avoid. As with all negative incentives, no one can be sure how the avoidance will be carried out.

Raising tax revenues is far from cost-free. Obviously, when tax rates on an activity are raised, the volume of that activity shrinks, leading to a revenue offset. There are also substantial collection costs to both the government and the taxpayer from raising taxes, which result in less money being collected than is paid. To the extent taxpayers seek to avoid, evade, or otherwise shelter and hide their taxable income, the amount of additional revenues is also greatly reduced and can, in fact, end up costing the government money directly as a consequence of raising taxes. Capital flight and labor flight, along with companies' going out of business, are classic responses to increased taxation.

If raising taxes actually were to improve the government's fiscal circumstances, it would do so by worsening the fiscal circumstances of those it governs. No phrase is more important for government to adhere to than *primum non nocere* (first do no harm). It makes no sense to balance the government's budget by unbalancing its citizens' budgets.

A flat tax eliminates much of the inefficiency in a convoluted tax system by broadening the tax base and sharply reducing marginal tax rates. Many of the distortions that exist with the current tax system are minimized. A flat-rate tax reduces the collection cost per dollar of tax revenue and eliminates much of the bureaucracy necessary to monitor and enforce numerous taxes. Its adoption leads to a surge in growth and creates a more competitive economy.

Changes to marginal tax rates are critical for growth because they change incentives to demand, and to supply, work effort, and capital. Firms base their decisions to employ workers, in part, on the workers' total cost to the firm. Holding all else equal, the greater the cost to the firm of employing each additional worker, the fewer workers the firm will employ. Conversely, the lower the marginal cost per worker, the more workers the firm will hire. For the firm, the decision to employ is based upon gross wages paid, a concept that encompasses all costs borne by the firm.

Workers, on the other hand, care little about the cost to the firm of employing them. Of concern from a worker's standpoint is how much the worker receives for providing work effort, net of all deductions and taxes. Workers concentrate on net wages received. The greater net wages received, the more willing a worker is to work. If wages received fall, workers find work effort less attractive and they will do less of it.

The difference between what it costs a firm to employ a worker and what that worker receives net is the tax wedge. A tax wedge separates effort from reward. It is intrinsically an economic variable that operates at the margin where incentives come into play and the decisions are made to, say, allocate capital between one project or industry and another. In this case, there is a separation between the incentives of the worker and the firm creating lost economic opportunities—potential gains to both firm and worker are lost.

A marginal tax-rate cut—ideally to a flat rate—has two types of effects. Because the decrease in marginal tax rates lowers the cost to the employer in the form of lower wages paid, firms will employ more workers. On the supply side, a reduction in marginal tax rates raises net wages received. Again, more work effort will be supplied. Therefore, tax cuts increase the demand for, and the supply of, factors of production. In dynamic formulations, as tax rates fall, output growth increases and vice versa.

Under a flat-rate tax, average tax rates will remain approximately constant for a given level of income or output. However, the rewards for incremental work by labor, the employment of additional capital, and the more efficient combination of the two will all be higher with the flat tax. As a result, more employment, output, and production are expected. Economic growth rates will accelerate until these effects are fully incorporated into the workings of the economy.

Theory Put into Practice

The tax base for both individuals and businesses has been eroded over the decades by the enactment of numerous exemptions, exclusions, and deductions. In addition, a profusion of tax credits has served to reduce the effective tax rate paid by some taxpayers on this already-reduced tax base while doing nothing to reduce the tax burden on individuals or businesses who are otherwise in identical economic circumstances. Such credits have reduced the government's tax receipts and the average tax rate while leaving marginal tax rates unchanged. In short, tax credits in virtually all forms are counterproductive.

In the realm of federal taxation, three taxes account for the bulk of revenues; personal income taxes, corporate profits taxes, and federal payroll taxes.

In recent politics, most attention has been paid to the current state of disarray of the personal-income tax. It is widely recognized that in spite of the statutory progressivity of the tax codes, deductions, exemptions, and exclusions of all sorts have rendered the actual income tax neither fair nor efficient. The superwealthy don't pay their fair share of taxes. The legislative process has made available tax shelters, deferrals, and various other tax-avoidance schemes to those with access to fancy accountants and high-priced lawyers. People struggling to become wealthy who can neither afford nor obtain access to such inequitable devices pay taxes after taxes, rarely getting the rewards they deserve. The current income tax does not redistribute income and would be more appropriately designated a lawyer's and accountant's employment act.

In today's economy, the personal income tax is not alone in its failure to serve its appointed task. The corporate-profits tax also has become a farce. Lobbyists have seduced a solicitous Congress time and again to substitute nonsense for common sense. Businesses that make highly desirable products and conserve our precious natural resources without adhering to the dictates of sophisticated tax counsel are taxed at incredibly onerous rates. If, on the other hand, a business squanders resources, makes a lousy product, retains gilded lobbyists and tax lawyers, and reports horrendous losses, it stands a good chance of qualifying for government subsidies and most assuredly doesn't pay for the government it uses. Just think of the recent Obama administration policies of bailing out General Motors, Chrysler, AIG, and others.

Equally flawed are Social Security (OASDHI) payroll taxes. These taxes are notoriously regressive and yet account for $900 billion in revenues and unmeasured lost opportunities. "Unearned income" is not subject to the payroll tax, nor in 2009 are annual incomes in excess of $106,800 for the Social Security portion of the payroll tax (12.4 percent)—there is no income limit for the Medicare portion of the payroll tax (2.9 percent). Any reform of the overall tax structure must redress the inequities of the payroll tax.

These three tax sources alone account for about 93 percent of total federal revenues (see Table 16-1). Therefore, any flat-rate tax proposal should incorporate all three forms of taxation.

Table 16-1 Tax Receipts by Major Category
(fiscal year 2008)

	Revenue (millions)	Percent of Total Revenue
Individual Income Taxes*	$1,145,747	45.4%
Corporate Income Taxes	304,346	12.1%
Old-Age Survivors, Disability and Health Insurance (OASDHI)	900,155	35.7%
Total Income and Federal Payroll Taxes	**$2,350,248**	**93.1%**
Estate and Gift Taxes	28,844	1.1%
Other Taxes and Budget Receipts	145,234	5.8%
Total Budget Receipts	**$2,524,326**	**100.0%**

*The latest estimate for capital-gains tax revenues (a subset of individual income-tax revenues) is 2006. In 2006, capital-gains taxes raised an estimated $117.8 billion. This was 11.3 percent of individual income tax revenues and 4.9 percent of total tax revenues.

Source: Department of the Treasury.

Adding to the list of ill-conceived and poorly executed taxes would be inheritance taxes, excess-profits taxes, and numerous others. Today, a summary of federal budget receipts requires page after page of entries in ever-smaller type to catalogue myriad specific taxes. In total, many of these taxes raise little revenue. Their cost to the economy in terms of recordkeeping and collection represents an unnecessary burden. In general, all these taxes should be eliminated forthwith.

Judicial fees, railroad and federal retirement funds, and the like, however, are revenues associated with the provision of a specific good or service to the payee. They are more analogous to a payment for a specific, identifiable service than to a tax and as such should be retained. Customs duties, which are an arcane code unto themselves involving international relations, fall outside the purview of this proposal. Yet even they should be considered in conjunction with the overall tax code.

The unemployment system, which varies from state to state in terms of both benefits and tax rates and also because of its state-specific nature, should be left intact in any purely federal tax reform. As a matter of practice, states, more often than not, use the federal tax codes as the starting point for developing their own statutes, so any federal tax reform will, perforce, lead to numerous state reforms.

Excise taxes on alcoholic beverages, tobacco products, firearms and munitions, as well as federal fines, other penalties, and the like, also should be retained. It must be presumed that Congress, when it passed these specific taxes, did so with the intent of discouraging the taxed activity rather than raising revenue. These are the so-called sin taxes.

One last major source of revenue is the Federal Reserve Bank. Because the Federal Reserve requires banks to hold low-interest-bearing deposits at Federal Reserve Banks, and then lends these funds at market rates of interest, the central bank's profits are absolutely enormous. What the Federal Reserve Bank doesn't spend it turns over to the Treasury. These policies are an integral part of monetary policy and, thus, are not included in this proposal. Because the Federal Reserve is in effect a public company, its expenses should be carefully scrutinized to make sure it serves the public and not special interests.

One last tax—a carbon-emissions tax—is discussed in detail in Chapter 18.

In total, the above categories designated as being outside the purview of a flat-rate tax base contributed $138.9 billion in federal revenues during fiscal year 2008 (Table 16-2).

Table 16-2 Revenue Categories Maintained

Classification	FY 2008 Revenues (millions)
Railroad Retirement Accounts	$4,443
Unemployment Insurance	39,527
Federal Employees' Retirement Contribution	4,125
Civil Service Retirement and Disability Fund	44
Excise Taxes:	
Federal Alcohol Tax	9,283
Federal Tobacco Tax	7,639
Other (Firearms, Motorboat Fuels,	
Miscellaneous Funds, etc.)	1,860
Customs Duties	27,568
Miscellaneous Receipts	44,384
Total Budget Revenues Maintained	**$138,873**

As part of an overall tax-simplification tax reform, all other taxes and sources of budgetary revenues should be repealed. These taxes are summarized in Table 16-3.

Table 16-3 Taxes to Be Repealed

	FY 2008 Revenues (millions)
Individual Income Taxes	$1,145,747
Corporate Income Taxes	304,346
Federal Payroll Taxes Old-Age Survivors, Disability, and Health Insurance	<u>900,155</u>
Total Income and Payroll Taxes Repealed	**$2,350,248**
Gift and Estate Taxes	28,844
Selected Excise and Other Taxes	<u>6,361</u>
Total Other Taxes Repealed	**<u>$2,429,366</u>**

To repeat, the complete flat tax eliminates all but a small number of federal taxes. Included among the taxes replaced are the personal income tax, corporate income tax, Social Security (OASDHI) payroll tax, and estate and gift taxes, as well as some lesser taxes.

In their stead would be two flat-rate taxes of equal rates: a flat-rate personal income tax and a flat-rate business value-added tax. With a minimum amount of deductions, a tax rate of 13.0 percent would immediately produce more revenue than all the excluded taxes and, in short order, would produce substantially higher revenues even without a Laffer Curve effect. Additionally, there would be increased revenues due to the Laffer Curve effect itself.

One real problem in our current tax code that desperately needs to be addressed encompasses true forms of income that are not taxed at all. One such untaxed form of income is unrealized capital gains. In fact, I outlined exactly how this form of income quite literally escapes taxation using the example of Warren Buffett.

The easiest way to rectify our failure to correctly tax unrealized capital gains is to require all increases in unrealized capital gains to be reported and taxed. Obviously, once taxed, the basis for the assets should be increased to allow for the taxed portion of the unrealized gains.

This taxation of unrealized capital gains needs to be analyzed carefully to avoid imposing undue burdens on people who can't or shouldn't sell all or part of their assets to acquire the liquidity to pay the tax. Unrealized capital losses should, like unrealized capital gains, be calculated as part of the tax base as well and be a deduction from the tax base. Some sort of five-year averaging process may well suffice to smooth sharp swings in taxable income and liquidity considerations.

A very nice benefit of taxing unrealized capital gains would be the removal of the locked-in effect that discourages asset holders from selling assets with untaxed unrealized capital gains. Our capital markets would function far more smoothly and our tax codes would be a lot fairer and simpler.

The potential addition to the U.S. tax base from taxing unrealized capital gains is enormous. According to the Federal Reserve, U.S. households and nonprofits owned $66 trillion in assets in 2008.[3] This is a reduction in total household assets from 2007 of nearly $11 trillion. Yet, even in these unprecedented times, taxing unrealized capital gains using a five-year averaging process is feasible.

Table 16-4 presents the rolling average annual change in the nominal value of assets over a five-year period held by households and nonprofits in the United States compared to realized capital gains over the same period.[4] Table 16-4 shows that the increase in the five-year moving average value of assets increases by around $2 trillion to $5.5 trillion a year while taxpayers realize only about 14 percent of the value of these assets. This leaves approximately $1.5 trillion to $5.0 trillion worth of unrealized capital gains that could be added to the annual tax base. Certainly, this tax base varies over time, with the current period being a particularly difficult time for asset holders. Additionally, as Figure 16-1 shows, after adjusting for inflation, the average five-year growth in assets follows predictable trends—growing more robustly during the late 1960s, 1980s, and 1990s when progrowth economic policies were being implemented. If implemented as part of my flat-tax proposal, continued growth in asset values and consequently the capital gains tax base would be expected. Of course, without the disincentive from selling contained in the current tax system, a large portion of the current unrealized capital-gains tax base may be shifted over to the realized capital-gains tax base, but for our purposes the distinction would become irrelevant.

One adjustment to these figures may be desired. The value of housing and other tangible illiquid assets is included in the above tax base. Currently, realized capital gains in housing are for all

3.　See Federal Reserve Statistical Release Z.1 Flow of Funds Accounts of the United States, http://www.federalreserve.gov/releases/z1/Current/.

4.　Department of Treasury, Office of Tax Analysis, http://www.treas.gov/offices/tax-policy/library/capgain1–2008.pdf.

Table 16-4 Realized Capital Gains Compared to Growth in Total Assets 5-Year Moving Average 2000–2008

(millions $)

	5-Yr. Change in Assets	5-Yr. Realized Capital Gains	Difference
2000	3,330,019.02	455,528.20	2,874,490.82
2001	2,918,765.76	473,277.20	2,445,488.56
2002	2,055,979.66	454,034.40	1,601,945.26
2003	2,573,507.70	427,651.00	2,145,856.70
2004	2,791,045.90	416,960.20	2,374,085.70
2005	4,152,850.16	426,133.60	3,726,716.56
2006	5,175,731.12	515,888.20	4,659,842.92
2007	5,520,802.34	N/A	N/A
2008	1,947,683.88	N/A	N/A

Figure 16-1 Growth in Inflation-Adjusted Assets 5-Year Moving Average 1960–2008

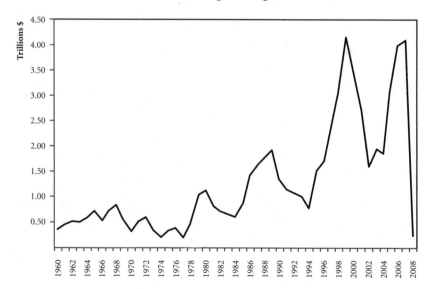

183

intents and purposes exempt from capital-gains taxes. Due to the uniqueness of housing, it may be desirable to perpetuate this policy and also exempt unrealized capital gains in housing from the tax base. Similarly, the difficulty of valuing tangible assets may make the inclusion of these assets impractical. Table 16-5 presents the increase in the five-year moving average value of financial assets only. It is assumed that all realized capital gains apply to financial assets, which is not the case, but a conservative estimate of the additional tax base achieved by taxing the unrealized capital gains on financial assets would vary between $200 billion and $2.5 trillion.

Table 16-5 **Realized Capital Gains Compared to Growth in Financial Assets 5-Year Moving Average 2000–2008**

(millions $)

	5-Yr. Change in Assets	5-Yr. Realized Capital Gains	Difference
2000	2,332,509.62	455,528.20	1,876,981.42
2001	1,725,841.76	473,277.20	1,252,564.56
2002	682,459.46	454,034.40	228,425.06
2003	1,023,795.50	427,651.00	596,144.50
2004	908,738.70	416,960.20	491,778.50
2005	1,931,174.36	426,133.60	1,505,040.76
2006	3,065,472.92	515,888.20	2,549,584.72
2007	3,951,523.14	N/A	N/A
2008	1,223,394.88	N/A	N/A

While contributions to tax-exempt organizations should be tax-deductible to the contributor and tax-free to the tax-exempt organization, income earned by the tax-exempt organizations should not be tax-exempt. Between 2005 and 2006, total cash, savings, and investments of charitable organizations grew by $824 billion.[5] This $824 billion increase in the assets of charitable organizations should

---

5.   IRS Statistics of Income Division, August 2009, www.irs.gov.

184

be part of the tax base and taxed at the same rates that for-profit businesses face. Likewise the income earned by employees of tax-exempt organizations should be fully taxable, like any other earned income. This is especially true for universities and other heavily en-dowed and subsidized tax-exempt organizations, including pension funds and endowments.

With a true flat tax at a low rate there's just no need for any of these exclusions, exemptions, and deductions.

The tax-exempt status of universities is worth special attention. I've spent a lot of my life intimately involved with universities as student, professor, father of students, and board member. Univer-sity endowments do not pay taxes on their capital gains, dividends, interest, royalties, and rent.[6] Rarely do universities pay state and local property taxes, and often, universities do not even pay sales taxes on their purchases of goods and taxable services. While the tax breaks ostensibly enhance the public good services universities provide—providing better education, subsequent employment op-portunities (especially for people of lesser means) and the positive benefits created by university-sponsored research—it seems to me that the purchase of a skybox at the football stadium fails to meet this criterion. Similarly, golden parachute provisions in the con-tracts of university presidents and football coaches also seem less worthy of taxpayer subsidies.

It is my view that the tax-exempt status of universities, other than for contributions, makes no sense under a true flat-tax system with low rates.

And the dollar value of these subsidies is not inconsequential. According to the National Association of College and University Business Officers (NACUBO), the total value of school endowment assets for the 791 college and university endowments represented by NACUBO for fiscal year 2008 (which ended June 30, 2008) was

---

6.   Richard Vadder, "Federal Tax Policy Regarding Universities Endowments and Beyond," Cen-ter for College Affordability and Productivity, February 2008.

$412 billion.[7] While for 2008, the average return was −3.0 percent (and was even worse for the first five months of 2009), based on a study by Richard Vedder, the average return for an endowment is much better—a positive inflation-adjusted 8.55 percent per year for the schools with the top fourteen endowments (endowments larger than $1 billion).[8] Including inflation, this equals an approximately 10 percent annual return. Taking into account the recent declines in the value of school endowments, a 10 percent annual return on investment income of university endowments would bring, in an average year, between $32 billion and $40 billion of previously untaxed income into the tax base, thereby allowing the overall flat-tax rate to be lowered for everyone.

In the spirit of making the tax base as broad as possible, virtually all deductions and tax credits for individuals and businesses should be repealed. In addition, the business tax base should include the value added of labor as well as the value added of capital and land. Great care, however, should be taken to make certain that value added, as it wends its way through numerous businesses, is taxed once and only once. Double, triple, and even higher multiples of taxation in our current business tax code, no matter how well concealed, have cost our society unconscionable quantities of lost output and lost employment opportunities.

All individual deductions and exemptions for individuals are no longer allowed. That holds for child allowances and tax credits, as well as for individual tax deductions. All that individual deductions do is help the more affluent of the poor and cause tax rates to be a lot higher by shrinking the tax base. They do not benefit the least affluent of the poor, that is, those people with no income. There is a huge deadweight revenue loss brought about by individual tax ex-

7.   "NACUBO Releases Results of the 2008 Endowment Study and Endowment Follow-up Survey." National Association of College and University Business Officers (NACUBO), January 29, 2009, http://www.nacubo.org/Research/News/NACUBO_Release_Results_of_the_2008_Endowment_Study_and_Endowment_Follow-up_Survey.html.
8.   Richard Vedder, "Federal Tax Policy Regarding Universities Endowments and Beyond," Center for College Affordability and Productivity, February 2008.

emptions. I may have missed this in Econ 1, but I never could figure out what the benefits of a tax deduction were for a person with no income. Help me!

Despite the seemingly uncomplicated nature of the theory behind the flat tax, practical application requires some unavoidable complications: A few adjustments and deductions need to be allowed. Before I explain exactly how I calculate the personal income-tax base and the business value-added tax base, I'd like to discuss some of these adjustments.

An example of a needed adjustment to personal income is the deductibility of mortgage interest. Mortgage interest has to remain deductible for individuals as long as interest income is taxable. To give an example, if someone borrows $100,000 at 7 percent and lends $100,000 at 7 percent, clearly that person should not be liable for taxation. That person is simply a conduit for a loan. And yet if a person borrows $100,000 at 7 percent and lends $100,000 at 10 percent, that person should be liable for taxation on the difference. Therefore, all interest income should be taxable and all interest expense should be deductible. To avoid fraud and manipulation, for individuals interest deductions should be limited to mortgage interest.

Also, homeowners effectively rent from themselves with pretax dollars. Renters, on the other hand, pay their rent in after-tax dollars. Therefore, to be kept on an even footing with homeowners, renters should be allowed to deduct rent on their primary residence from their overall tax base. No longer would there be an economic distortion between homeowners and renters.

Imagine you catch your neighbor looking covetously at your home while at the same time you're jealous of your neighbor's home. Recognizing that each of you likes the other's house better than your own home, you decide to switch houses. You rent your neighbor's house, and your neighbor rents your house. Both of you still live in the same two houses. The question is, under our current tax code, does switching houses constitute a taxable event? The answer is yes.

If you rent your neighbor's house, you have to pay rent in after-tax dollars. Likewise, the rent your neighbor pays you is also in after-tax dollars. Whereas if each of you stays in your own home, there is no tax. Basically, what happens is the rent you effectively pay yourself is in pretax dollars.

To account for homeownership correctly from a tax standpoint, homeowners should be taxed on the imputed rental value of the owner-occupied home. Such a solution, however, really is impractical as well as impolitic. But there is an inequity to renters.

To rectify the failure to tax the imputed rental value of owner-occupied homes, renters should be allowed to deduct their rent on their primary residence. Thus all people will be treated fairly and equally under the tax codes. Distortion will be held to a minimum.

One can make a case that some charitable contributions at least should not be tax-deductible. For example, if I make a contribution to a private school in exchange for an equal reduction in my child's tuition, clearly that contribution should not be tax-deductible. On the other hand, if someone gives anonymously to a charity that helps the sick, it would be hard to argue against a tax deduction. Charitable contributions have many motives, but the law should have only one answer. In deference to politics, it would be hard to go against charitable deductions even if a case could be made for only partial deductibility. Therefore, allowances should also be made for personal charitable contributions.

For business value-added there shouldn't be any specific deductions other than all purchases from other companies. One unusual feature of business value-added under the flat tax is that all purchases from other companies—including capital equipment—would be expensed when purchased. This has the effect of leaving a lot of undepreciated capital on the books of firms. Therefore, during a transition period this proposal would allow businesses to continue their depreciation of undepreciated capital over time, leaving the tax rate a little higher than it otherwise would be.

Specifically, the tax base for individuals, businesses, and independent contractors is calculated as follows.

Personal-Income Tax

A. Taxable income for all individuals, save independent contractors.

1. Take income from all sources . . . wages, salaries, interest income, dividends, capital gains (short term and long term), royalties, fees, and so on.
2. Subtract charitable contributions.
3. Subtract mortgage interest payments.
4. Subtract receipts of Social Security, unemployment benefits, and other transfer payments specifically designated as tax-exempt.
5. Subtract rent payments for primary residence.
6. The resultant figure is the taxable income base.

B. Taxable income for independent contractors. To receive a business taxpaying identifying number for an individual requires explicit state permission, which should be based on the recipient's demonstrated special employment circumstances that would warrant such treatment.

1. For the independent contractor possessing a taxpaying identifying number, the tax base for personal income-tax purposes is the dollar value of total sales (including, but not restricted to, personal services) less:
   - Purchases from other businesses and independent contractors bearing taxpaying identifying numbers of items used exclusively to generate sales and revenues.
   - Purchases of imported goods or services, with the requisite import taxpaying identifying number, used exclusively to generate sales and revenues.

- Depreciation of pre-flat-rate tax depreciable assets at their regular depreciation schedules.
2. Subtract charitable contributions.
3. Subtract mortgage interest payments.
4. Subtract receipts of Social Security, unemployment benefits, and other transfer payments specifically designated as tax-exempt.
5. Subtract rent payments for primary residence.
6. The resultant figure is the independent contractor taxable personal income tax base.

Business Value-Added Tax

C. Taxable value-added for businesses.
1. For all entities possessing a business taxpaying identifying number, including independent contractors, the tax base is the total dollar value of all sales during the period less:
   - All purchases including interest payments from entities that possess a taxpaying identifying number (including independent contractors).
   - All purchases of imported goods with the requisite import taxpaying identifying number.
   - Depreciation of pre-flat-rate tax depreciable assets at their regular depreciation schedules.
   - Bad debts incurred.
   - Charitable contributions.
   - No other deductions are permitted.
2. The resultant figure is the business value-added tax base.

My calculations of the U.S. personal income and business value-added tax bases are shown in Table 16-6. My calculation results in an estimated personal income-tax base for 2007 (the most recent year for which we have complete data) of $9.1 trillion. My calculation for the business value-added tax base for 2007 is $9.9 trillion.

Table 16-6 Estimated Personal-Income and Value-Added Tax Base 2007

(dollars in millions)

Personal Income	**11,894,100**	**Gross Product**	**14,077,600**
Plus Capital Gains	895,674	Less Business Investment	
Less Charitable Contributions	(193,604)	Fixed Nonresidential	(1,640,200)
Less Mortgage Interest Payments	(491,432)	Business-Fixed Residential	(629,000)
Less Transfer Payments (Tax-Exempt)	(1,687,800)	Depreciation	(1,760,000)
Less Monetary Rent	(299,100)	Less Business Transfers	(102,200)
Less Imputed Rent	(1,063,300)		
Equals Tax Base for Personal Income	**$9,054,538**	**Equals Business Value Added Tax Base**	**$9,946,200**

The tax rate is derived by dividing targeted revenues by the total tax base. On a static basis, with no increase in average tax rates and using fiscal year 2007 as a guide, requisite flat-tax revenue would be $2.4 trillion on a combined tax base of $19.0 trillion (Table 16-7). On this basis, a flat-tax rate of 13.0 percent applied to both taxable personal income and business value-added would provide more than enough revenue. The appropriate tax rate for independent contractors would be 26.0 percent applied to their tax base.

The net sales tax base (some may wish to call it a VAT) is approximately the same dollar magnitude as that of the flat income tax base. Therefore, as a first-order approximation, my proposal is a flat tax on approximately twice the stated personal income-tax base.

Table 16-7 Calculation of Flat-Tax Rate

(dollars in millions)

Tax Bases:

Personal-Income	9,054,538
Business Value-Added Tax	9,946,200
Total Tax Base	**$19,000,738**
FY 2007 Targeted Budget Revenue	**$2,429,366**

Flat-Tax Rate = Revenues/Tax Base =
$2.4 trillion/$19.0 trillion ≈ 13.0 percent

My flat-tax proposal is designed to minimize the disincentives induced by tax rates and yet still provide the requisite amount of revenue for the services we all want government to provide. This static revenue-neutral proposal will, by definition, raise the same amount of revenue as the current system. But, in truth, the United States has everything to gain from its implementation. The broad-based, low-rate flat-tax system minimizes distortions and maximizes efficiency gains.

Economists in general acknowledge that reduced tax rates will have long-term beneficial effects. However, they tend to underestimate how quickly the economy responds to economic incentives. Ignoring the substitution effects may be perilous and lead to incorrect forecasts. The reality is that tax revenues would soon exceed the most optimistic projections. The longer this new tax system is in place, the greater will be these gains. In addition, prosperous times have the added benefit of reducing demand for government social-spending programs (unemployment, welfare, and so on).

Revenue-Neutrality Considerations

The decision of what the actual tax rate should be is political. The tax rate I have calculated is approximately static revenue-neutral, based on the size of the federal government before the massive economic collapse and huge increases in federal spending over the past year. I first proposed the flat-rate tax for the United States back in 1984. The size of the government relative to the economy back then was smaller—a flat-rate tax of 11.5 percent was necessary for a static revenue-neutral tax. Nearly twenty-five years later, for 2007, the revenue-neutral flat-rate tax is 13.0 percent. In 2009, given the fall-off in federal revenues, the number would be somewhat lower.

The unfunded liabilities that have been incurred by the Bush and Obama administrations (described previously) for all intents and purposes doubled the annual expenditures of the U.S. federal government. It follows that it would take a tax rate that is twice as high in order to support these expenditures, which don't even include the possible additional expenditures associated with the Obama administration's health and energy policies.

As I argued previously, the programs and expenditures of the Obama administration are not financially realistic and need to be scaled back. A flat-rate tax needs to be implemented based on the historic government expenditure levels—not on the levels that exist today. Instead, that portion of the stimulus bill that has not been spent yet—much of the stimulus bill spending will occur in 2010 and beyond—should be rescinded. Other budget cuts will also need to be implemented to restore fiscal sanity to the federal budget.

17

TAX AMNESTY

The dream of tax reform has always been to reduce the perceived immorality of the tax codes. By implementing a flat-rate tax the benefits of evading taxes would be reduced and yet the penalties for evading taxes would remain unchanged. With less benefit accruing to the tax cheat and yet the same penalty facing that tax cheat, there will be fewer tax cheats. But transforming tax cheats into law-abiding taxpayers requires careful planning.

There is a striking parallel between the people who operate in the underground economy (the market that functions without regard to standard law, regulation, or taxation) and asset holders with unrealized capital gains. In both instances, the potential taxpayers are locked into their current holding behavior. This holding behavior in the case of tax evaders results from an accumulation of "accrued" taxes. The total amount of the accrued tax liability is a direct result of all previous and current tax evasion activities.

A program of temporary tax amnesty with an offer-in-compromise option is the mechanism for unlocking the "accrued" tax liabilities of the underground economy.[1] The historical record

---

1.   "The Offer in Compromises (or OIC) program, in the United States, is an Internal Revenue Service (IRS) program under 26 U.S.C. § 7122 which allows qualified individuals with an unpaid tax debt to negotiate a settled amount that is less than the total owed to clear the debt. A taxpayer uses the checklist in the Form 656, Offer in Compromise, package to determine if the taxpayer is eligible for the offer in compromise program. The objective of the OIC program is to accept a compromise when acceptance is in the best interests of both the taxpayer and the government and promotes voluntary compliance with all future payment and filing requirements." *Wikipedia*, September 25, 2009.

of changes in the tax rates on capital gains strongly suggests that total tax receipts from capital-gains realizations are also very sensitive to "temporary" tax-rate changes.

The beauty of tax amnesty programs is that they raise revenues not by burdening existing hardworking honest taxpayers but by giving those who've strayed from the straight and narrow a chance to get back on track. Because these programs are voluntary, it's obvious that through noncomplier participation the former noncompliers—in addition to the government—will be better off. And the lower and fairer tax rates are, the less tax evasion, avoidance, and noncompliance there will be.

A federal tax amnesty program would raise lots and lots of money quickly and give the economy a supply-side jump-start as well. Tax amnesty now is just what the doctor ordered. It's one of the few tax increases that actually stimulate the economy. It truly is a win-win for everybody.

The tax burden is reduced on existing taxpayers. Critical programs can continue to be funded. Fiscal solvency to government is restored. But most of all, those people caught in a web of deceit and deception can be brought back into the mainstream of law-abiding taxpayers of their own volition. And with fewer scofflaws after a full tax amnesty program is completed, enforcement efforts can be directed in a more concentrated manner at the hard-core noncompliers.

By notifying individuals and businesses that an amnesty program will soon be in effect, that there will be no criminal prosecution or tax penalties for those who come forward and pay their fair back taxes, and that after the amnesty period there will be a redoubled effort to track down the tax cheaters, we will create a huge outpouring of amended returns. At the discretion of the specific amnesty program is the assessment of interest charges and the willingness of the government to negotiate specific circumstances through an offer-in-compromise program (the settling of a tax liability for less than full payment).

195

The State and Local Experience

Tax amnesty is a fairly common practice for state and local governments. Over the past twenty-five years there have been no fewer than sixty-two separate state tax amnesty programs in forty different states (see Table 17-1 at the end of this chapter for detailed information). Connecticut, Massachusetts, New Jersey, and New York have had a full three amnesty programs each and Louisiana has had four. Most of these state tax amnesty programs have also included local governments and have encompassed all forms of taxation.

Past state tax amnesty programs have raised far more revenue for fiscally strapped state and local governments than even their most vocal advocates projected. One such example is the amnesty program in Connecticut between 2002 and 2004. This program was hailed as a "whopping success" and raised an estimated $109 million,[2] far above the legislated goal of $24 million. Delinquent tax payments flowed in from virtually every tax category, including the sales and use tax (55 percent), income tax (19 percent), corporation tax (16 percent), gross earnings tax (1 percent), gift tax (1 percent), and miscellaneous taxes (8 percent).

"The 2002 Tax Amnesty Program is one of the bright spots in the state's current budget situation," Governor John Rowland said. "The money raised through this unusually successful program will allow us to make a fair sized dent in the state budget deficit." Connecticut tax commissioner Gene Gavin added, "The money collected above the statutory goal will be applied, dollar-for-dollar, against the budget shortfall. It is not only good news for the tax delinquents who took advantage of this program, it is also good news

---

2.   "Tax Amnesty Brings In More Than $109 Million," Press Release, Connecticut Department of Revenue Services, December 10, 2002; "Governor Rowland, Commissioner Gavin Hall Whopping Success of 2002 Tax Amnesty," Press Release, Connecticut Department of Revenue Services, December 3, 2002.

for the law-abiding taxpayers of Connecticut who will benefit from the success of amnesty."

Other states have also experienced similar success. Kentucky's second-ever amnesty program ended in September 2003. Data show collections totaled just over $100 million.[3] According to Governor Paul Patton, "We continue to be delighted with the results of the Tax Amnesty program. These funds are badly needed to maintain vital state government services without having to make significant cuts."

"My Dog Ate My Tax Return"

Many delinquent taxpayers begin their nefarious pattern through relatively innocent circumstances. A 1994 IRS study suggested that a significant portion of federal tax noncompliance is unintentional.[4] A unique state-level study conducted during Arkansas' 1997 tax amnesty program surveyed participants and provided insight into the reasons behind taxpayer delinquency.[5] Covering a wide range from the understandable to the outrageous, these survey responses read like a student's excuses for missing homework:

- "The reason I didn't pay my taxes is plainly because I clearly forgot them. No excuses."
- "This tax is both morally and constitutionally wrong."
- "I didn't file in 1989 and it kept getting worse. I was afraid after the first year."
- "My ex-wife lied about mailing the return. She took the money out of the bank and kept it."
- "I did not have money at the time. The refinery where I was employed exploded."

---

3.   "Tax Amnesty Receipts Exceed $100 Million," Press Release, Kentucky Revenue Cabinet, October 24, 2002.
4.   Christina Ritsema, Tracy S. Manly, and Deborah W. Thomas, "Why Taxpayers Are Noncompliant: Comments From 1997 Arkansas Tax Amnesty Participants," *State Tax Notes*, Tax Analysts, January 27, 2003.
5.   Ibid.

Categorizing and compiling the responses reveals that the percentage of noncompliers who reach that status unintentionally (56 percent)—due to forgetfulness, inability to file due to complexity of the tax system, or error—is greater than the percentage of those who intentionally don't pay their taxes (44 percent) due to personal circumstances or their opinion of the tax system.

Of course, once delinquent, taxpayers feel trapped and continue to cheat on their taxes quite intentionally.

Things to Consider

There are several critical elements to a federal tax amnesty program. First, programs at the federal level and the state and local levels are more effective if they are authorized and conducted at the same time. What are the chances that a noncomplier has duped only the state tax collectors and not the IRS? Slim to none. And given that the noncomplier has duped both the IRS and the state tax authorities and simultaneously knows that his admission to the IRS must be divulged to the state authorities (which have not granted amnesty), why would that noncomplier still want to come forth?

Second, the tax amnesty must be effectively publicized. A publicized amnesty at the federal, state, and local levels would clearly be unprecedented.

Finally, higher levels of enforcement and greater penalties for noncompliers following the conclusion of the amnesty program would increase the cost-benefit ratio of avoidance and evasion and encourage increased future compliance. Putting all these points together indicates a far larger payout if the federal and state authorities cooperate.

The Potential Windfall

Accurately estimating the total amount of receipts from a nation-wide federal tax amnesty program is fraught with uncertainty. Looking at past results, state program recoupments as a percentage of tax bases range all over the board, depending on the breadth of the program (which tax categories were granted amnesty), the severity of the state laws, and publicity of the program. But one feature seems to be shared by all the state tax amnesty experiences: Revenues to be collected are grossly underestimated. On top of that, the expense of collecting these delinquent taxes is relatively low.

Past IRS studies on the issue of noncompliance under the individual income tax suggest that the noncompliance rate—defined as the amount of tax liability for a given year not paid voluntarily and in timely fashion as a percentage of the total "true" tax liability—is in the range of 16.9 percent to 18.8 percent.[6] This rate covers the sins of all nonfilers, underreporters, and underpayers.

The total tax receipts in fiscal year 2008 were just over $2.5 trillion.[7] Using the IRS percentage above, this would put underpayment on the income tax alone at about $200 billion annually. The IRS estimate for the total is $345 billion. Tax amnesty, however, doesn't just affect the amounts of noncompliance for one year. Tax amnesty programs reach far back into the tax delinquents' pasts. Therefore, the base upon which tax amnesty operates is some cumulative historical moving sum far larger than one year's tax collections.

My best estimate is that a federal, state, and local tax amnesty program, combined with an aggressive offer-in-compromise out-

---

6. Elinor Convery, Dennis Cox, Chih-Chin Ho, and Wayne Thomas, "Federal Tax Compliance Research: Individual Income Tax Gap Estimates for 1985, 1988 and 1992," Internal Revenue Service, April 1996. Michael Brostek, "Tax Compliance: Multiple Approaches Are Needed to Reduce the Tax Gap," January 23, 2007, GAO-07-391T.

7. Tax data from Historical Tables: Supplements to 2009 President's Budget, Table 2.1.

reach, could immediately increase total tax revenues by between $750 billion and $1.0 trillion. This range represents an immediate realization of a little over 10 percent of total federal tax collections for the past five years. In addition, due to former noncompliers' now being aboveground and paying future taxes, I believe the government could expect continuing increments to federal tax receipts of $100 billion in the first year, resulting from about $750 billion higher total income (VAT and personal) at the 13 percent rate. These revenues would grow rapidly over the years. State and local governments would be enormous beneficiaries as well.

Looking at the big picture, tax amnesty programs alone are only a short-term palliative. But they do provide revenues to pay off some of the national debt that has been put on the nation's books by Presidents Bush and Obama. But when this proposal is combined with my flat-tax reform, scofflaws, delinquents, and other noncompliers will have a reduced incentive to be back to their old tricks. The fairer and lower tax rates are, the less tax evasion, avoidance, and noncompliance there will be. This is why the combination of the flat-rate tax and a tax amnesty holds such promise for the United States.

Even if my estimates are off by a large amount, a federal tax amnesty program would still be a huge win for everybody. And, who knows, my estimates may very well be like previous state estimates and significantly underestimate the revenue recoupment. It's surely better than a sharp stick in the eye.

Table 17-1 Historical State Tax Amnesty Programs

(in $millions)

State	Start Date	End Date	Major Taxes Covered	Amnesty Collections	State and Local Tax Base Used	Tax Base	Collections, % of Tax Base
California	1/1/04	4/15/04	Tax Shelter Abuse	$1,345.0	FY2002 Total Taxes*	$114,015	1.18%
New York	11/18/02	1/31/03	All	$582.7	FY2002 Total Taxes*	$88,394	0.66%
New York	11/1/96	1/31/97	All	$253.4	FY1997 Total Taxes	$75,468	0.34%
Texas	3/11/04	3/31/04	All	$438.0	FY2002 Total Taxes*	$53,464	0.82%
New York	11/1/85	1/31/86	All	$401.3	FY1986 Total Taxes	$45,129	0.89%
Florida	7/1/03	10/31/03	All	$268.9	FY2002 Total Taxes*	$41,935	0.64%
Illinois	10/1/03	11/17/03	All	$532.0	FY2002 Total Taxes*	$39,927	1.33%
Ohio	10/15/01	1/15/02	All	$48.5	FY2002 Total Taxes*	$34,692	0.14%
New Jersey	4/15/02	6/10/02	All	$276.9	FY2002 Total Taxes*	$33,019	0.84%
Pennsylvania	10/13/95	1/10/96	All	$96.0	FY1996 Total Taxes	$30,280	0.32%
New Jersey	3/15/96	6/1/96	All	$359.0	FY1996 Total Taxes	$27,449	1.31%
California	12/10/84	3/15/85	Ind. Income, Sales	$197.0	FY1985 Ind. Income, Sales	$26,432	0.75%
Massachusetts	10/1/02	11/30/02	All	$138.0	FY2002 Total Taxes*	$24,042	0.57%
Massachusetts	1/1/03	2/28/03	All	$34.0	FY2002 Total Taxes*	$24,042	0.14%
Michigan	5/15/02	6/30/02	All	$81.9	FY2002 Total Taxes*	$22,712	0.36%
Virginia	9/2/03	11/3/03	All	$98.3	FY2002 Total Taxes*	$21,216	0.46%
Florida	1/1/88	6/30/88	All	$30.5	FY1988 Total Taxes	$18,773	$0.16%
Maryland	9/1/01	10/31/01	All	$39.2	FY2002 Total Taxes*	$18,756	0.21%

State	Start Date	End Date	Major Taxes Covered	Amnesty Collections	State and Local Tax Base Used	Tax Base	Collections, % of Tax Base
Texas	2/1/84	2/29/84	All	$0.5	FY1984 Total Taxes	$17,834	0.00%
Wisconsin	6/15/98	8/14/98	All	$30.9	FY1999 Total Taxes	$17,418	0.18%
New Jersey	9/10/87	12/8/87	All	$186.5	FY1988 Total Taxes	$17,116	1.09%
Illinois	10/1/84	11/30/84	All	$160.5	FY1985 Total Taxes	$17,007	0.94%
Michigan	5/12/86	6/30/86	All	$109.8	FY1986 Total Taxes	$15,577	0.70%
Connecticut	9/1/02	12/2/02	All	$109.0	FY2002 Total Taxes*	$14,513	0.75%
Georgia	10/1/92	12/5/92	All	$51.3	FY1993 Total Taxes	$13,774	0.37%
Missouri	8/1/02	10/31/02	All	$76.4	FY2002 Total Taxes*	$13,471	0.57%
Missouri	8/1/03	10/31/03	All	$30.1	FY2002 Total Taxes*	$13,471	0.22%
Colorado	6/1/03	6/30/03	All	$18.4	FY2002 Total Taxes*	$13,064	0.14%
Connecticut	9/1/95	11/30/95	All	$46.2	FY1996 Total Taxes	$12,543	0.37%
Virginia	2/1/90	3/31/90	All	$32.2	FY1990 Total Taxes	$11,728	0.27%
Louisiana	9/1/01	10/30/01	All	$173.1	FY2002 Total Taxes*	$11,712	1.48%
Louisiana	10/1/96	12/31/96	All	$1.6	FY1999 Total Taxes	$10,533	0.02%
Kentucky	8/1/02	9/30/02	All	$100.0	FY2002 Total Taxes*	$10,453	0.96%
Arizona	9/1/03	10/31/03	All ex. Property	$73.0	FY2002 Total Taxes*, ex. Property	$10,101	0.72%
Maryland	9/1/87	11/2/87	All	$34.6	FY1988 Total Taxes	$9,673	0.36%
Massachusetts	10/17/83	1/17/84	All	$86.5	FY1984 Total Taxes	$8,984	0.96%
South Carolina	10/15/02	12/2/02	All	$66.2	FY2002 Total Taxes*	$8,911	0.74%
Connecticut	9/1/90	11/30/90	All	$54.0	FY1991 Total Taxes	$8,776	0.62%

State	Start Date	End Date	Major Taxes Covered	Amnesty Collections	State and Local Tax Base Used	Tax Base	Collections, % of Tax Base
Wisconsin	9/15/85	11/22/85	All	$27.3	FY1986 Total Taxes	$8,279	0.33%
North Carolina	9/1/89	12/1/89	All	$37.6	FY1990 State Total Taxes	$7,871	0.48%
Kansas	10/1/03	11/30/03	All	$53.7	FY2002 Total Taxes*	$7,576	0.71%
Minnesota	8/1/84	10/31/84	All	$12.1	FY1985 Total Taxes	$7,407	0.16%
Oklahoma	8/15/02	11/15/02	All ex. Property	$38.8	FY2002 Total Taxes*, ex. Property	$7,161	0.54%
Nevada	2/1/02	6/30/02	All	$7.3	FY2002 Total Taxes*	$6,053	0.12%
Louisiana	10/1/87	12/15/87	All	$0.3	FY1988 Total Taxes	$5,857	0.01%
Louisiana	10/1/85	12/31/85	All	$1.2	FY1988 Total Taxes	$5,640	0.02%
Kentucky	9/15/88	9/30/88	All	$100.0	FY1989 Total Taxes	$5,174	1.93%
Missouri	9/1/83	10/31/83	All	$0.9	FY1984 Total Taxes	$5,070	0.02%
Colorado	9/16/85	11/15/85	All	$6.4	FY1986 Total Taxes	$4,852	0.13%
New Mexico	8/16/99	11/12/99	All	$45.0	FY2000 Total Taxes	$4,801	0.94%
Iowa	9/2/86	10/31/86	All	$35.1	FY1987 Total Taxes	$4,336	0.81%
Maine	9/1/03	11/30/03	All	$34.7	FY2002 Total Taxes*	$4,228	0.82%
South Carolina	9/1/85	11/30/85	All	$7.1	FY1986 Total Taxes	$3,844	0.18%
Alabama	1/20/84	4/1/84	All	$3.2	FY1984 Total Taxes	$3,654	0.09%
New Hampshire	12/1/01	2/15/02	All	$13.5	FY2002 Total Taxes*	$3,479	0.39%
Kansas	7/1/84	9/30/84	All	$0.6	FY1985 Total Taxes	$3,324	0.02%
Arizona	11/22/82	1/20/83	All	$6.0	FY1983 Total Taxes	$3,154	0.19%
New Hampshire	12/1/97	2/17/98	All	$13.5	FY1996 Total Taxes	$2,863	0.47%

State	Start Date	End Date	Major Taxes Covered	Amnesty Collections	State and Local Tax Base Used	Tax Base	Collections, % of Tax Base
Rhode Island	4/15/96	6/28/96	All	$7.9	FY1996 Total Taxes	$2,711	0.29%
Arkansas	9/1/87	11/30/87	All	$1.7	FY1988 Total Taxes	$2,665	0.06%
Mississippi	9/1/86	11/30/86	All	$1.0	FY1987 Total Taxes	$2,599	0.04%
Maine	11/1/90	12/31/90	All	$29.0	FY1991 Total Taxes	$2,510	1.16%
Oklahoma	7/1/84	12/31/84	Income, Sales	$13.9	FY1985 Income. Sales	$2,461	0.56%
West Virginia	10/1/86	12/31/86	All	$15.9	FY1984 Total Taxes	$2,335	0.68%
New Mexico	8/15/85	11/13/85	All	$13.6	FY1986 Total Taxes	$1,836	0.74%
North Dakota	10/1/03	1/31/04	All	$6.9	FY2002 Total Taxes*	$1,713	0.40%
Rhode Island	10/15/86	1/12/87	All	$0.7	FY1987 Total Taxes	$1,696	0.04%
South Dakota	4/1/99	5/15/99	All	$0.5	FY1999 Total Taxes	$1,653	0.03%
Vermont	5/15/90	6/25/90	All	$1.0	FY1990 Total Taxes	$1,131	0.09%
North Dakota	9/1/83	11/30/83	All	$0.2	FY1984 Total Taxes	$915	0.02%
Florida	1/1/87	6/30/87	Intangibles	$13.0	FY1987 intangibles**	$360	3.61%
Idaho	5/20/83	8/30/83	Ind. Income	$0.3	FY1983 Ind. Income	$226	0.13%

Equal-Weighted Average: 0.54%

Tax-Base Weighted Average: 0.64%

Note: Due to very limited scope, amnesties in Arizona (1/1/02–2/28/02) and New York City (10/20/03–1/23/04) were excluded. *Estimate based on most recent available data (actual FY2002 state and estimated FY2002 local tax revenue). **Estimate. *Source:* Federation of Tax Administrators, state revenue departments, U.S. Census Bureau.

18

ADDRESSING GLOBAL WARMING WHILE GROWING THE ECONOMY

The current scientific consensus contends that economizing on our fossil fuel use could have a positive impact on the environment and, in fact, may even avert a global crisis. Based on this current scientific consensus and the potential environmental benefits from reducing carbon emissions, it would surely seem prudent to do what we can to reduce global carbon emissions. I am concerned, though, by what the secondary impact on the economy of policies enacted to reduce carbon emissions will be.

The debate over the current environmental consensus boils down to three general positions. First there are those who believe the earth is warming, and man-made greenhouse gas emissions are the primary cause. Next, there are those who believe the earth is warming, and other phenomena are the primary cause; and last there are those who do not believe evidence that the earth is warming.

For those who believe the earth is warming, and man-made greenhouse gas emissions are the primary cause, global-warming policies must be implemented to minimize the significant economic damage these policies can create. Only by addressing the deleterious consequences on the economy of a carbon tax can the electoral consensus be guaranteed.

Those who question the notion of man-made global warming, or do not believe in the phenomenon of global warming at all, should recognize that in order to take action against the threat of global warming, one does not have to believe that we are in fact facing a crisis, or that man has caused that crisis. Today all one needs to assume is that burning less fossil fuel and burning what we do burn more efficiently will not hurt the planet. Regarding global warming, the appropriate questions are:

1. Is there a risk that global warming is happening?
2. If so, is there a less risky solution that can address the potential hazard while safeguarding against the potential adverse economic consequences of global warming policies?

While I am not an environmental scientist, it seems to me that there is a risk that man-made global warming is real. And there are some basic economic truths that, if followed, would ensure that our response to the risk of global warming does minimal harm to the world's economy. Our problem, if there is one, is with carbon emissions into the atmosphere. A solution to carbon emissions that causes a depression is not only not necessary, it's downright ignorant.

There is one common, but serious, mistake made when designing global-warming policies, especially with regard to President Obama's cap-and-trade policy. With respect to a carbon tax, proponents, especially proponents of a tax on gasoline, often argue that the tax incidence affects both the consumers (U.S. drivers) and the producers of oil (Saudi Arabia and Venezuela are often mentioned). Consequently, they argue Saudi Arabia, Venezuela, and other oil suppliers would in effect be paying part of the gasoline tax. You can almost hear the crowds yelling "Yippee!"

However, as we discussed earlier, based on the Bhagwati theorem, a trade distortion should be addressed with appropriate trade policies; a production distortion should be addressed with appropriate tax or incomes policies on production; and a consumption distortion should be addressed with appropriate tax or incomes policies on consumption.

In the case of carbon emissions, there is a consumption problem. When consumers use energy, or products created from energy, the prices do not reflect the costs of the carbon emissions to the environment; consequently consumption is higher than optimal once the full costs of the product are taken into account.[1] The appropriate policy response is a tax on carbon emissions themselves, which for practical purposes boils down to a tax on the consumption of oil, other fossil fuels, or products where carbon gases are emitted as a by-product, the source of the market distortion, but not on trade or production, the source of the adverse economic impacts.

Swapping a tax on carbon with an across-the-board marginal income-tax cut meets these criteria. From my standpoint, even if there were no global warming, I still would opt for an across-the-board income-tax swap every day of the week and twice on Sundays. But even more to the point, my proposal for a complete flat tax easily accommodates a carbon tax as a so-called sin tax. Whatever the revenue projections are for a carbon tax, the overall flat-tax rate would be reduced pari passu for a perfect revenue offset. Voilà!

To give a concrete example, if the carbon tax were expected to raise $600 billion—around the static estimate for the current cap-and-trade legislation—then the 13 percent flat-tax rate could be lowered to 9.75 percent from 13 percent. Not too bad, eh?

The carbon tax increases the relative price of carbon-producing activities, thereby discouraging the use of carbon. Consumers and producers will feel both an income effect and a substitution effect from the new carbon tax. The income effect arises because the higher carbon tax reduces people's after-tax income. A lower after-tax income decreases people's ability to spend and save. The carbon tax simultaneously burdens production with higher taxes that effectively lower the price suppliers receive from selling carbon-based products—the tax raises the costs of doing business. As a result,

---

1.   Ronald Coase, "The Problem of Social Cost," *The Journal of Law and Economics* 3 (1), 1960, pp. 1–44.

either profits will fall, wages will fall, consumer prices will increase, or some combination of the three will occur.

The substitution effect arises because the price that people pay for products that either emit carbon or require carbon emissions in their production will rise relative to the price of all other products and services. The higher relative price discourages consumers and producers from purchasing "carbon-emitting" products—which is consistent with the goal of addressing global warming.

The adverse economic impact arises due to the carbon tax's impact on production and on lower after-tax income for consumers. Whether there are adverse economic impacts, on net, from a carbon tax depends on what the government does with the money. If the government were to spend this revenue windfall, then the amount of inefficiencies in the economy would increase.[2]

In a properly designed policy, the carbon tax encourages the consumer substitution effect without imposing undue production and consumer income effects. The correct carbon tax recognizes the real adverse economic impacts the proposal can create and appropriately adjusts for these impacts through a static dollar-for-dollar reduction in the marginal income-tax rate.

The lower flat-tax rate offsets the negative effects on consumers by providing an equal and opposite impact on people's ability to earn higher yields elsewhere. Simultaneously, the lower flat income-tax rate provides an equal and opposite offset for the effect of producing other products on the cost of doing business, thereby offsetting the negative impact on profits, wages, and/or prices. What is not offset is the higher relative price of products that either emit carbon or require carbon emissions in their production. The price of these goods and services will rise relative to the price of all other products and services, thereby encouraging the reduction in carbon emissions.

---

2.   See James Gwartney and Richard Stroup, "Labor Supply and Tax Rates: A Correction of the Record," *American Economic Review,* 1983.

The net impact is precisely what the policy is designed to do: decrease overall carbon emissions while not creating adverse economic impacts.

Calculating the revenue offset on a static basis is crucial. In the dynamic world, the carbon tax will discourage the products and technologies that emit carbon. The reduced tax base lowers the government's tax revenues.

It is important that the risk that global warming represents be addressed. A carbon tax coupled with a static dollar-for-dollar flat tax-rate cut is the most efficient way to address global warming without wreaking havoc on the economy. The combination of a carbon tax and the flat-rate income tax will simultaneously reduce overall carbon emissions and significantly increase the incentives in the economy to work, invest, and innovate.

And it is here that I have been quite impressed by Al Gore's proposal of reducing the payroll tax to accompany his proposed increase in the carbon tax:

> For the last fourteen years, I have advocated the elimination of all payroll taxes—including those for Social Security and unemployment compensation—and the replacement of that revenue in the form of pollution taxes—principally on CO_2. The overall level of taxation would remain exactly the same. It would be, in other words, a revenue-neutral tax swap. But, instead of discouraging businesses from hiring more employees, it would discourage business from producing more pollution.[3]

In principle my proposal is very little different from Al Gore's, even though our assessment of the risk may be very different, remembering that I know little about global warming.

---

3.   Al Gore, Speech at New York University Law School, September 16, 2001.

19

FIGHT POVERTY AND THE POVERTY TRAP WITH ENTERPRISE ZONES

The "safety net" designed to help the disadvantaged and unemployed in our society is a complex web of services (such as employment placement), in-kind payments (such as medical care coverage and food stamps), and direct income supplements (such as Aid to Families with Dependent Children [AFDC]) that are available to alleviate the worst hardships of poverty. Since 1965, transfer payments to persons have increased nearly 900 percent (adjusted for inflation) to $1.8 trillion. On average transfer payments to individuals increased 5.5 percent each and every year since 1965, which outpaced the inflation-adjusted economic growth rate of 3.1 percent per year.

Much of the increase in transfer payments has occurred in Social Security and other government-funded retirement programs. But the growth in transfer payment programs aimed specifically at the poor and disadvantaged tells the same story. In 2008, expenditures for AFDC, food stamps, and the like[1] totaled $590.7 billion, nearly 1,240 percent larger than the amount spent in constant 2008 dollars in 1965 (Figure 19-1), or an annual growth rate of 6.2 per-

---

1. These expenditures include: Unemployment Insurance, Supplemental Nutrition Assistance Programs (SNAP), Supplemental Security Income, Earned Income Tax Credit, Medical Assistance including Medicaid, Aid to Families with Dependent Children (AFDC), Assistance Programs Operating Under the Personal Responsibility and Work Opportunity Reconciliation Act of 1996, General Assistance, Energy Assistance, and Women's Infants and Children (WIC) programs.

Figure 19-1 **Growth in Inflation-Adjusted Transfer Payments Total and Total Income Support Payments 1965–2008**

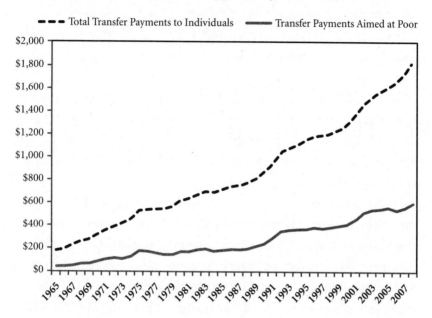

cent per year. And these numbers don't include policies such as the Earned Income Tax Credit (EITC).

In order to achieve parsimony in conjunction with fairness and equity, each of these programs has stringent criteria for its recipients.

Back in 1983, I wrote a paper called "The Tightening Grip of the Poverty Trap."[2] In this paper I described how "income" tests for welfare, while designed to ensure that *only* the truly needy would receive the help they so desperately lacked, have marked, perverse effects on the economic incentives of the poor.

Needs tests, means tests, and income tests exclude people as their incomes progressively increase, ensuring that funds are not squandered on those who are less in need. While "needs" tests may

---

2.   Arthur B. Laffer, "The Tightening Grip of the Poverty Trap," AB Laffer Associates, April 29, 2003.

be rationalized on both moral and budgetary grounds, when combined with payroll and income taxes, the phased reduction of welfare benefits has meant that spendable income actually rises very little as gross wages increase, and for some income thresholds, spendable income (total spending power) actually declines as gross wages increase.

Specifically, I examined the net effect on spendable income of the combination of "needs" tests and taxes for an inner-city family of four (one adult and three dependents) in Los Angeles that avails itself of the maximum city, county, state, and federal welfare benefits to which it is entitled given its income.

What was clear from this analysis is that marginal tax rates for inner-city inhabitants were prohibitively high—in some cases, the poorest people actually faced the highest marginal tax rates of all income groups. Over the entire range from no wages to wages of $1,300 per month, the family in my analysis faced marginal tax rates (net increases in spendable income) that ranged from a low of 53 percent (a poor family gained only $47 in spendable income when its gross monthly wages increased from $0 to $100) to a high of 314 percent (a poor family lost $214 in spendable income when its gross monthly wages increased from $1,000 to $1,100 a month).

My conclusion was straightforward: Why would anyone increase work effort if for every dollar earned, the government took away three? It makes no sense. Unfortunately, the situation today is much the same as in the 1980s. In 1996 President Clinton signed a welfare reform bill pushed by the Republican Congress that reduced many disincentives to work. The work requirements and time limits for welfare worked like a charm: The percentage of Americans on welfare fell dramatically in most states. But starting in 2002, Congress began to whittle away at those reforms, and we are essentially back where we started.

A 1996 study by Linda Ginnarelli and Eugene Steuerle at the Urban Institute examined the changes in what we are calling spendable income for different hypothetical families currently on welfare if they were to become employed in a minimum-wage job.[3] The tax implications include actual taxes paid, lost welfare benefits, and any expenditure necessary for the job (such as commuting expenditures) for both part-time and full-time employment. Much like my 1983 piece, the Urban Institute study found that the marginal tax rates facing the poorest people ranged from 70 percent to 101 percent (families could actually lose spendable income by taking a job). Summarizing their findings, Ginnarelli and Steuerle concluded that:

> *A significant portion of the population faces tax rates of 100 percent or more for work at a full-time minimum wage job or for increasing their work effort beyond some minimal level. The net impact of this system, in our view, is pernicious. Whatever the ability of statistical techniques to discover changes in work behavior with changes in tax rates, very high rates breed discontent and disrespect for the law, violate basic notions of equity, and go against the work ethics of society. The average tax rate on work at full-time at minimum wage or twice minimum wage is so high, moreover, that the individual merely needs to work a small fraction of that time, or at only $1 or so an hour, in the informal sector to do better.[4]*

The evidence shows that the poverty trap continues today. A story from the weblog of Jeff Frankel (James W. Harpel Professor of Capital Formation and Growth at Harvard University's Kennedy School of Government) pretty much says it all.[4] The story (a

---

3. Linda Ginnarelli and Eugene Steuerle, "The Twice-Poverty Trap: Tax Rates Faced by AFDC Recipients," Urban Institute, 1996.
4. Jeff Frankel, "Effective Marginal Tax Rates on Lower Income American Workers," *Jeff Frankels Weblog*, February 8, 2008, http://content.ksg.harvard.edu/blog/jeff_frankels_weblog/2008/02/08/8/.

retelling of one told by a colleague, Jeff Liebman) tells of a single mother who

> *had moved from a $25,000 a year job to a $35,000 a year job, and suddenly she couldn't make ends meet any more. . . . She really did come out behind by several hundred dollars a month. She lost free health insurance and instead had to pay $230 a month for her employer-provided health insurance. Her rent associated with her section 8 voucher went up by 30% of the income gain (which is the rule). She lost the ($280 a month) subsidized child care voucher she had for after-school care for her child. She lost around $1600 a year of the EITC. She paid payroll tax on the additional income. Finally, the new job was in Boston, and she lived in a suburb. So now she has $300 a month of additional gas and parking charges. She asked me if she should go back to earning $25,000.*[5]

Another study by the National Center for Children in Poverty followed the financial incentives for Becky Evans, a single mother with two children living in Philadelphia.[6] This study also comes to the same conclusion as my 1983 study—as a low-wage family earns more income, the total amount of resources (spendable income) does not necessarily increase. Taking into account a full array of income-support programs (both monetary and in-kind), the study finds that:

> *Even with the help of government work supports, Becky can't cover her family's basic expenses until her earnings reach about $23,000, which would require full-time work at $11.05 an hour. She can almost make ends meet at about $19,000 in*

---

5.   Ibid.
6.   Nancy K. Cauthen, "When Work Doesn't Pay: What Every Policymaker Should Know," National Center for Children in Poverty, June 2006.

earnings, but by $20,000, her family is no longer eligible for food stamps and falls farther behind.

If her earnings increase beyond $23,000, Becky will have a small cushion in her budget that could be saved or used to cover an emergency. But if her income reaches $36,000, she will lose her child care subsidy. Subsequent earnings gains will be reduced as her children lose their health insurance, and Becky begins to pay premiums. Becky's earnings will have to increase to $40,000 before she breaks even again. The bottom line is that Becky's family is no better off financially if she earns $40,000 than if she earns $23,000.[7]

The overall effect of these high effective tax rates on the poor and disadvantaged has been nothing short of tragic.

To an economist, however, these results are a fully predictable consequence of the dramatically increased economic disincentives and other legislated barriers that have disenfranchised the poor from participation in America's economic prosperity.

The disenfranchisement costs cannot be fully expressed in dollars. They must also include the personal degradation of continually seeking work and being told that their services are unwanted, which adds to the victims' feelings of resentment and social anomie.

An individual's decision not to participate in the labor force is an active statement of how that person sees his abilities relative to society's values. The individual might well say that one's chances of finding a job are so low that it is not worth trying. He might be saying that the wage he could be paid for his work would be so low relative to welfare opportunities that it is not worthwhile to seek work. One way or another, nonparticipation is tantamount to having no hope of engaging in the productive activity that is a central part of most people's lives.

The tragedy of the unemployment problem is not fully reflected

---

7.   Ibid.

in the average figures. The average unemployment rate misses the growing concentration of high unemployment rates among those groups that are being left behind. These people are developing habits and a lifestyle in which productive activity is absent. They are missing the training and experience that have been used by past generations as the stepping-stone to a better life for themselves and their children.

Disruption of the family unit is another aspect of welfare disincentives that might have been expected from a careful study of the benefit structure. Benefits from public assistance agencies are generally directed toward family units, and these benefits increase less than proportionately as family size increases. Two families of three members each will generally be eligible for more benefits than one family of six members when there is no outside income. This incentive toward divisiveness increases as the family begins earning income. As the family of six earns income, its benefits fall at a faster rate than that for two families of three each earning half as much.

The incentives to divide a family go further when one considers that in a family unit with two adults, one of the two must be working unless he is disabled or has been unsuccessful in his job search. In a family unit with only one adult, it is unnecessary that the one adult work or search for a job as long as there are school-age children at home. Separating the family can simultaneously increase welfare benefits and eliminate the need for one adult to work.

Rewards for family division are most pressing when one member is fully employed. The income of one adult may sufficiently reduce benefits so that the family's spendable income suffers. By keeping himself separate from the rest of the family through lack of marriage or other legal connection, the employed adult allows the other parent to be eligible for the full array of entitlement programs. Thus the eligibility requirements may make family desertion a parental duty, not an act of cowardice.

A Positive Plan: Enterprise Zones

Programs that ignore the enormous disincentives for the poorest Americans to supply work effort are doomed to failure. Excessive effective tax rates on low-income families have distorted the economy and produced a poverty trap. Only after these effective tax rates are reduced will the economic standing of the poorest Americans reach their full potential.

The lessons from history are clear. The success stories of Americans from humble origins were written because economic shackles were loosened. The sharp decline in unemployment and the rapid rise in real incomes during the Kennedy, Reagan, and Clinton tax-cutting eras were directly a consequence of the improved economy associated with enhanced private incentives.

What is needed is a reversal of those policies that have tightened the grip of the poverty trap by turning the safety net of a moral society into an immoral labyrinth that uses poverty to entrap the poor. Policy must be directed toward ensuring that the fruits of economic recovery can be harvested by the least advantaged in our society. The following five-point program would be a first and necessary step in that direction.

In order for business to be attracted to poorer areas, firms need to anticipate after-tax profits. A halving of the business flat income tax rates for firms operating in a designated "enterprise zone" would go a long way toward providing socially constructive incentives. Given the current absence of business in these areas, such a big reduction in tax rates would have little effect on business tax revenues. To the extent that some unemployed found work and some welfare recipients earned more, federal, state, and local spending would fall.

Equally important is the need to ensure something other than "absentee businesses," or firms located in the enterprise zone but employing people elsewhere. This requires elimination of the entire flat tax on all personal income for individuals who live and work in

217

the enterprise zone for a period of time until these neighborhoods catch up. Such a dramatic reduction in the flat-tax tax rates would mean little net revenue loss. Every person newly employed would save the government much more in welfare and unemployment compensation than he would cost in forgone taxes. Higher property values would raise city revenues. Higher income, sales, and other tax receipts would also occur because of more output. Less poverty and despair would ultimately lead to more efficient educational spending, less need for police protection, and so on.

The third part of an effective enterprise zone program would be to exempt teenagers from the minimum-wage law (see section one). This change would have some immediate beneficial effects. It would, to the extent teenagers actually found jobs from the increased business activity levels in the enterprise zone, also reduce deficits. Its most important effect, however, would be long-run. Teenagers would be able to become apprentices and learn the requisite skills to allow them to become productive members of the workforce. This step is crucial for a permanent solution.

The fourth part of a comprehensive enterprise zone would be to relax major new and existing regulations and other forms of government strictures that apply to businesses and individuals operating in the enterprise zone. The purpose of these statements is to identify regulations that might constrain economic activity and employment in the enterprise zones.

Last, regardless of whether an individual is located within a designated enterprise zone or not, effective tax rates in excess of 100 percent should be relaxed. Increased income from work should never lead to a net reduction in spendable income. This can be achieved through the relaxation of means, needs, and other "income" tests.

20

OTHER FLAT-TAX PROPOSALS

There are other flat-rate tax proposals, and let me say upfront, these are far better than our current tax system.

Robert Hall and Alvin Rabushka first introduced their flat-rate tax proposal in the *Wall Street Journal* on December 10, 1981. And it is a good proposal. The original proposal had two income-tax rates: 15 percent and 28 percent.

As it now stands, the Hall-Rabushka plan taxes both business and personal income (similar to my plan) at 19 percent. The 19 percent rate is higher than my rate because the Hall-Rabushka plan exempts income below $25,500 (as of 1995, which is indexed to inflation). The Hall-Rabushka proposal also does not include payroll taxes in the flat-tax base.

Back in 1995, Dick Armey (former congressman from Texas, and the current chairman of FreedomWorks) introduced legislation that would have implemented the Hall-Rabushka flat-tax concept, with a tax rate of 17 percent and an $11,350 exemption for a single person, $22,700 for a married couple, and a per-dependent credit of $5,300.[1]

In his classic book *Capitalism and Freedom*,[2] Milton Friedman proposed a negative income tax. Friedman's negative income tax established one simple flat-rate tax, but an income-tax threshold

---

1.   See http://www.pbs.org/newshour/bb/congress/armey's_flat_tax.html.
2.   Milton Friedman, *Capitalism and Freedom*, The University of Chicago Press, 1962.

such that at the tax threshold, a family would owe no income tax. Any family with annual income below the income-tax threshold would receive a tax payment from the government. Any family with annual income above the threshold would pay income taxes on the differences between the actual income earned and the tax threshold.

Income thresholds are problematic, however, and a flat-rate tax system without thresholds is able to leverage more of the benefits from a flat tax—the lowest possible tax rate, over the broadest tax base, with the simplest possible rules for administration. And it is for this reason that including payroll taxes in the flat-tax revenue base is so important. Social Security expenditures are expenditures of the federal government that are no different than expenditures on Medicare, defense, or any other federal program. Removing this special "tax" distinction for Social Security will help with the necessary financial reforms that must occur. More important for our purposes, the payroll tax is a regressive tax. Eliminating this tax allows my flat-tax plan to address regressivity concerns without having to implement an income threshold that reduces the effectiveness, and increases the complexity, of a flat-rate tax.

Another popular proposal is a national sales tax, commonly referred to as the FairTax. If fully implemented, the FairTax would repeal the Sixteenth Amendment to the U.S. Constitution, which would remove the federal government's ability to levy an income tax. According to FairTax.org, the tax would eliminate "all federal personal and corporate income taxes, gift, estate, capital gains, alternative minimum, Social Security, Medicare, and self-employment taxes."[3] Instead, the FairTax would impose a national retail sales tax that would be 30 percent added on to the cost of goods sold at the point and time of sales. This number would be the equivalent of a 23 percent income tax (30/130).

Just like the Hall-Rabushka tax, if implemented, the FairTax

---

3.   See http://www.fairtax.org/site/PageServer?pagename-about_main.

would have significant progrowth effects. However, like the Hall-Rabushka plan, the FairTax addresses regressivity concerns (because the tax is based on consumption) by giving monthly payments to U.S. households that fall below a specified income threshold in the form of an advanced rebate termed a "prebate." The inclusion of this prebate creates unnecessary complexities and leads to a higher-than-necessary tax rate.

Also, the high sales-tax rate creates issues that are not created with my flat-rate tax plan. For instance, the retail sales tax in some localities in California under the FairTax would approach 40 percent. The simplicity of my flat-rate tax avoids sticker shock by dividing the tax across two very broad tax bases.

While any of the proposed tax reforms would be a marked improvement over our current tax system, the simplicity and maximum progrowth incentives of the proposal outlined here make this proposal the most desirable.

Part Three

Monetary and Trade Policies: Interest Rates, Exchange Rates, and Inflation

As is common practice in my profession, the world of political economics is composed of four all-inclusive grand kingdoms: fiscal policy, incomes policies, monetary policy, and trade policy. We're all more or less familiar with each of these categories of public policy, but to reiterate:

- Fiscal policy encompasses government spending and taxation.
- Monetary policy is more narrowly focused on Federal Reserve policies *in re* money supply, prices, interest rates, exchange rates, and other such arcana.
- Trade policy, of course, has to do with imports, exports, comparative advantage, the gains from trade, and the terms of trade along with tariffs, quotas, and other impediments to the free flow of goods and services across national boundaries.
- Income policies is generally a catchall category for anything missed in the other three categories. Income policies includes all sorts of government actions that indirectly affect the economy, such as regulations, restrictions, and requirements like the minimum wage, wage and price controls, and health-care reform.

There's considerable overlap and ambiguity when it comes to the details of which policy goes in which category, but the broad boundaries should be fairly understandable. In this book I've already covered a number of incomes policies and fiscal policy in Parts One and Two. Part Three will cover monetary and trade policies.

As is only natural, the reason I concern myself with public economic policy is that I believe these policies matter and matter a lot to the health and welfare of our nation. And they do! We really have come a long way over the past half century. But all those gains are now at risk. So, whether you are agnostic, dyslexic, or insomniac, please stay up all night with me and see if there really is a Dog.

21

MONETARY POLICY

The story of monetary policy is the story of wisdom lost, then reacquired. Using *Star Trek* vernacular, the prime directive of monetary policy is to stabilize prices, thereby eliminating inflation. Just how monetary policy achieves this price stability is open to debate, but suffice it to write that inflation is basically too much money chasing too few goods. Inflation is everywhere and at all times a monetary and goods phenomenon.

If you think about exactly what inflation is, it is the rate of decline in the purchasing power of the monetary unit—here in the United States that monetary unit is the dollar—or alternatively, inflation is the rate of increase of the number of dollars it takes to purchase a given bundle of goods. It is as elementary as that, my dear Watson. Looking at both the price level and the rate of inflation as measured by the consumer price index, you can see from Figure 21-1 and Figure 21-2 that we've had a lot of variation in inflation here in the good old U.S. of A.

And, with this concept of inflation in mind, it is easy to see that more goods with the same amount of money or less money with the same amount of goods leads to lower prices, holding everything else the same. Higher prices are the direct consequence of less goods and/or more money. Stable prices require a continuous balance between the quantity of goods and the quantity of money.

After World War II, the United States was one of a number of countries on a gold exchange standard known collectively as the

Bretton Woods agreement. This agreement was signed in Bretton Woods, New Hampshire, in 1944, and also included the formation of the International Monetary Fund. As a result of this agreement, monetary policy in the early part of the post–World War II era was global in scope, as opposed to national or regional as it is today.

Figure 21-1 U.S. Consumer Price Index

(monthly, through Jul 09)

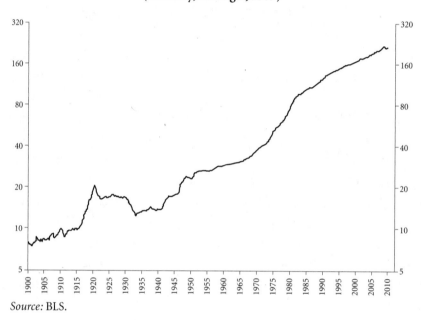

Source: BLS.

The United States was singled out to have a special role in the Bretton Woods agreement. We were responsible for maintaining a fixed dollar price of gold, which we were able to maintain by agreeing to buy or sell gold at thirty-five dollars per troy ounce with a small bid/ask spread. The logic underlying this U.S. obligation was as simple as it was correct.

When there's too much money, markets sense higher inflation and people turn to gold. Because the U.S. Treasury supported the price of gold, any upward pressure on its price would force the Treasury to be a seller of gold. The very fact that gold was purchased from the Treasury automatically took money out of circulation, thereby bringing the quantity of money back in balance with goods. The process was simple, automatic, and elegant. In fact, the gold standard of the eighteenth and nineteenth centuries basically relied on this same mechanism, only back then Britain was the guarantor of the price of gold. Under Bretton Woods the United States was the guarantor.

Figure 21-2 U.S. Inflation, 1900 to present
(monthly)

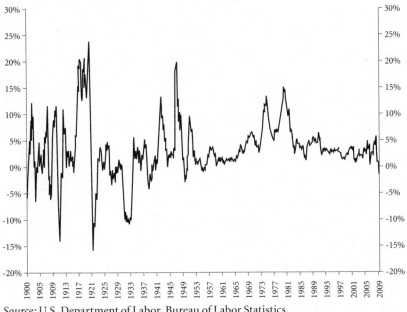

Source: U.S. Department of Labor, Bureau of Labor Statistics.

Other countries under the Bretton Woods agreement were responsible for guaranteeing the value of their individual currencies against the U.S. dollar, much in the same way as the U.S. dollar price of gold was guaranteed. These other countries were expected to keep their currencies from either appreciating or depreciating against the U.S. dollar. There were, of course, intermittent breakdowns in the Bretton Woods system, but during its heyday it worked

227

pretty well. In my view, Bretton Woods' two biggest shortcomings were, first, its reliance on each and every country's good intentions to keep domestic inflation in check and, second, its reliance on gold as an appropriate indicator of the general price level. Neither of these reliances turned out to be as enduring as the creators of Bretton Woods had anticipated.

Addressing the good intentions of each and every country that was a party to the agreement, we find that even in the early 1960s French president Charles de Gaulle used the Bretton Woods system as a hostile tool to have his way with President Kennedy.[1] But that was only the beginning. By the mid to late 1960s foreign governments routinely engaged in mischievous shenanigans with the international monetary system. By the late 1960s and early 1970s the system had become irreparably damaged, and monetary policy devolved into a collection of unhinged paper currencies administered by unprincipled, incompetent political hacks. The era from, say, 1970 to 1980 was the period in history where we experienced the awesome destructive power of a monetary system gone awry—a veritable monetary tsunami.

It was during this period of U.S. economic history that I wrote a series of editorials for the *Wall Street Journal* outlining the unpleasant consequences I foresaw from bad U.S. monetary and trade policies. The United States had devalued the dollar not only against gold but also against many other currencies. This was the time of the Smithsonian accord.

In my first editorial on trade, money, and devaluations, February 5, 1973, titled "Do Devaluations Really Help Trade?"[2] I argued that, both from a theoretical perspective and from past experiences, it was clear that devaluations do not improve trade balances; in fact, devaluations usually made trade deficits larger for the devaluing country.

---

1.   Ruud Van Dijk, *Encyclopedia of the Cold War,* Vol. 1, p. 99; New York: MTM Publishing, 2008.

2.   Arthur B. Laffer, "Do Devaluations Really Help Trade?" *Wall Street Journal,* February 5, 1973.

My second editorial was on January 10, 1974, with the heading "The Bitter Fruits of Devaluation."[3] The key statement was: "The mystery of the current bout of inflation is readily solvable; it is as much a direct consequence of the dollar's devaluation as any other cause." Basically this conclusion results from the Law of One Price, whereby prices are arbitraged across national boundaries and currency conversions. If a ton of steel sells for £200 in London and the dollar price of the pound (the exchange rate) is $1.60 then the price of a ton of steel in dollars will be $320 plus or minus. If the dollar devalues against the pound, say, to $2.40 per pound, then the dollar price of steel will have to rise versus the pound price of steel by 50 percent for the Law of One Price to hold. Devaluations cause fully offsetting price movements and inflation in the devaluing country's currency.

My third editorial extended monetary policy to the world at large. Its title was "Global Money Growth and Inflation,"[4] and it was published on September 23, 1975. In this editorial I looked at how Eurodollars, foreign currencies, and changes in exchange rates can offset, magnify, or change domestic monetary policy. The period I was writing about then was not all that different from today with the Federal Reserve headed by Ben Bernanke.

While it was acceptable as an indicator of overall prices in the eighteenth and nineteenth centuries, the price of gold in the last half of the twentieth century just didn't cut the mustard. In the early 1930s, even though the price of gold was fixed, overall prices fell sharply (see Chapter 24). In the 1950s and 1960s, the opposite was the case. Gold's central role in monetary policy had been eroded. The price of gold no longer was a good proxy for the overall price level. A change was needed.

In the early 1980s under gifted Federal Reserve chairman Paul Volcker (1979–87), the United States once again returned to a price

---

3.   Arthur B. Laffer, "The Bitter Fruits of Devaluation," *Wall Street Journal*, January 10, 1974.

4.   Arthur B. Laffer, "Global Money Growth and Inflation," *Wall Street Journal*, September 23, 1975.

rule, only this time the dollar wasn't pegged to gold. Following a meeting I had with Chairman Volcker in 1982, I cowrote an article for the editorial page of the *Wall Street Journal*.[5] In this article Charles Kadlec and I outlined in detail Chairman Volcker's vision of a price rule, a vision that is as relevant today as it was in 1982. Volcker essentially said, "Look, I have no idea what prices are today. Or what inflation is today. And we won't have those data for months. But I do know exactly what the spot prices of commodities are."

In short, what Chairman Volcker did was to base monetary policy on the secular pattern of spot commodity prices (the market price of a commodity for current delivery). During boom periods, spot commodity prices rise relative to all prices. During a recession, they fall relative to all prices. But in the long run there is a stable relationship between spot commodity prices and all prices. It's very similar to a gold standard, except that Chairman Volcker was using twenty-five commodities instead of just one. Every quarter from 1982 on, monetary policy has been guided by the spot price of a collection of commodities (Figure 21-3), save for our present period.

If spot commodity prices rose above their cyclically adjusted long-term level—outside a band, of course—the Fed would then start selling bonds in the open market, thus removing monetary base (bank reserves plus currency in circulation) from the banking system and thereby taking money out of the economy. The Fed would continue selling bonds until spot commodity prices once again came back in line with their historical level, money again being in balance with goods. Obviously, if spot commodity prices fell below the cyclically adjusted lower band the Fed would buy bonds.

Following Volcker, this policy has been meticulously adhered to by Alan Greenspan. I had hoped it would also be adhered to by our current Fed chairman, Ben Bernanke.[6] But it hasn't been.

---

5. Arthur B. Laffer and Charles W. Kadlec, "Has the Fed Already Put Itself on a Price Rule?" *Wall Street Journal*, October 28, 1962.

6. Arthur Laffer, "Ben Bernanke is the Right Person at the Right Time," *Wall Street Journal*, October 26, 2005.

Figure 21-3 The Fed "Price Rule": Dow Jones
Spot Commodity Index vs. the Fed Funds Rate
(monthly through 5/5/06)

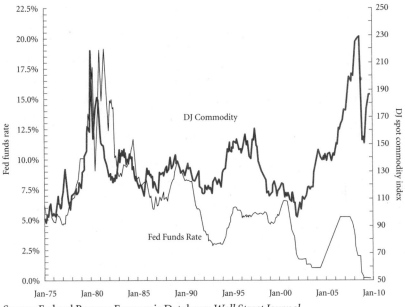

Source: Federal Reserve Economic Database; *Wall Street Journal.*

In my view, the Fed had arrived at a monetary system that, while it does have flaws, is better than any system ever before designed by man. The scenario I've described of the United States moving from the price rule of a gold exchange standard to an unhinged paper currency and then back to a rock-solid price rule based on spot commodity prices really comes to life when one examines the historical record of inflation in the United States. Just look at Figure 21-2. What pops out of that figure is the stability of inflation around a very low mean in the years following Volcker's ascension to the chairmanship of the Fed. This is what I mean when I write a price rule of twenty-five commodities. It really doesn't get any better. Unfortunately, the most recent year or two's inflation numbers are quite disturbing.

Thanks to the success of the Fed and Paul Volcker (and later,

Alan Greenspan), we saw a 180-degree turnaround in interest rates in the early 1980s. Take a look at the ten-year government T-note yield (Figure 21-4). Today, the ten-year T-note yield stands at 3.50 percent and, breaking down that yield using the ten-year Treasury Inflation-Protected Security (TIPS) yield, we can see that the nominal yield of 3.50 percent is composed of a healthy real yield of 1.7 percent and inflation expectations of 1.7 percent. I don't know if any of you will remember, but when Reagan took office on January 20, 1981, the prime interest rate was 21.5 percent and the ten-year yield was close to 13 percent.

Figure 21-4 10-Year T-Note Yield

(constant maturity, monthly through 5/5/06)

Source: St. Louis Federal Reserve Bank.

Perhaps the purest expression of the effectiveness of the policies we have discussed to this point is the performance of the stock market. While trade policies to be discussed shortly do matter—and matter a lot—no three factors play a bigger part in equity performance than corporate profitability, tax rates (both corporate and personal), and the market's discounting mechanism, interest rates. And those factors are direct results of fiscal policy and monetary policy.

In Figure 21-5 I have plotted the S&P 500 Index deflated by the consumer price index. The chart and the inflation-adjusted equity returns in the figure paint quite a picture! Most recently, however, the picture has become bleak. We truly are in a new era of diminished expectations. A lot of people are going to have to learn to live with less.

Figure 21-5 Inflation-Adjusted S&P 500 Index
(semi-log, Jan 06 = 100, through Aug 09)

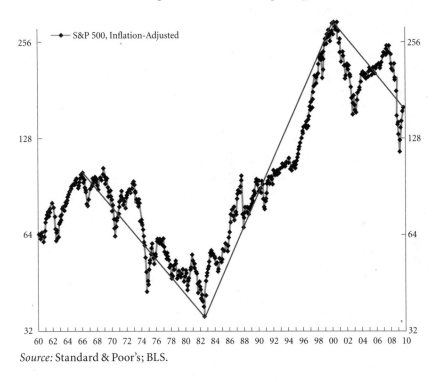

Source: Standard & Poor's; BLS.

S&P 500: 1,016.4

	Nominal	Real
Jan 66 to Present	5.6%	1.1%
Jan 66 to Jul 82	0.5%	−6.1%
Jul 82 to Aug 00	16.1%	12.5%
Aug 00 to Present	−4.3%	−6.6%

In February 1966, not too long after the Kennedy tax cuts, the Dow Jones Industrial Average peaked at 995 (intraday it climbed briefly over 1,000). In August 1982, the Dow hit a low of 777.

Now just think about that. The nominal value of the Dow went from 995 in February 1966 to 777 in August 1982. Thus, over a period of a little more than sixteen years the Dow fell 22 percent in nominal terms, or at an average annual *loss* of 1.5 percent. And that's the performance in nominal terms—keep in mind this period was a high-inflation environment. If you adjust those nominal returns for inflation you end up with a real *loss* of 74 percent from February 1966 to August 1982, or a compound annual loss of 7.9 percent for sixteen-plus years. Now, that's a bear market!

This was the record of equity returns when Reagan took office. When the "Real President's" tax cut finally took place, do you remember what happened? Once the bulk of the phased-in tax cuts were in place in 1983, the economy soared, and so did asset values. From the low point in August 1982 to August 2000, the Dow Jones Industrial Average rose 1,343 percent, or at an average annual rate of 16.1 percent. Adjusted for inflation, these figures are 714 percent, or 12.5 percent per year—all the result of progrowth, supply-side policies put into action.

22

THERE IS NO CONNECTION
BETWEEN GROWTH AND INFLATION

The objective of monetary policy should be to establish a currency that is, as the old phrase goes, "as good as gold." In fact, good monetary policy should make the currency better than gold. Money is only a "veil." The only true objective of monetary policy is to produce price stability. With that objective in mind, the design of an optimal monetary policy is fairly straightforward, as I described a few pages earlier, under a twenty-five-commodity price rule.

While many economists define money in empirical terms such as currency in circulation plus demand deposits (M1) and others add time deposits (M2) and so on, my preference is to consider the concept of money first and why that concept is important. Once the concept is clear its empirical counterpart should be easier to determine.

To me, money is important because it is a conduit between any one good and any other good. Money is that entity through which you have to traverse to obtain another good. Households, for example, sell their services to businesses in the marketplace for money and then use that money to pay taxes and buy other goods and services. In fact, it is money that allows households to convert work effort into consumption. In the same way businesses sell their products again for money, and then use that money to pay land, labor, and capital. Money is the sine qua non of an advanced market economy. Money is the means of payment. But even with this concept there are still lots of difficulties in measuring exactly what is the empirical counterpart of money.

If you're a boy who trades baseball cards with his friends, those cards may well be money in that milieu. In other circumstances, subway tokens in New York or cigarettes in Germany right after World War II were also money. These are just a few examples that demonstrate the diversity of what money really is. If you're in a men's room with a pay toilet, and you don't have a dime, you don't have money. Hundred-dollar bills just don't cut it. I wrote an article in the *Journal of Political Economy* in 1971[1] that postulated that money also included unused trade credit available.

Money can also be credit in some instances, but credit is usually not money. Credit is the means by which savers (lenders) transfer resources to investors (borrowers). Credit is the means by which savings are allocated to investing. Money is that narrow channel that facilitates transactions, pure and simple.

There's a poem I just absolutely love about money by the economist Kenneth Boulding, which goes like this.

We must have a good definition of Money,
For if we do not, then what have we got,
But a Quantity Theory of no-one-knows what,
And this would be almost too true to be funny.
Now, Banks secrete something, as bees secrete honey;
(It sticks to their fingers some, even when hot!)
But what things are liquid and what things are not,
Rests on whether the climate of business is sunny.
For both Stores of Value and Means of Exchange
Include among Assets a very wide range,
So your definition's no better than mine.
Still, with credit-card-clever computers it's clear

---

1.   Arthur B. Laffer, "Trade Credit and the Money Market," *Journal of Political Economy*, Vol. 78, No. 2 (March–April 1970), pp. 239–67.

That money as such will one day disappear;
Then, what isn't there we won't have to define.[2]

But all these conceptual issues notwithstanding, one can't stick with a conceptual definition of money that has no empirical counterpart. Theories, to be meaningful, have to be testable. My preference in today's economy is to use M1 as the appropriate counterpart to the theoretical concept of money. M1 includes currency in circulation, demand deposits and other checkable deposits, and traveler's checks. Now back to an optimal monetary policy.

The primary objective of monetary policy, as I wrote earlier, is to achieve price stability. But economists are often stuck on a mistaken notion of the cause of inflation. Therefore, my first step in designing such an optimal policy is to dispel some basic monetary policy myths, the most prevalent of which is the idea that growth causes inflation. Consider this recent statement from Fed chairman Ben Bernanke:

> *Even after a recovery gets under way, the rate of growth of real economic activity is likely to remain below its longer-run potential for a while, implying that the current slack in resource utilization will increase further. We expect that the recovery will only gradually gain momentum and that economic slack will diminish slowly. In particular, businesses are likely to be cautious about hiring, and the unemployment rate is likely to rise for a time, even after economic growth resumes. . . . In this environment, we anticipate that inflation will remain low. The slack in resource utilization remains sizable, and, notwithstanding recent increases in the prices of oil and other commodities, cost pressures generally remain subdued. As a consequence, inflation is likely to move down some over the next year relative to its pace in 2008.[3]*

---

2. Kenneth E. Boulding, "Economics as a Moral Science," *American Economic Review,* 1969, Vol. 59, No. 1, pp. 1–12.
3. Chairman Bernanke's testimony in front of the House of Representatives, June 3, 2009.

The quotation above illustrates that the governors of the Federal Reserve are firmly wedded to the notion that with strong growth at full resource utilization comes inflation. And as long as the economy performs well below full resource utilization we have little to fear from inflation. The enormous popularity of this view that growth causes inflation notwithstanding, nothing is further from the truth: Growth actually *reduces* inflation. In order to understand why growth reduces inflation and why the rival theory endorsed by Fed chairman Bernanke is not correct, I start by examining a staple of modern macroeconomics, the Phillips Curve.

The Phillips Curve in its modern context postulates that growth causes inflation, and the closer the economy is to full employment, the more inflation a given amount of growth will cause. The Phillips Curve itself originated with an empirical study published in the academic journal *Economica* by British economist A. W. Phillips in 1958.[4] Phillips analyzed U.K. wage changes and unemployment rates for the period 1861–1957 and found a negative relationship. During periods with large increases in nominal wages, according to Phillips's study, unemployment tended to be low. Periods of stable or falling wages generally had high unemployment. Although Phillips himself was quite circumspect about the policy implications of his findings, later economists such as Paul Samuelson and Robert Solow postulated a tradeoff between unemployment and inflation and used Phillips's study as empirical justification.

The postulated Phillips Curve tradeoff between inflation and unemployment would lead one to conclude that policies implemented to get an economy out of a slump will do so only by also causing prices to rise; policies implemented to rein in inflation will have the undesirable consequences of slowing growth and increasing unemployment. Sad but true: In this Phillips Curve world, "There is no free lunch."

---

4.   A. W. Phillips, "The relationship between unemployment and the rate of change of money wages in the United Kingdom, 1861–1957," *Economica*, 1958, Vol. 25, pp. 283–99.

The Phillips Curve: Intuitive—Yet Incorrect

The Phillips Curve logic is enormously appealing to academics and members of the financial press.[5] One can't watch a business show on television for five minutes without hearing some analyst warn of "inflationary pressures" brought on by larger-than-expected growth. The Phillips Curve also has broad appeal because it seems to make perfect sense to the average businessman, who can see a parallel between the Phillips Curve logic and the realities of operating his own company.

From a businessman's perspective, to accommodate an increase in demand, a company can either increase quantity, increase price, or do some of each. The company's decision whether to increase quantity or increase price depends upon the current state of its business. If business has been slow and the company has excess capacity and an underused labor pool, it probably will satisfy the increase in demand primarily by increasing quantity. If business is slow enough, the company may well cut its prices to attract customers. Slow times warrant stable or even reduced prices. However, if business is really good and capacity is stretched and there's a shortage of labor, it's only logical that the company will ration demand and increase profits by raising prices.

To a businessman, it would seem a small step to extend his knowledge of his business to the economy at large. Aggregating over all businesses, the conclusions are simple: High unemployment and excess capacity keep inflation at bay while growth is inflationary—especially when the economy is close to full employment. Despite the completely straightforward application of Phillips Curve logic to an individual business, there is a subtle flaw that creeps in

---

5.   Before the Phillips Curve, Keynesian economists really had no way of explaining inflation. In his book *A General Theory of Employment, Interest and Money*, Professor John Maynard Keynes focused on many things, but not inflation.

whenever the Phillips Curve principle is aggregated from an individual business to the whole economy.

When a businessman talks about lowering prices because demand is weak, he's not talking about dollar prices so much as he is talking about lowering the prices of his products to attract business away from other products. To attract business away from other companies, the businessman lowers his product prices relative to the prices of other products, thus making his goods more competitive in a price-sensitive marketplace. In turn, when a businessman talks about his company raising its product prices, he also means that the company raises those prices *relative* to the prices of other goods and services so that he can increase profits, pay workers more, and pay his suppliers more in order to increase output. Therefore, when a company raises prices, demanders of the company's products substitute away from the now-higher-priced products into *relatively* less expensive substitutes—a movement along the demand curve.

Likewise, higher *relative* prices of a company's products at full capacity provide incentives to the company to bid workers, capital, and raw materials away from other firms—a movement along the supply curve. Higher relative prices for a company's products raise the relative prices of factor inputs intensive in the production of this now-higher-priced product by proportionally more than the product price rose, thus attracting those critical factors away from alternative uses. In a downturn the exact reverse occurs. So far so good.

Where the analogy between a company and the economy breaks down is in aggregation. While a company can raise the prices of its products relative to the prices of all other goods and services, an economy cannot raise the relative price of all goods and services relative to all goods and services. As intuitive as the analogy between a company and the whole economy may seem to even an astute businessman, it's still silly. Not everyone can be above average. What is true for a company is most definitely not true for an economy—it's impossible for *all* prices to rise relative to all prices. What, then, is true for an economy, given that we all know inflation exists?

The True Nature of Inflation

A price is nothing more or less than the ratio of two goods in exchange. In a barter exchange of apples for oranges, the price of an apple is so many oranges and the inverse of that price is the apple price of an orange. Inflation, no matter what the numéraire, is the rate of increase of the exchange ratio. A businessman who talks in terms of dollars is really referring to the relative price of his products vis-à-vis other products.

The inflation we talk about, however, for the economy as a whole is literally a general rise in the prices of all goods and services measured in units of money. Stated somewhat differently, inflation is the rate of decline of the purchasing power of money. When it comes to comparing individual businesses with an entire economy, a price is not a price which is not a price. For a business, prices are relative prices of one good for another, while for an economy, prices are dollar prices of all goods and services.

Therefore, it only makes sense that for the macroeconomy, the money (dollar) price of a basket of goods reflects the relative scarcity of money versus the scarcity of goods. The scarcer money is, the lower the price of goods measured in money; the more plentiful money, the higher the money price of goods. But to our point, the more plentiful goods are, holding money constant, the lower (not higher) the money price of a representative good will be; conversely, the scarcer goods are (as in a recession), the higher the money price for goods and services. More goods mean lower prices; fewer goods mean higher prices. It's as simple as that.

Just imagine what would happen to U.S. prices if output fell dramatically and the quantity of money didn't change. Let's imagine output fell all the way down to the output level of Luxembourg. What do you think would happen to Luxembourg's price level if it had the quantity of money of the United States? It would go through the roof.

Inflation is in part caused by recession and cured by growth. For an economy, inflation results from an oversupply of money (relative to goods) or an undersupply of goods (relative to money). Holding the quantity of money constant, an increase in the quantity of goods will lower prices and a reduction in the quantity of goods will increase prices.

Just as a bumper crop of apples lowers the price of apples, so, too, does a bumper crop in the production of goods and services—an increase in output, employment, and production—lower the price of goods and services. Output growth—economic expansion—reduces inflation. Recession, contraction, and increased unemployment actually increase inflation. Ironically, the Phillips Curve, as used by its modern adherents, has it exactly backward. Putting people back to work doesn't cause inflation. Period!

For the astute reader who is searching memory banks to intuitively confirm or reject the empirical content of my conjectures, I will remind him of the inflation and high unemployment of the 1970s. When President Reagan took office on January 20, 1981, inflation was well in the double digits, the dollar was collapsing in the foreign exchanges, the prime interest rate was 21.5 percent, and the unemployment rate was high and rising. Once our policies were in place the dollar rose and inflation fell as the economy soared and interest rates tumbled.

So much for the Phillips Curve!

Indeed, in the early post–World War II period the two fastest-growing economies were those of Germany and Japan, and they also happened to be among the lowest-inflation countries with strong currencies. Italy, the United Kingdom, and the United States, on the other hand, were slow-growth, high-inflation countries with weak currencies.

Yet a classic example of how traditional economists of the time viewed the Reagan tax cuts is Walter Heller's article in the *Wall Street Journal* of July 12, 1978.

To summarize, then, nothing in the history of tax cuts, econometric studies of taxpayer responses, or field surveys of incentives suggests that the effects of a big tax cut on the supply of output even begin to match its effects on the demand for output. A $114 billion tax cut in three years would simply overwhelm our existing productive capacity with a tidal wave of increased demand and sweep away all hopes of curbing deficits and containing inflation. Indeed, it would soon generate soaring deficits and roaring inflation.[6]

Money—Getting the Theory Right

In the world of economics, everything is ruled by the law of demand and supply and price and quantity. The amount of goods and services people are willing to buy or hold depends on price, and the amount of goods and services people are willing to supply also depends upon price. At any moment in time there's a unique price equilibrating the amount demanded with the amount supplied. Making the same point in another way, there's a unique quantity equilibrating the price demanders are willing to pay and the price suppliers are willing to accept.

That having been written, an increase in demand (a change in demand resulting from anything other than a change in price) will by itself lead to upward price pressure and upward quantity pressure. A reduction in demand will do just the reverse; it will put downward pressure on both prices and quantities.

Take apples, for example. If we were to discover that apples have definite aphrodisiacal qualities—or, in the specific case of Californians, if we were to discover that apples have hallucinogenic attributes previously unknown—the demand for apples would increase,

---

6.   Walter Holler, "The Kemp-Roth-Laffer Free Lunch," *Wall Street Journal*, July 12, 1978.

causing the price of apples to rise. This is an example of an increase in demand. The increase in the price of apples will then induce apple growers to pick their trees cleaner and to grow more apples. This is a movement along the supply curve. Thus, with an increase in demand there will be more apples at higher prices. Symmetrically, if apples were found to cause cancer or infertility, the demand for apples would fall, leading to lower apple prices and fewer apples produced.

Disturbances can occur not only in the demand for products but also in their supply. For spontaneous increases in supply there is an analogous set of responses. An increase in supply will lead to downward pressure on price and upward pressure on quantity, while reductions in supply will do just the opposite. Those reductions in supply will result in higher prices and lessened quantity. It's really straightforward.

Continuing our apple example, if apple growers have an unexpected bumper crop of apples, there will be an excess supply of apples, leading to lower apple prices, which will induce apple buyers to buy more apples (movement along the demand curve). To wit: more apples and lower prices. With a crop failure (a reduction in supply), there will be an excess demand for apples and fewer apples sold at the resulting higher prices. Increases and decreases in the supply of apples lead to greater quantities at lower prices and lesser quantities at higher prices. When there are supply changes, prices and quantities move in opposite directions. Increases and decreases in demand, however, lead to greater quantities at higher prices and lesser quantities at lower prices. When there are demand changes, prices and quantities move in the same direction.[7]

The important point in this discussion is that for changes in supply, prices and quantities will move in opposite directions, while for changes in demand, prices and quantities will move in

---

7.   This relationship was made famous in the economics profession by Holbrook Working in a seminal paper: "The Statistical Determination of Demand Curves," *Quarterly Journal of Economics*, 1925, Vol. XXXIX.

the same direction. Therefore, though we know what happens to quantity, we still have no idea what happens to price. An increase in quantity can result from an increase in either supply or demand. In the former case prices will fall, while in the latter case prices will rise.

Money, as magical as some people think it may be, is not different from any other commodity in the realm of economics. It has to obey the laws of supply and demand just like everything else. If the quantity of money increases because of an increase in supply, we find ourselves in the familiar terrain of monetarists where increases in quantities of money are associated with higher inflation, higher interest rates, higher gold prices, and a weaker currency. It is in this arena that the old saw "inflation is everywhere and at all times a monetary phenomenon" comes into play.

If, however, the quantity of money increases as a result of an increased demand for money, things start getting a little weird; inflation, interest rates, and the price of gold will fall and the currency will strengthen as quantities of money grow faster. Fast money growth can, conceptually at least, imply lower interest rates and inflation, just as well as higher inflation and interest rates. An analogous discussion could be had about reductions in the quantity of money resulting in higher inflation and interest rates. Now let's see where all this takes us.

The Historical Debate

In the late 1970s, I explained increases and decreases in the demand for money by asking people to imagine what would happen if everyone knew with perfect certainty that twenty years from now the value of one dollar—in terms of the goods and services it could buy—would be exactly the same as it is today. Interest rates, of course, would tumble, as would the price of gold, and the dollar would soar in the foreign exchanges, as would stock prices. But, in addition, the quantity of dollars would increase because the demand for dollars would rise, eliciting greater supplies (a movement along the supply curve). Other factors being equal, wouldn't you be more willing to hold a stable-valued currency than one that is depreciating rapidly? Of course you would. And this is exactly what happened in the early to mid-1980s in the United States under the able leadership of President Ronald Reagan and Federal Reserve chairman Paul Volcker.

During the early 1980s, Milton Friedman and I had a number of lively discussions in our meetings with the president. In each of those discussions, Milton warned that rapid growth in the quantity of money would soon lead to much higher inflation, while I said just the opposite. My view was that the rapid growth of money in the early 1980s was due to increases in the demand for money, while Friedman held that the quantity of money was the same as the supply of money. To this point, here is a statement from Milton in an article he wrote for the *Wall Street Journal* in 1989:

> It is a truism, expressed in what is called the quantity equation of money, that the quantity of money (M) times the velocity of circulation of money (V) equals the price level (P) times output (y) or $MV = Py$.
>
> It is an empirical generalization expressed in the quantity theory of money that over any appreciable period, independent changes in V play a minor role, compared with the changes in the other variables. As a result, changes in prices (inflation or deflation) are dominated by changes in the quantity of money per unit of output. It is also an empirical generalization for the U.S. and similar countries that it takes something like two years for a change in the rate of monetary growth to affect significantly the behavior of prices.[8]

---

8. Milton Friedman, "Whither Inflation?" *Wall Street Journal,* July 6, 1981, p. A12.

The above paragraph is the crux of our debate. Monetarists believe that inflation and higher interest rates occur whenever the *quantity* of money grows faster than real output. I believe that the demand for money is equally significant, and that we could witness—and, in fact, have witnessed—periods of low inflation and low interest rates when the quantity of money per unit of output was rising, as in the 1980s.

On the point of disagreement, the results did not support Milton's claim. If he were correct in writing that changes in the quantity of money per unit of real output cause price changes, then we would expect the ratio of M1 to real GDP to move in lockstep with changes in interest rates. Yet some of the most pronounced jumps in the quantity of money per unit of output—as for example in 1985, 1991, and 2000—coincided with some of the lowest inflation rates and biggest drops in interest rates over the entire period (see Figure 22-1).

My argument, on the other hand, is that we would not expect to see any specific relationship between changes in the quantity of money per unit output and inflation or interest rates. During periods when the demand for money dominates money growth we would expect to see changes in money per unit output be negatively related to inflation and changes in interest rates, yet during periods when the supply of money dominates money growth, we would expect to see changes in money per unit output be positively related to inflation and changes in interest rates. And what we would expect is what happened.

The monetarist explanation didn't work very well even in the 1970s. While the Fed created way too much money, the demand for money didn't keep pace with the inflationary growth in nominal GDP. But the monetarist explanation breaks down completely in the 1980s and beyond. The reason is that monetarists ignore the role played by money demand.[9]

Many economists, especially Milton Friedman, postulate that

---

9.   Arthur Laffer, "The Bitter Fruits of Devaluation," *Wall Street Journal*, January 10, 1994.

there are long lags in the effects of monetary policy. I ask the reader to imagine what would happen if Fed chairman Ben Bernanke announced tomorrow that he was going to expand the monetary base by $1 trillion starting immediately (by the way, that's almost exactly what he has done). It really wouldn't take up to two years for prices to respond to that bombshell. Especially in this age of professional Fed-watchers, changes in monetary policy should show up almost instantaneously, not only in the nominal T-note yield but also in the current purchasing power of the dollar. In a paper I wrote in 1972 titled "A Formal Model of the Economy" (coauthored with R. David Ranson), I was unable to find any lag between money and GNP or inflation.[10]

Figure 22-1 Velocity (GDP/Sweep Adjusted M1) vs. 10-Yr. Treasury

(quarterly, average of months, actual through Q2-09, estimated through Q3-09)

Source: St. Louis Federal Reserve Bank, BEA.

---

10. Arthur B. Laffer and David R. Ranson, "A Formal Model of the Economy," *Journal of Business*, 1971, 44(3), pp. 247–70.

Major changes in fiscal and monetary policies definitely affect the willingness of people to hold money per unit of output—that is, the demand for money is affected. Consequently, the monetarist framework, which assumes the demand for money per unit of output never changes, ignores changes in velocity and thus sets itself up to make systematic forecasting errors in an environment with major policy shifts.

Just look at the late 1960s and 1970s versus the 1980s and 1990s. The Reagan era had a very noticeable impact on the velocity of money, and that impact lasted for years and years. If one had understood the role played by the demand for money, one could have predicted the fall in inflation and interest rates.

The idea that the demand for money cannot be ignored is the crucial point in my argument. Monetarists believe excessive growth in the *quantity of money* (M1 for our purposes) leads to higher inflation and higher interest rates, while I believe excessive growth in the *monetary base* leads to higher inflation and higher interest rates. To clarify, it's not that Milton and the monetarists were crazy. The monetarists are completely correct when there are no shifts in the demand for money.

If there is a sharp rise in the demand to hold U.S. dollars, the equilibrium quantity of money *and* the purchasing power of the dollar will increase and interest rates will fall. What happens in the money market is no different from what happens in the apple market when people learn that apples are excellent aphrodisiacs or hallucinogens—the heightened demand leads to more apples *and* a higher price for apples.

To summarize, monetarists ignore the demand for money and therefore conclude that excessive money growth relative to real output is a good predictor of inflation and interest rates. In contrast, I maintain that inflation and interest rates are better predicted by excess base growth, that is, how much more the monetary base grows relative to growth in M1.

23

Setting the Stage for Financial Collapse: The Alchemy of 2003–2009

The monetary base is made up of currency in circulation in the nonbanking sector, vault cash held by banks, and reserves held by member banks at the Fed. This is the supply of money controlled by the government. The Fed can change that number by buying or selling bonds net in the market. It can do that through the primary dealers. The central bank increases the monetary base when it buys bonds. To better illustrate my points, let's say the Fed buys $100 worth of bonds. It pays for those bonds by issuing a check on itself, by opening up a $100 account, which is a liability on itself. So now on the Fed's balance sheet, it owns $100 worth of bonds that it did not own before, and it has $100 worth of liabilities that it did not have before. It's a perfectly balanced account.

There is no money more ultimate than the monetary base; it is literally the base of the financial pyramid. It is the final say, the final arbiter. In the old days you could take gold and silver certificates into the central bank and demand that they give you the underlying gold or silver. That's not the case today. Today if you have a dollar bill you cannot cash it in for anything. You can exchange it for other forms of the monetary base. You can exchange it for four quarters, or for a deposit at your bank, but you cannot get something else entirely for your dollar.

Member banks hold Fed liabilities as assets on their balance sheet. These assets determine how much lending a bank can do, essentially how many liabilities a member bank can issue. There are also reserve requirements based upon all the deposits held at member banks—member bank liabilities, demand deposits, traveler's checks, and so on. Based on these liabilities, member banks can calculate what their reserve requirements are. If their reserves required are greater than the reserves they actually hold, they have to borrow reserves. Once a bank has hit its reserve requirement, once its reserves equal the reserves required based upon its liabilities, that bank is restricted in how much it can grow and how many new loans it can make.

A member bank, however, can go out into the federal funds market and borrow reserves from another member bank. It's a zero-sum game, but at times some member banks have excess reserves and some others have a demand for extra reserves. This creates a very active federal funds market in which member banks can borrow reserves from one another. But for the entire Federal Reserve System, there is no way that all member banks can increase their liabilities without an increase in reserves coming forth from the Fed. Once they've all hit their reserve requirements, the member banks are restricted in any new loans they can make. That is how the Fed controls member banks, by the amount of reserves it puts into the system.

Now, for you and me, the monetary base is not liquidity. We hold our checking accounts at member banks, in money market accounts, or at other entities. Liquidity for a company may be its checking account at the bank, which is a liability of the bank. As I mentioned before, these liabilities are restricted by the reserve requirements and the amount of reserves that a bank holds. So the monetary base is essentially the reserves of the reserves of the system. That's how the liquidity pyramid goes, and the Fed controls that quantity 100 percent.

The Fed also controls the federal funds target rate, which is the rate at which member banks can borrow and lend with one another. If the federal funds target rate is well above the ninety-one-day T-bill, that acts as a tax on lending reserves, which means that banks will be much less willing to lend reserves to each other. This effectively constricts the monetary base, or at least the effectiveness of the monetary base. If the federal funds target rate is way below the ninety-one-day T-bill, it's effectively a guaranteed return on lending and it causes banks to try to expand the system as fast as they can. That's why the Federal Reserve has historically tried to keep the federal funds target rate very close to the ninety-one-day T-bill. So we've now fully established that the Fed controls the monetary base and the federal funds target rate.

Federal Reserve changes in the monetary base are literally changes in the supply of money. If the Fed increases the monetary base by buying bonds, that's an expansion of liquidity in the overall system and that's an increase in the supply of money. If the Fed decides to sell bonds and contract the monetary base, that is a reduction in the supply of money. Monetary analysis should always begin with the monetary base and the supply of money.

The demand for money is a little different. The demand for money depends upon two things: the transactions demand for money and the speculative demand for money. Economists look at the transactions demand for money as being related to nominal income. In the old equations, it was $MV = PY$, where PY was nominal income, nominal GNP, or nominal GDP. Whether you're a Keynesian or a monetarist, the level of demand for money is based upon the level of transactions, or on the level of GDP in nominal terms. That's the transactions demand.

Basically banks hold reserves in order to match deposit and withdrawal flows. If there's an excess of withdrawals in one day, they'll run down their reserves a little bit. If there's an excess of deposits one day, they'll build up their reserves. Banks would like to hold reserves purely and simply for transactions reasons and the meshing of deposits and withdrawals. The same is true for families and for businesses. They don't use reserves, but they do use deposits at member banks and deposits at other banks in the system. Families and businesses alike try to mesh their income and expenditure streams. Checks come in at different times from when they go out, so you hold deposits to balance the flow between revenue and expense. If you have a lot of checks to write, you can work down your checking account. If you receive a lot of payments, you build up your checking account. You can hold it in demand deposits, time deposits, traveler's checks, or money-market accounts. Demand for money is predicated on the meshing of income and expenditure streams, whether for an individual, a business, or a bank.

The second demand for money is what we call the speculative demand for money, and it is based upon interest rates. Keynes put it this way: When interest rates are low people expect those interest rates to go up, and if interest rates are low and rising, people will hold a lot of cash waiting for them to get high so they can then invest in the bond market. When interest rates finally do rise, everyone invests in bonds, because they are now relatively cheap. When this happens, the price of bonds will then rise, interest rates will fall, and the speculative demand for money will fall. That's a little specious for me, but it works all the same.

My way of looking at the speculative demand for money is a little different. The one-year bond yield is the opportunity cost of holding cash. If you have a $100 bill, the cost of holding that bill for a year is the lost interest rate that you could have made had you invested that in a one-year bond. So the nominal interest rate over a year is the opportunity cost of holding money for a year. Obviously, when interest rates are very low, you'll hold more money per unit of transactions. And when interest rates are high you're going to hold less money per unit of transactions. This is the demand for money based upon interest rates. So as I stated above, you have two components for the demand for money: the transactions demand and the speculative demand. The transactions demand I relate to GDP, and the speculative demand I relate to short-term interest rates.

In the beginning of 2003, real GDP growth was very high. Real growth averaged about 5 percent in the second and third quarters of 2003, and nominal growth was far greater than that. Meanwhile, the ninety-one-day T-bill was quite low, hovering between 80 and 100 bps for most of 2003. So not only were transactions growing at a very rapid rate, but interest rates were very low. Due to the low interest rates, the speculative demand for money was high, causing people to hold a lot of money per unit of transactions.

Over the next four and a half years, you saw two things happen with regard to the demand for money. Income growth, while still positive, declined throughout the entire period, stalling to where real GDP growth in the first quarter of 2007 was 0.1 percent. So number one, the transactions demand for money increased at an ever-slower rate. Number two, nominal interest rates rose dramatically. The ninety-one-day T-bill yield went from about 1.19 percent in the beginning of 2003 to 5.11 percent in early 2007. With rapidly rising interest rates decreasing the speculative demand for money and slowing growth in the transactions demand for money, the overall growth in the demand for money declined sharply. People were holding less and less money per unit transactions. From the beginning of 2003 until about May 2007 there was effectively a collapse in the growth of the demand for money. That's a long period for the demand growth for money to fall.

During this period, the Fed very, very diligently tried to keep inflation from taking a foothold in the United States. It started reducing the rate of growth of the monetary base to ensure that the supply of money did not exceed the demand and cause inflation. And it did a good job. But in spite of its diligence, interest rates rose, as I mentioned before. Also during that period, spot commodity prices such as gold, wheat, and oil rose, while the dollar fell in the foreign exchanges. Basically, all sorts of inflation harbingers entered the picture. Yet the expected rate of inflation, derived from the ten-year bond yield and the ten-year TIPS yield, remained within a steady band.

In early 2007 things started changing. First there was a resurgence of real GDP growth in the second and third quarters, meaning the growth rate in the transactions demand for money stopped declining. Second, the ninety-one-day T-bill leveled off and started to fall, leading to a huge increase in the speculative demand for money. The monetary base, however, did not grow at all. What happened was money became scarcer and scarcer. And when you combine this increase in the demand for money with the Fed's tight monetary policy over a long period of time, something's going to happen that will trigger a financial collapse.

To illustrate my point I'll use the old story of the late Iben Browning, who, despite having been a climatologist from the University of New Mexico, was the darling of Wall Street. He said if you take a boiler and turn the heat up all the way and turn off all the safety valves, you've guaranteed that the boiler will explode. But furthermore, if you go into that boiler every fifteen minutes with a little brass tap hammer and go tap-tap-tap on the side of that boiler, you've guaranteed that you'll be there when it happens.

So unless the Fed had changed its policy on the issuance of liquidity and the supply of money in order to accommodate the increased demand for money in the beginning of 2007, sooner or later the boiler was going to explode, and there would be a liquidity crisis of world-class proportions. This is exactly what has happened in the United States. The triggers of the liquidity crisis, the housing debacle, subprime mortgages, and so on, didn't cause it, they were merely the tapping on the side of the boiler. In 2007, we had a horrendous housing market, but GDP growth stayed fine. It was in 2008 that the lowering led to a macrophenomenon, because that's when you have the liquidity crisis. We have argued time and time again that the Fed should have increased the supply of money by increasing the monetary base. The Fed waited until late 2008 and then it way overdid the increase.

In late 2008, the Fed injected the most liquidity into the monetary base probably ever, at least that I'd seen. From September 10 to September 24 the monetary base went from a sweep-adjusted $873.9 billion to $949.9 billion. Up until that time, that was the biggest percentage increase in the monetary base that I know of. Over the next ten months, however, the Fed proceeded to add over $800 billion more to the monetary base, eclipsing $1.8 trillion at its highest point in May 2009. In December 2008, the Fed cut the Fed funds rate to a range of 0–25 bps, and has held it that low ever since. This marks the easiest monetary policy and the largest increase in the monetary base in both absolute and percentage terms ever. It's bigger than the Y2K increase in the last half of 1999. It's also bigger than the 9/11/01 increase, when the Fed did a great job under Alan Greenspan of increasing the base to make sure we avoided a credit crunch. It's just too bad that we've been calling for this type of action since spring 2007. We are currently in a liquidity crisis and the consequences are exactly what you see outside. Member banks are not being provided enough liquidity to be able to issue enough liabilities, which causes a liquidity crisis for the depositors at member banks. Companies that are short of liquidity are forced to sell off assets, thereby causing the price of those assets to fall as they are marked-to-market. All of a sudden there is a solvency problem as well, and that is exactly what has happened. The Fed was able to create a liquidity crisis and then turn it into a full blown economic collapse.

Solvent entities have become insolvent because of the liquidity crisis and the resulting fire sale and drop in asset prices. We've seen this type of liquidity crisis only four times since 1970—1974, 1998, 2000, and today. But that is exactly why we have the problems we have today in the United States.

Recent Times

As bad as the fiscal picture is, panic-driven monetary policies portend even more dire consequences. We can expect rapidly rising prices and much, much higher interest rates over the next four or five years, and a concomitant deleterious impact on output and employment not unlike that of the late 1970s.

About eight months ago, starting in early September 2008, the Bernanke Fed did an abrupt about-face and radically increased the monetary base, which is composed of currency in circulation, member bank reserves held at the Fed, and vault cash, by a little less than $1 trillion. The Fed controls the monetary base 100 percent and does so by purchasing and selling assets in the open market. By such a radical move, the Fed signaled a 180-degree shift in its focus from an anti-inflation position to an antideflation position.

The percentage increase in the monetary base is the largest increase in the past fifty years by a factor of ten (see Figure 23-1). It is so far outside the realm of our prior experiential base that historical comparisons are rendered difficult if not meaningless. The currency-in-circulation component of the monetary base—which before the expansion had constituted 95 percent of the monetary base—has risen by a little less than 10 percent, while bank reserves have increased almost twentyfold. Following those increases, the currency-in-circulation component of the monetary base has fallen to a smidgen less than 50 percent of the monetary base. Yikes!

Figure 23-1 **Monetary Base, % Change from a Year Earlier**

(monthly, seasonally adjusted, Jan 50 through May 09)

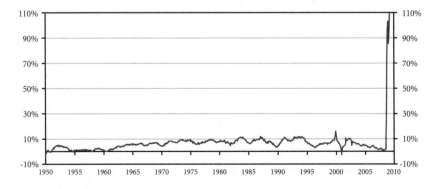

Bank reserves are crucially important because they are the foundation upon which banks are able to expand their liabilities and thereby increase the quantity of money.

Banks are required to hold a certain fraction of their liabilities—demand deposits and other checkable deposits—in reserves held at the Fed or in vault cash. Before the huge increase in bank reserves, banks had been constrained from expanding loans by their reserve positions. They weren't able to inject liquidity into the economy, which had been so desperately needed in response to the liquidity crisis that began in 2007 and continued into 2008. But since last September, all that has changed. Banks now have huge amounts of excess reserves, enabling them to make lots of net new loans.

The way a bank or the banking system makes new loans is conceptually pretty simple. Banks find an entity that they believe to be creditworthy that also wants a loan, and in exchange for the new company's IOU (loan) the bank opens up a checking account for the customer. For the bank's sake, the hope is that the interest paid by the borrower more than makes up for the cost and risk of the loan. The recently ballyhooed "stress tests" on banks are nothing more than checking how well a bank can weather differing levels of default risk.

What's important for the overall economy, however, is how fast these loans are made and how rapidly the quantity of money increases. For our purposes, money is the sum total of all currency in circulation, bank demand deposits, other checkable deposits, and traveler's checks (economists call this M1). When reserve constraints on banks are removed, it does take the banks time to make new loans. But given sufficient time, they will continue to make new loans until they are once again reserve-constrained. The expansion of money, given an increase in the monetary base, is inevitable, and will ultimately result in higher inflation and interest rates. In shorter time frames, the expansion of money can also result in higher stock prices, a weaker currency, and increases in commodity prices such as oil and gold.

At present, banks are doing just what we would expect them to do. They are making new loans and increasing overall bank liabilities (money). The twelve-month growth rate of M1 is now in the 15 percent range, and close to its highest level in the past half century.

With an increased trust in the overall banking system, the panic demand for money has begun to and should continue to recede. The dramatic drop in output and employment in the U.S. economy will also reduce the demand for money. Reduced demand for money combined with rapid growth in money is a surefire recipe for inflation and higher interest rates. The higher interest rates themselves will also further reduce the demand for money, thereby exacerbating inflationary pressures. It's a Catch-22.

It's difficult to estimate the magnitude of the inflationary and interest-rate consequences of the Fed's actions because, frankly, we haven't ever seen anything like this in the United States. To date what's happened is potentially far more inflationary than were the monetary policies of the 1970s, when the prime interest rate peaked at 21.5 percent and inflation peaked in the low double digits. Gold prices went from $35 per ounce to $850 per ounce, and the dollar collapsed on the foreign exchanges. It wasn't a pretty picture.

Now the Fed can, and I believe should, do what it must to mitigate the inevitable consequences of its unwarranted increase in the monetary base. It should contract the monetary base back to where it otherwise would have been, plus a slight increase geared toward economic expansion. Absent this major contraction in the monetary base, the Fed should increase reserve requirements on member banks to absorb the excess reserves. Given that banks are now paid interest on their reserves and short-term rates are very low, raising reserve requirements should not exact too much of a penalty on the banking system, and the long-term gains of the lessened inflation would many times over warrant whatever short-term costs there might be.

Alas, I doubt very much that the Fed will do what is necessary to guard against future inflation and higher interest rates. If the Fed were to reduce the monetary base by $1 trillion, it would need to sell a net $1 trillion in bonds. This would put the Fed in direct competition with Treasury's planned issuance of about $2 trillion worth of bonds over the coming twelve months. Failed auctions would become the norm and bond prices would tumble, reflecting a massive oversupply of government bonds.

In addition, a rapid contraction of the monetary base as I propose would cause a contraction in bank lending, or at best limited expansion. This is exactly what happened in 2000 and 2001, the last time the Fed contracted the monetary base. The economy quickly dipped into recession. While the short-term pain of a deepened recession is quite sharp, the long-term consequences of double-digit inflation are devastating. For Fed chairman Ben Bernanke it's a Hobson's choice. For me the issue is how to protect assets for my grandchildren.

24

LESSONS FROM THE
GREAT DEPRESSION

People who disagree with the preceding analysis of recent monetary policy point to the Great Depression as their counterexample. Indeed, the 1930s has become the sole object lesson for today's monetary policy. Even with this huge increase in the monetary base, Fed chairman Ben Bernanke has reiterated his goal not to repeat the mistakes made back in the 1930s by tightening credit too soon, which he says would send the economy back into recession. Former Dallas Fed president Bob McTeer shares this view and attributes the sharp downturn in the economy in 1937 to the Fed's doubling of bank reserve requirements from August 1936 to May 1937.

What many professionals take away from the U.S. experience of the 1930s is the inverse relationship between inflation and unemployment, as shown in Figure 24-1. The conclusion they reach is that tight money crashed the U.S. economy and caused deflation as well. Therefore we need really easy money now and there is no risk of inflation. They couldn't be more wrong if they tried.

While Fed policy was undoubtedly important in the 1930s, it was not the primary cause of the Great Depression or the economy's relapse in 1937. The Smoot-Hawley tariff of 1929–30 was the catalyst that got the whole process going. It was the largest single increase in taxes on trade during peacetime and precipitated massive retaliation by foreign governments on U.S. products. Huge federal and state tax increases in 1932 followed the initial decline in the economy, thus doubling down on the impact of the Smoot-Hawley tariff. There were additional large tax increases in 1936, which were the proximate cause of the economy's relapse in 1937.

Figure 24-1 CPI Index vs. Unemployment Rate

(monthly, seasonally adjusted, Jan 25–Dec 42)

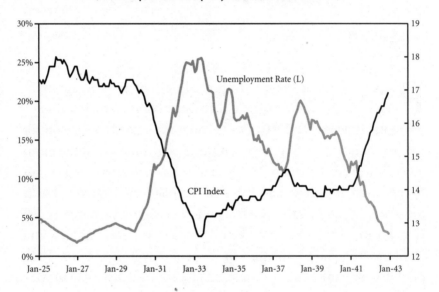

In the years 1930 and 1931 there was a very slight increase in tax rates on personal income at both the lowest and highest brackets. The corporate tax rate was also increased from 11 percent to 12 percent. But beginning in 1932 the lowest personal income-tax rate was raised from less than one half of one percent to 4 percent and the highest rate was raised from 25 percent to 63 percent (that's not a misprint!). The corporate rate was raised to 13.75 percent. And federal excise taxes too numerous to list were raised as well. The highest inheritance-tax rate was also raised in 1932, from 20 percent to 45 percent, and the gift tax was reinstituted, with the highest rate set at 33.5 percent.

In 1934 the highest estate-tax rate was again raised, from 45 percent to 60 percent, and then to 70 percent in 1935. The highest gift-tax rate went from 33.5 percent in 1933 to 45 percent in 1934 and 52.5 percent in 1935. The highest corporate tax rate was raised to 15 percent in 1936 and 1937 with a surtax on undistributed profits up to 27 percent. Finally, in 1936 the highest personal income-tax rate was raised to 79 percent. Starting in 1937, with the passage of the Social Security Act in 1935, the payroll tax levy was first implemented at a rate of 2 percent (one-half directly levied on the employee and one-half levied on the firm) on the first $3,000 of an employee's salary or wage.

Because of the number of states and their diversity I'm going to aggregate all state and local taxes and express them as a percentage of GDP. This measure of state tax policy truly understates their contribution to the tragedy we call the Great Depression, but I'm sure the reader will get the picture. In 1929 state and local taxes were 7.2 percent of GDP and then rose to 8.5 percent, 9.7 percent, and 12.3 percent for the years 1930, 1931, and 1932 respectively.

The damage caused by high taxation during the Great Depression is the real lesson we should learn. A government quite simply cannot tax a country into prosperity. If there were one warning I'd give to all who will listen, it is that U.S. federal and state tax policies are on an economic crash trajectory today, just as they were in the 1930s.

Inflation

Before 1933 the United States was on a true gold standard where gold coins, gold certificates, and silver certificates actually circulated in the economy as money. A consequence of this monetary system was that the Federal Reserve had little power to control either bank reserves or interest rates, the primary tools by which the Fed executes monetary policy. Fed policy was reactive, not proactive, as so many

experts argue today. As a result of the Smoot-Hawley tariff and the
1932 tax increases, people panicked and increased their holdings of
gold by converting fiat money and checking accounts into physical
gold holdings. By mid-1932 there were public fears of a change in
the gold-dollar relationship. Milton Friedman and Anna Schwartz
wrote, "Fears of devaluation were widespread and the public's preference for gold was unmistakable."[1] Converting fiat money and
checking accounts into gold caused the supply of money to contract, even though the monetary base continued to grow. Panic en-
sued (see Figure 24-2).

Figure 24-2 **Gold Coin in Circulation Outside the Treasury
and Federal Reserve Banks vs. M1 Money Growth Yr/Yr**

(monthly, seasonally adjusted, Jan 29–Dec 34)

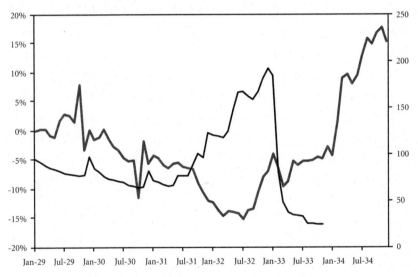

Following this panic, in early 1933 the federal government (not
the Fed) declared a bank holiday, prohibiting banks from paying
out gold or dealing in foreign exchange. An executive order made

1.   Milton Friedman and Anna Jacobson Schwartz, *A Monetary History of the United States, 1867–
1960*, Princeton: Princeton, 1960.

it illegal for anyone to "hoard" gold and forced everyone to turn in gold and gold certificates to the government at an exchange value of $20.67 per ounce of gold in return for unbacked paper currency and bank deposits. All gold clauses in contracts private and public were declared null and void and by the end of January 1934 the price of gold, most of which had been confiscated by the government, was raised to thirty-five dollars per ounce (Figure 24-3). In less than a year, the government confiscated as much gold as it could at $20.67 an ounce and then devalued the dollar in terms of gold by almost 60 percent. That's one helluva tax.

Figure 24-3 Gold Spot Price $/Oz

(monthly, semilog, through Dec 37)

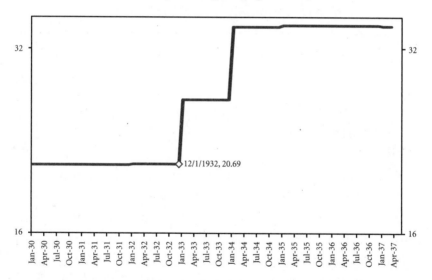

Following the devaluation of gold in early 1933, the monetary base proceeded to jump up substantially (Figure 24-4) as did stocks (Figure 24-5), which rallied nearly 100 percent in the subsequent three months.

The increase in the demand for gold not only had the quantity effect mentioned above but also put upward pressure on the price of gold. But since the price of gold was fixed at $20.67 an ounce, this meant that the prices of all goods and services had to fall for the relative price of gold to rise. Gold then as now is the first refuge of the cautious, only then the dollar price of gold couldn't rise as it can today.

Figure 24-4 Monetary Base

(monthly, semilog, through Dec 37)

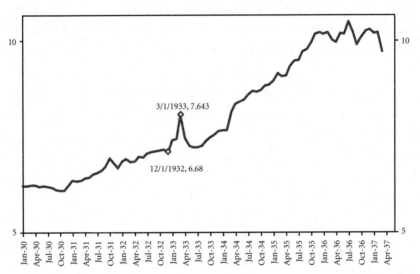

If you look at the level of the Consumer Price Index depicted in Figure 24-6, there was a mild decline during the last half of the 1920s until early 1930. Thereafter, the price level tumbled until early 1933, just when the administration declared a bank holiday, confiscated gold holdings, and then devalued the dollar by almost 60 percent. From early 1933 until mid-1937 the CPI rose by about 15 percent. And that's the story.

The lessons here again are pretty straightforward. A country can experience inflation during a depression, and that inflation is strictly a monetary phenomenon.

My hope is that those people who are running our economy do look to the Great Depression as an object lesson. My fear is that they will misinterpret the evidence and attribute high unemployment and the initial decline in prices to tight money, while increasing taxes to combat budget deficits.

Figure 24-5 S&P 500

(monthly, semilog, through Dec 37)

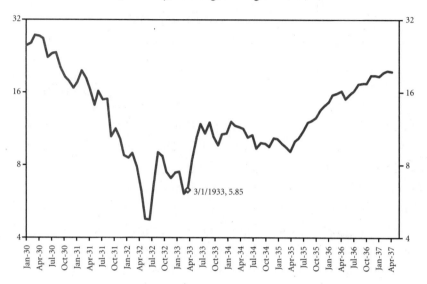

Figure 24-6 CPI Index Level

(monthly, seasonally adjusted, Jan 25–Dec 42)

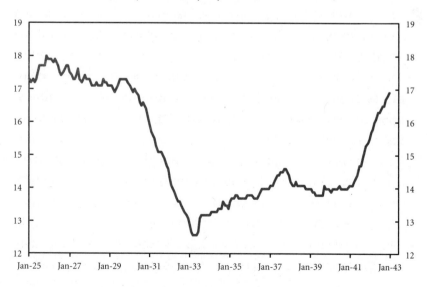

25

TRADE POLICY

Trade policies today are unquestionably freer than they have been for many centuries. Back in the sixteenth, seventeenth, eighteenth, and even nineteenth centuries, tariffs provided the lion's share of government revenues and customs were a major government activity. Government's focus on trade peaked at the end of the third decade of the twentieth century when the United States imposed a huge set of tariffs on imported goods collectively known as the Smoot-Hawley tariff. The pattern of stock-market collapse as this tariff legislation wended its way through the U.S. House and Senate demonstrates beyond reasonable doubt the prescience of markets.[1] What followed this massive intervention against free trade was the biggest stock-market crash in history, a period of unimaginable economic contraction and ubiquitous misery called the Great Depression.

World War II, which immediately followed the Great Depression, was also a period of highly restrictive trade policies where enemy combatants were literally embargoed—that is, all trade stopped. Following World War II there were lots of policies aimed at rebuilding the world's economies, including massive foreign aid and freer trade, but trade was still far from free. In fact, it wasn't until 1958 that the continental European economies actually had convertible

---

1.   For discussion of this topic and many others, I highly recommend Jude Wanniski, *The Way the World Works*, Regnery Publishing Inc., 1978.

currencies. Before convertibility, each government had to grant special permission if one of its citizens wished to buy foreign currencies. Such policies are inconceivable today. But they may not be inconceivable in the future.

While President Kennedy pushed for dramatically lower tariffs on traded products with the Trade Expansion Act of 1962 and with the Kennedy Round tariff negotiations (1964–67), his policies on trade were not universally pro–free trade. He imposed the Voluntary Foreign Credit Restraint Program, for example, and initiated the Interest Equalization Tax, each of which was intended to restrict the free flow of capital across national boundaries. Given how fungible money is, it still astounds me that governments back then actually thought that capital controls would work.[2]

President Johnson, too, had a checkered record. In January 1965 the Canada–United States Automotive Agreement was signed by President Johnson and Canadian prime minister Lester B. Pearson and represented one of our biggest steps in the direction of free trade. The auto pact removed tariffs on cars, trucks, and automotive parts sold between the United States and Canada and was the precursor of the North American Free Trade Agreement (NAFTA). Yet President Johnson also made the theretofore voluntary capital flow restriction programs mandatory, expanded the Buy America program, and prohibited U.S. citizens from engaging in private transactions in gold—not all that enlightened, eh?

President Nixon was pretty much an across-the-board protectionist. In 1971 he imposed a 10 percent import surcharge and excluded foreign-made capital goods from his investment tax credit. President Ford's trade policies weren't all that memorable. President Carter, on the other hand, was protectionist, especially when it came to energy.

President Reagan was exceptionally pro–free trade, successfully

---

2.   This was in fact the subject of my dissertation, which was also published as a book: Arthur Laffer, *Private Short-term Capital Flows*, New York, M. Dekker, V. 5, 1975.

backing several major rounds of tariff reductions, but did from time to time impose one-off protectionist measures. President Reagan proposed NAFTA but was unsuccessful in winning Congress over to his view. President Bush 41 continued President Reagan's push to get NAFTA through Congress but was equally unsuccessful.

The surprise was President Clinton. During his entire tenure in office President Clinton maintained a consistent position favoring free trade. President Clinton went against his own party, defied the unions, and became the champion of NAFTA. He was able to bring enough Democrats on board to actually get NAFTA passed by Congress—no small feat. This was a huge success for free trade and President Clinton deserves a lot of credit.

Following on the heels of President Clinton, President Bush 43 continued America's efforts to make global trade more free. He not

Figure 25-1 **Average U.S. Tariffs: Duties Collected as a % of All Imports**

(annual through 2006)

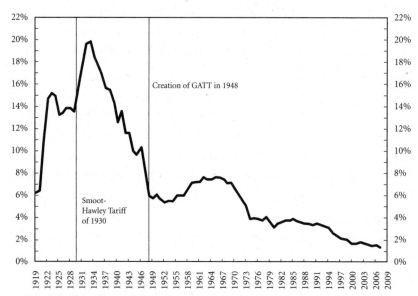

Source: U.S. International Trade Commission.

Figure 25-2 Total U.S. Merchandise Trade (Imports + Exports of Goods) as a % of U.S. GDP

(annual through Q2-2009)

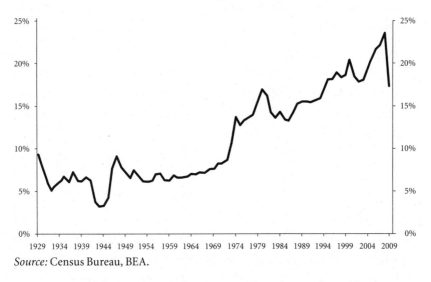

Source: Census Bureau, BEA.

only backed the Doha Round of tariff reductions but actually sponsored DR-CAFTA (the Dominican Republic–Central America Free Trade Agreement) and got it passed by the skin of its teeth. None of the prior presidents in the postwar era was completely consistent when it came to free trade, and President Bush, too, had some notable setbacks in the form of the Agricultural Bill, a Canadian lumber tariff, and steel tariffs.

Borrowing from the Heritage Foundation, I've plotted the average level of tariffs on all U.S. imports going back to 1929 (Figure 25-1). Thanks to ever-declining duties and restrictions, trade in the United States has never been freer. The results of this move toward free trade have been impressive. Perhaps the best reflection of the benefits from freer trade is a simple plot of total U.S. trade (U.S. exports plus U.S. imports) as a share of U.S. GDP (Figure 25-2). Just look at how large a share of the U.S. economy trade represents today. It is absolutely spectacular! The United States is the one country that has really opened up its doors to trade with China. Over just the past ten years, U.S. total trade with China as a share of U.S. GDP has risen from 0.8 percent to 2.4 percent! For a real-life example of the impact of free trade on the standard of living of everyday Americans, make a comparison of the prices of items between shops in Europe versus those same items in U.S. shops. Wow, what a difference. Without China, there is no Wal-Mart. And without Wal-Mart, Americans would all be a lot poorer.

Unfortunately, as you can see from the very latest data in Figure 25-2, total trade for the United States has taken an ominous U-turn. I fear this U-turn is not an aberration.

Another measure that goes hand-in-hand with trade is immigration. If our country hasn't been doing so well relative to the rest of the world, then why have more and more people been trying to move here, both legally and illegally? In Figure 25-3 I've plotted legal immigration into the United States as a percentage of U.S. population from 1950 to the present. Over the past fifty-five years the immigration rate relative to the total population has doubled! For obvious reasons, reliable illegal immigration data are difficult to come by, so we won't plot them here. But the Pew Hispanic Center estimates that the total illegal alien population in the United States has risen from 3 million in 1980 to 11.1 million in 2005. We have been a "people magnet" because we're so good, not in spite of it. The latest indications, however, are that the attractiveness of the United States to foreigners may be waning.

Not only did we attract people from all over the world based on supply-side policies, but we also attracted their money. Everyone has been trying to invest in the United States. *We're where it's at.* Just ask yourself this question: Would you rather have capital lined up on our borders trying to get into America, or capital lined up on our borders trying to get out of America? Of course, we'd all much prefer to have capital trying to get in.

Figure 25-3 Legal Immigration into the
U.S. as a % of U.S. Population

(annual through 2008)

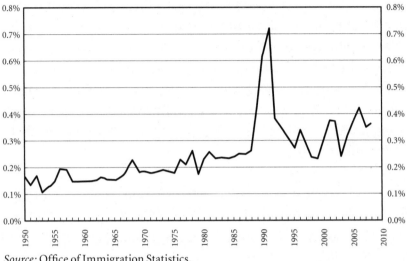

Source: Office of Immigration Statistics.

In a country where good things are happening, such as tax cuts, fiscal responsibility, a sound currency, and regulatory reform, you'll find more rapid economic growth, and you'll also find that everyone wants to invest in that country, whether those investors are foreign or domestic. The only way foreigners can generate a net domestic currency cash flow to carry out their investment desires is if the domestic country runs a trade deficit. The trade deficit, in point of fact, is the counterpart to the capital surplus. And capital surpluses are unambiguously good. They provide rapidly growing countries with the real resources to increase output, employment, and productivity. Growth countries, like growth companies, don't lend money—they borrow it. Without capital surpluses (read trade deficits), the prospects for growth would be reduced and prosperity would be constrained. Trade deficits are per se good.[3]

---

3.   Two papers that cover this topic in depth are: Arthur B. Laffer, "A Supply-Side Perspective on Trade, Part II," Laffer Associates, December 15, 2003; Arthur B. Laffer, "Whither the Dollar," Laffer Associates, July 6, 2005.

We have been the quintessential growth country for some twenty-five years. A faster-growing country will have increased imports and reduced exports—the components of the trade deficit. The trade deficit is caused by those same good things that caused more rapid growth. Rapid growth will be associated with a worsening of the trade accounts; slower growth will be associated with an improvement in the trade accounts. To the supply-side economist, a trade deficit is a surefire sign that the domestic economy is healthy. In our nation's history, periods of healthy economic growth have gone hand-in-hand with relatively large trade deficits (Figure 25-4). It's as simple as that.

Figure 25-4 Trade Deficit (+)/Surplus (–) as a % of GDP vs. Real GDP Growth

(quarterly, GDP through 2Q2008, trade through 2Q2009)

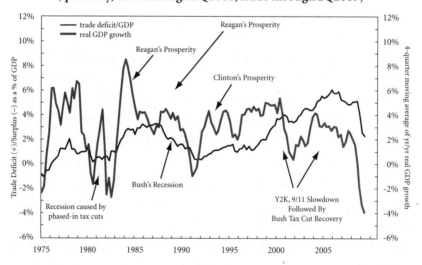

Unfortunately, all the positive results of good economics appear to be coming to an end. But this reversal of trends shouldn't surprise anyone who knows what is going on. If there are two locations, the United States and the rest of the world, and the United States is raising taxes while the rest of the world is lowering taxes, it's obvious that capital will move from the United States to the rest of the world. Trade deficits (capital surpluses) as a share of GDP are way down and are expected to fall further. The dollar is weak and U.S. trade as a share of GDP is down as well. We need to reverse this trend right away by implementing good trade and monetary policies.

Trade: The Ricardian Epiphany

English economist David Ricardo in the early nineteenth century developed the theory of comparative advantage to explain trade flows among nations. In a nutshell, his theory postulated that countries export those products and services where the domestic costs of production are *relatively* low and import products and services where domestic production costs are *relatively* high. His insights encompassed many aspects of international economics and are as applicable today as they were in his own time.

To extend the Ricardian concepts to today's world, imagine we have a schedule of the dollar costs of each and every product produced in the United States and the euro costs of each and every product produced in Euroland. It's one helluva long list for both areas. Stretch your imagination a smidgen further and calculate the ratio of the dollar-to-euro costs of each and every product. Now arrange all those products and services from the highest to the lowest ratio of dollar cost to euro cost. What results is a schedule of all products and services ranked from those products at the top, where the United States has the least comparative advantage, down to those products and services at the bottom, where the United States has the greatest comparative advantage. According to Ricardo, the United States will tend to import those goods and services at the top of the list because they're more cheaply produced in Euroland and will export those goods at the bottom of the list because those goods are more inexpensively produced in the United States. It's all pretty straightforward and simple.

Ricardo's theory of comparative advantage went on to make the point that there exists a unique cost ratio corresponding to the dollar/euro exchange rate where each country pays for its imports with the proceeds it earns from selling its exports. At that exchange rate the value of all U.S. imports of goods and services exactly equals the value of all U.S. exports of goods and services. In static terms, that exchange rate is referred to as the equilibrium exchange rate.

If costs in the United States and Euroland don't change and we hypothetically raise the exchange rate above the equilibrium rate—that is, we assume the dollar depreciates against the euro—then all U.S. goods become more competitive. The United States will export more of those goods it already exports to Euroland and will import less of every good and service it imports from Euroland. In fact, conceptually at least, some goods that were imported into the United States from Euroland at the Ricardian equilibrium exchange rate will now be exported from the United States to Euroland at the now-devalued dollar/euro exchange rate. The U.S. trade accounts will go from a perfect zero, where dollar exports exactly equaled dollar imports, to a position of U.S. trade surplus, where dollar exports exceed dollar imports, at the new lowered-value dollar exchange rate. In theory, at least, we can derive a hypothetical schedule of U.S. trade surpluses and deficits corresponding to a continuum of dollar/euro exchange rates. The cheaper the dollar as measured in euros, the greater will be the U.S. trade surplus—Euroland's trade deficit. And, likewise, the more expensive the dollar as measured in euros, the greater will be the U.S. trade deficit—Euroland's trade surplus. And this is where we find Ricardian trade theory at the dawning of the twenty-first century.

In the discussion above I have taken considerable liberties with the real world and made lots of assumptions that are to a greater or lesser extent realistic. But the basic principles of the theory hold and still serve us well even though we all are aware that significant modifications are in order. Ricardian trade theory is a useful tool. No one would deny the *argumentum ad absurdum* that if we in the United States could buy all of Europe's goods and services for ten dollars, we would do it, or if Europeans could buy everything in the United States for ten euros, they would do it. It's obvious.

What evolves from this Ricardian synthesis is the interesting point that the further the exchange rate moves from the equilibrium rate—either above or below—the more difficult it is to move it further away. The cheaper the dollar gets in euro terms, for example, the more pressure there is for the dollar to appreciate back toward the mean. It is almost as if the exchange rate were attached to the equilibrium rate by an elastic band. The more the exchange rate strays from the equilibrium rate, the more the elastic band pulls on it to bring it back. There are very natural upper and lower limits on just how far exchange rates can move when each region's price levels are set by domestic monetary policy.

Another critical modification of the Ricardian framework has to do with the rate of change of the exchange rate in addition to the level of the exchange rate. As stressed earlier, the level of the exchange rate determines the relative competitiveness of the various regions of the world. That's true. But even if foreign goods are cheaper than domestic goods, domestic purchasers of foreign products will restrain their purchases if they believe foreign products will become even cheaper in the very near future. If you know that the prices of foreign goods will be lower next month than they are this month, you'd buy the bare minimum this month and save the larger purchases for a time when foreign prices are lower yet. When looking at the trade accounts, a full Ricardian analysis should consider not only the exchange rate, but also changes in the exchange rate.

Putting all this together, I have plotted the inflation-adjusted exchange rate between the U.S. dollar and a composite of all foreign currencies all the way back to the 1970s (Figure 25-5). The effects I discussed earlier are easily discerned.

Figure 25-5 Trade Deficit as a % of GDP vs. Value of the Dollar
(through 2Q2009)

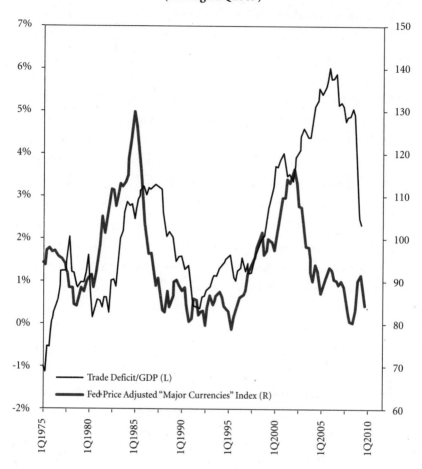

Capital Flows and Trade Imbalances

Imagine a world composed of a finite number of countries, each with its own tax code, regulations, laws, customs, monetary policy, and trade barriers. Investors trying to earn the highest after-tax returns will diversify their portfolios by country. Now, if one, and only one, country lowers its tax rates, reduces its inflation, reduces unnecessary regulations, and reduces its trade barriers, each and every investor will want to increase the portion of his assets located in the now more progrowth country. It's just common sense.

If there were only one world currency (not unlike the many states of the United States), then investors would physically move some of their assets from all the other countries into the now-freer economy. Investors, in other words, would take advantage of the new progrowth policies in the one country. Each asset moved out of a country would be that country's export and trade surplus and, of course, the now more progrowth country into which those assets moved would have net imports and a trade deficit. In economic and accounting terms the now-freer country would have a trade deficit corresponding to its capital surplus, while the sum of all the rest of the countries of the world would have trade surpluses corresponding to their aggregate capital deficit.

Bringing exchange rates, separate currencies, and comparative advantage back, the picture begins to clarify dramatically.

The Late 1970s/Early 1980s

For example, take the U.S. economy and politics of the late 1970s and early 1980s. In 1978 alone U.S. capital-gains tax rates were slashed (Steiger/Hansen), California property-tax rates were more than halved (Proposition 13), and in 1979 Paul Volcker was appointed chairman of the Federal Reserve. All in all it was a very good couple of years. And then in 1980 Ronald Reagan was elected president of the United States and promised tax-rate cuts, deregulation, free trade, and a sound monetary policy. Compared to the late 1960s and all of the 1970s, this was a 180-degree turnaround.

Virtually everyone in the world was optimistic about America, and for good reason. Americans took advantage of the policy changes through appreciating asset values and higher profits. The only way foreigners could avail themselves of the greater opportunities in the United States was to invest more net in the United

States. And to do that they had to generate a dollar cash flow by selling more goods to the United States and buying fewer goods from the United States. The trade surplus generated by foreigners was one and the same as the foreign capital deficit. Symmetrically, the U.S. trade deficit was the U.S. capital surplus.

If those who constantly fret over the persistence of the U.S. trade deficit were correct that the emerging and continuing trade deficits were a result of indulgent consumption-driven overspending by Americans financed by "credit cards," then clearly the dollar should have fallen in the foreign-exchange markets. It didn't. Not only did the dollar not fall, but from late 1978 through February 1985 the dollar increased in value by more than 50 percent versus the average of all foreign currencies. The changes wrought in the global economy resulted from an increased demand for dollars rather than an increased supply of dollars. That's Econ 1. The U.S. trade accounts went further and further into the red and the dollar just kept getting stronger and stronger. By the end of the Reagan/Volcker era the U.S. trade deficit/capital surplus remained high, but the dollar witnessed a sharp decline. In fact, it wasn't until the dollar had fallen mightily that the trade balance even started to turn around. But, then again, people won't buy any more goods from the United States than they have to if they believe U.S. goods' prices will be even lower in the near future.

The Late 1980s/Early 1990s

The decline in the dollar followed later by the reduction in the trade deficit and capital surplus fully reflected the change in U.S. investment prospects as the curtain fell on both Ronald Reagan and Paul Volcker. Optimism continued to fall right along with the capital surplus and the dollar. President H. W. Bush had raised taxes and had backpedaled from Reaganomics. President Bill Clinton's first two years in office weren't much better. First, there was the 1993

280

tax increase and then Hillary's health-care scare. Yikes! The dollar stayed weak and the capital surplus and trade deficit stayed low. Investors were far less enthusiastic about the United States.

Another Turnaround

But then came the 1994 election with its "Contract with America." The Democrats lost the House, the Senate, and state governorships. It was a political rout of biblical proportions. Clinton did an about-face and became more Reagan than Reagan. Robert Reich was out and Dick Morris was in. It was a new era with a born-again, pro-growth Democratic president—shades of JFK.

President Clinton reappointed Reagan's Fed chairman twice, pushed NAFTA through Congress, signed welfare reform into law, cut government spending as a share of GDP by three and a half percentage points, left office with budget surpluses, and signed the biggest capital-gains tax rate cut in our nation's history. The United States was back with an ambitious supply-side agenda.

President Clinton was replaced by George W. Bush, who continued the extraordinarily ambitious progrowth policies. Bush cut personal income tax rates, abolished the inheritance tax, and dropped the tax rates on capital gains and dividends to their lowest levels in my lifetime. Bush pressed for tort reform, Social Security reform, lifetime savings accounts, and the elimination of the Alternative Minimum Tax. When faced with his father's dilemma of deficits, the need for greater spending, and a sluggish economy, he didn't cave in. He actually cut tax rates and increased defense spending. He simply didn't want to raise taxes on the last three people working.

The period starting in the first quarter of 1995 on through the second quarter of 2002 was not only a period of U.S. supply-side economic policies, it was also a period when the rest of the world, with a couple of notable exceptions, was recaptured by the dirigiste policies of income redistribution and demand management. Ping-Ponging back and forth between Alain Juppé, Jacques Chirac, and Lionel Jospin, France raised its VAT by two percentage points, instituted its notorious thirty-five-hour workweek, and sank into the quagmire of prounion, antigrowth rhetoric. Gerhardt Schroeder, Oskar Lafontaine, and the rest of the redistributionist crowd did all they could to hobble business in what was once a proud Germany. Wim Duisenberg was a disaster at the ECB and Prime Minister Yoshiro Mori could not have been worse for Japan.

Within lesser countries, the antibusiness sentiment surged as well. Carlos Salinas was replaced by Ernesto Zedillo in Mexico, and Jean Chrétien reigned supreme in Canada. It was a sad day for the non-U.S. world. Everyone wanted out of their asset positions in the non-U.S. world and into assets in America. Capital was lined up on the U.S. border trying to get into the United States. And into the United States capital came.

The U.S. capital surplus once again soared. Or, if you are captured by the deep root canal theorists, the trade deficit skyrocketed, ultimately to a figure close to 6 percent of U.S. GDP—the highest figure ever recorded for the United States.

SUMMARY:

A PRESCRIPTION FOR AMERICA

O ur prescription for America covers a wide range of targets but can be summed up quite simply: All the panicked decisions that have been made since the start of the financial crisis must be repealed. As we have shown, the consequences of these decisions have been ugly and the sooner we correct these mistakes the better.

Beyond fixing past mistakes, we need to implement proactive reforms that strengthen each of the four grand macroeconomic kingdoms: fiscal policy, monetary policy, trade policy, and incomes policies. These proactive reforms will establish the positive incentives necessary for sustained economic prosperity for us and our children. Reviewing our suggested reforms, the United States needs to do the following things.

Make the Bush Tax Cuts Permanent, and Ideally Implement a Flat-Rate Tax

As we have shown throughout this book, tax policies are on the wrong track. President Obama and this Congress should immediately eliminate the Alternative Minimum Tax and make all President Bush's tax cuts that are set to expire in 2011 permanent.

But, what the United States really needs, and what will help establish a new era of economic prosperity in the United States, is a flat-rate tax that imposes the lowest possible tax rate on the broadest possible tax base. Such a tax provides the fewest incentives to evade, avoid, or otherwise not report taxable income and the fewest ways in which people can escape taxation. If the marginal tax rate is lowered, the incentives to produce, invest, and save are all increased. Greater economic growth will follow. For the government, a more stable revenue source will be created that will improve the government's ability to budget. An increased ability to budget will lead to an increased efficiency in the manner that the government spends the taxpayers' money.

A revenue-neutral flat-tax rate would be approximately 13 percent on business net sales (VAT) and personal unadjusted gross income—the two tax bases. A flat-rate tax will also provide a more stable revenue source.

One important adjustment to a flat-rate tax should be included. Due to the scientific consensus that global warming is occurring, the United States should implement a carbon-emissions tax. But, and this is critical, in order to avoid the negative economic consequences a carbon-emissions tax would create, the flat-tax rate should be reduced dollar for dollar on a static revenue-neutral basis. If a carbon-emissions tax is implemented along with the flat-rate tax, the actual flat-rate tax rate will be even less than 13 percent.

Address the Looming Unfunded Liabilities Crisis

The spending spree of 2008 and 2009 and the subsequent economic collapse have worsened an already insurmountable problem facing the United States—total unfunded liabilities of the U.S. federal government. The grand total of federal net debt based on our current actions has now become about 100 percent of GDP.

Putting this in perspective, every household in the United States today owes $557,745 due to the current federal unfunded liabilities! And these don't even include the potential unfunded liabilities that could arise due to the government's explicit backing of Fannie Mae's, Freddie Mac's, and Ginnie Mae's mortgage portfolios or the potential costs to the Federal Reserve's balance sheet due to all the risky assets it has purchased.

Addressing the unfunded-liabilities problem requires a combination of progrowth policies to grow our economy and sound budget changes to help manage the current unfunded-liabilities crisis.

There are many good governance and sound budgeting practices that will help. For instance, the federal government should be prohibited from deliberately running a budget deficit larger than 5 percent of GDP, including, and this is crucial, increases in unfunded liabilities. All federal programs, to the extent possible, should be based on defined-contribution characteristics, not defined-benefit characteristics. Government accounting should be subjected to the same accounting standards private industry is currently required to adhere to, with similar penalties for malfeasance.

Put Government on a Low-Fat Diet

Addressing our long-term unfunded liabilities also requires addressing our current spending habits. The government is simply spending too much money. More troubling, much of this spending is being wasted on corporate bailouts and ineffective tax rebates that are worsening the unfunded-liabilities crisis.

To lessen the burden immediately, all stimulus and bailout funds that have not been spent should be impounded. Any ownership rights government has acquired in private companies via bailouts should be sold as quickly as is feasible, and the government should refrain from any exercise of control on those companies. Fannie Mae, Freddie Mac, and Ginnie Mae should stop buying and guaranteeing mortgages immediately and should develop a plan to sell their current inventory of mortgages they own in the private market. The Federal Reserve should be admonished not to acquire any major stakes in private firms save for very short-term stabilization reasons. These actions will have the effect of stopping the growth in our unfunded liabilities and will eventually begin to bring these liabilities down.

Longer-term, structural changes are required that will help prevent a recurrence of our current spending crisis. There are several simple reforms that will change the tax-and-spend incentives of Washington, D.C.

First, Congress and all government employees should be required to live by the letter of the law, and all the provisions that apply to other citizens for whom the laws apply. They should be required to retire on Social Security like everyone else and have no other retirement benefits provided separately by the government. They should be provided with health care and other perquisites commensurate with those given to other citizens. All laws should be applicable to all politicians.

Second, Congress should not be allowed to place earmarks on legislation and thereby circumvent the congressional vetting process. A bill in its final form should be allowed to be voted on only after two full weeks have elapsed to allow Congress to fully understand and assess the implications of all legislation.

Last, the president should be granted the authority for a line-item veto that would require a two-thirds majority vote of Congress to override.

Reinstate a Sound and Stable Monetary System

A good monetary policy requires policy decisions to be made on a deliberative and purposive basis devoid of erratic rapid changes. The current policy of the Federal Reserve does not meet this definition. Recent policy has been nothing but erratic and panicked, leading to an imminent inflation problem in the United States. The implications will be rising interest rates at home and a falling dollar on foreign-exchange markets.

To regain a stable dollar, the Federal Reserve should be put on an explicit price rule. Under a price rule, the Federal Reserve adds reserves to the banking system when the relevant price measures are under downward pressure and removes reserves from the banking system when the relevant price measures face upward pressure. Spot commodity prices, interest rates, exchange rates, and the price of gold are good indicators of inflationary pressures and should be used to anchor monetary policy.

Support Free Trade for All

Since the end of World War II the globalization of the world economy has been the greatest poverty alleviation program in the history of mankind. The Obama administration has lost its way, and leadership, on free-trade issues. The United States is no longer the global leader. Free-trade agreements with South Korea and Colombia sit in limbo while the administration engages in trade skirmishes with China. More troubling, the Doha Round of global trade talks are languishing without strong U.S. leadership.

The ideal global economic environment is very straightforward: All trade of goods, services, people, and investments is unencumbered by impediments such as tariffs and quotas, save a few exemptions such as sensitive military technology.

At a bare minimum, the United States must reaffirm its commitment to free trade and take back the leadership for a successful completion of the Doha Round of free-trade talks. We must live up to the spirit and letter of all past free-trade agreements, such as NAFTA, and all pending free-trade agreements should be passed by the Senate.

Every quota or tariff imposed by the United States hurts residents of the United States. Because all restrictions hurt the United States regardless of what our trading partners do, ideally, the United States would commit to a unilateral reduction in all U.S. tariffs and the elimination of all unnecessary secondary restrictions on

U.S. imports. Such a momentous policy shift would create substantial momentum for the Doha Round of free-trade talks, while simultaneously improving the welfare of Americans—a clear win-win and a giant step toward improved U.S. prosperity.

Repeal Ill-Conceived Regulations

The Obama administration is rapidly trying to change the regulatory landscape in the United States. Examples include pushing for a major increase in the role of government in health care, creating a giant bureaucracy to watch over people's use of carbon emissions, and strengthening current policies that inhibit developing beneficial energy sources (such as nuclear power and offshore oil drilling). Such actions unequivocally worsen U.S. incomes policies and reduce our country's economic prosperity. While it is unknown which regulation, mandate, or restrictions will ultimately pass, the key to prosperity is to ensure that as many of these burdensome proposals as possible do not pass, and to repeal those that have passed.

The incomes policies we focused on in this book, and there are others, would require the government to:

- If passed, repeal cap-and-trade regulations and require the government to repurchase all carbon-emission allowances from the current owners of those rights, regardless of whether the original emission allowance was sold or given away.
- Greatly reduce all current restrictions on nuclear power generation to enable a major expansion of nuclear power generation in the United States.
- Remove, in an orderly fashion, all explicit support of specific industries—housing, autos, insurance, or anything else.
- Plans for health-care reform as currently outlined in legislation in the House and Senate should be abandoned. If passed, these reforms should be subsequently repealed.

288

- Effective health-care reform requires rational economic decision-making based on accurate prices. Health-care services should be treated like any other product where purchases are not subsidized through the tax code. Income supplements (such as vouchers for low-income individuals to purchase health insurance) are a far preferable method for helping people who can't help themselves.

- Repeal the policies that have been skewing the economic environment in favor of unions as opposed to the health of the economy. U.S. economic policy should neither encourage nor discourage the formation of unions. Additional requirements should be imposed on government unions—such as schoolteachers, police and fire, nurses, and prison guards—who are public servants. They should not be allowed to strike and should be subject to antitrust supervision. By their very nature, government unions should also be nonpartisan and uninvolved as unions in the political process.

- The minimum-wage law should be repealed in its entirety. If complete repeal of the minimum wage is not possible, the second-best policy would be to exempt teenagers and lock in the current nominal dollar value of the minimum wage.

A Renewed Prosperity

I hope that the reader now has an appreciation that sound economic policy is not difficult. In fact, much of it is just pure common sense. Tax policies that punish work, saving, and investing create less work, saving, and investing. Monetary policies that devalue the dollar create high inflation, high interest rates, and a weak dollar. The list goes on.

Regaining our economic prosperity begins and ends with creating economic policies that encourage growth. Throughout this book we have shown the many areas where our current policies have strayed from the path to prosperity. As long as this is the case, our economic growth will be weak and volatile, and our standard of living will grow below its potential.

Reversing the antigrowth bent of our current policies and fully embracing the progrowth prescriptions outlined throughout this book will put us back on the path to prosperity. The result will be a resumption of strong economic growth, interrupted only occasionally by short and shallow recessions. The U.S. standard of living will regain its growth potential and we can regain the vision of that "shining city on a hill."

Appendix:
The Laffer Curve

The story of how the Laffer Curve got its name isn't one of the *Just So Stories* by Rudyard Kipling. It began with a 1978 article published by Jude Wanniski in *The Public Interest* titled "Taxes, Revenues, and the 'Laffer Curve.' " As recounted by Wanniski (associate editor of the *Wall Street Journal* at the time), in December 1974 he had been invited to have dinner with me (then a professor at the University of Chicago), Don Rumsfeld (chief of staff to President Gerald Ford), and Dick Cheney (Rumsfeld's deputy and my former classmate at Yale) at the Two Continents Restaurant at the Washington Hotel in Washington, D.C. (just across the street from the Treasury). While discussing President Ford's WIN (Whip Inflation Now) proposal for tax increases, I supposedly grabbed my napkin and a pen and sketched a curve on the napkin illustrating the tradeoff between tax rates and tax revenues. Wanniski named the tradeoff "The Laffer Curve."

I personally don't remember the details of that evening we all spent together, but Wanniski's version could well be true. I used the so-called Laffer Curve all the time in my classes and to anyone else who would listen to illustrate the tradeoff between tax rates and tax revenues. My only reservation about Wanniski's version of the story concerns the fact that the restaurant used cloth napkins and my mother had raised me not to desecrate nice things. Ah well, that's my story and I'm sticking to it.

The Historical Origins of the Laffer Curve

The Laffer Curve, by the way, was not invented by me; it has its origins way back in time. For example, the Muslim philosopher Ibn Khaldun wrote in his fourteenth-century work *The Muqaddimah*:

> *It should be known that at the beginning of the dynasty, taxation yields a large revenue from small assessments. At the end of the dynasty, taxation yields a small revenue from large assessments.*

A more recent version of incredible clarity was written by none other than John Maynard Keynes:

> *When, on the contrary, I show, a little elaborately, as in the ensuing chapter, that to create wealth will increase the national income and that a large proportion of any increase in the national income will accrue to an Exchequer, amongst whose largest outgoings is the payment of incomes to those who are unemployed and whose receipts are a proportion of the incomes of those who are occupied, I hope the reader will feel, whether or not he thinks himself competent to criticize the argument in detail, that the answer is just what he would expect—that it agrees with the instinctive promptings of his common sense.*
>
> *Nor should the argument seem strange that taxation may be so high as to defeat its object, and that, given sufficient time to gather the fruits, a reduction of taxation will run a better chance than an increase of balancing the budget. For to take the opposite view today is to resemble a manufacturer who, running at a loss, decides to raise his price, and when his declining sales increase the loss, wrapping himself in the rectitude of plain arithmetic, decides that prudence requires*

him to raise the price still more—and who, when at last his account is balanced with naught on both sides, is still found righteously declaring that it would have been the act of a gambler to reduce the price when you were already making a loss.[1]

Theory Basics

The basic idea behind the relationship between tax rates and tax revenues is that changes in tax rates have two effects on revenues: the arithmetic effect and the economic effect. The arithmetic effect is simply that if tax rates are lowered, tax revenues per dollar of tax base will be lowered by the amount of the decrease in the rate. And the reverse is true for an increase in tax rates. The economic effect, however, recognizes the positive impact that lower tax rates have on work, output, and employment and thereby the tax base by providing incentives to increase these activities. Raising tax rates achieves the opposite economic effect by penalizing participation in the taxed activities. The arithmetic effect always works in the opposite direction from the economic effect. Therefore, when the economic and the arithmetic effects of tax-rate changes are combined, the consequences of the change in tax rates for total tax revenues are no longer quite so obvious.

Figure A-1 is a graphic illustration of the concept of the Laffer Curve—not the exact levels of taxation corresponding to specific levels of revenues. At a tax rate of 0 percent, however, the government would collect no tax revenues, no matter how large the tax base. Likewise, at a tax rate of 100 percent, the government would also collect no tax revenues because no one would be willing to work for an after-tax wage of zero—there would be no tax base. Between these two extremes there are two tax rates that will collect

---

1.   John Maynard Keynes, *The Collected Writings of John Maynard Keynes,* London: Macmillan Cambridge University Press, 1972.

the same amount of revenue: a high tax rate on a small tax base and a low tax rate on a large tax base.

Figure A-1 The Laffer Curve

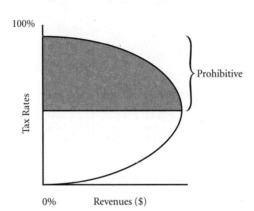

The Laffer Curve itself doesn't say whether a tax cut will raise or lower revenues. Revenue responses to a tax-rate change will depend upon the tax system in place, the time period being considered, the ease of moving into underground activities, the level of tax rates already in place, the prevalence of legal and accounting-driven tax loopholes, and the proclivities of the productive factors. If the existing tax rate is too high—in the "prohibitive range" shown in Figure A-1—then a tax-rate cut would result in increased tax revenues. The economic effect of the tax cut would outweigh the arithmetic effect of the tax cut.

Moving from total tax revenues to budgets, there is one expenditure effect in addition to the two effects tax-rate changes have on revenues. Because tax cuts create an incentive to increase output, employment, and production, tax cuts also help balance the budget by reducing means-tested government expenditures. A faster-growing economy means lower unemployment and higher incomes, resulting in a reduction in unemployment benefits and other social welfare programs.

Over the past hundred years in the United States, there have been three major periods of tax-rate cuts: the Harding/Coolidge cuts of the mid-1920s, the Kennedy cuts of the mid-1960s, and the Reagan cuts of the early 1980s. Each of these periods of tax cuts was remarkably successful in terms of virtually any public policy metric.

Before we discuss and measure these three major periods of U.S. tax cuts, three critical points have to be made, one regarding the size of tax cuts, one regarding their timing, and one regarding their location.

1. Size of Tax Cuts

People don't work, consume, or invest to pay taxes. They work and invest to earn after-tax income and they consume to get the best buys—after tax. Therefore, people are not concerned with taxes per se—their concern is focused on after-tax results. Taxes and after-tax results are very similar but have crucial differences.

Using the Kennedy tax cuts of the mid-1960s as our example, it is easy to show that identical percentage tax cuts when and where tax rates are high are far larger than when and where tax rates are low. When Kennedy took office in 1961, the highest federal marginal tax rate was 91 percent and the lowest rate was 20 percent. For every dollar earned pretax, the highest-bracket income earner would receive nine cents after tax (the incentive), while the lowest-bracket income earner would receive eighty cents after tax. These after-tax earnings were the relative after-tax incentives to earn the same amount (one dollar) pretax.

By 1965, after Kennedy's tax cuts were fully effective, the highest federal marginal tax rate had been lowered to 70 percent (a drop of 23 percent or twenty-one percentage points on a base of 91 percent) and the lowest tax rate was dropped to 14 percent (30 percent lower). Now, for every dollar earned pretax, the person in the highest tax bracket would receive thirty cents after tax, or a 233 percent increase from the nine cents after-tax earned when the tax rate was 91 percent, and the person in the lowest tax bracket would receive eighty-six cents after tax, or a 7.5 percent increase from the eighty cents earned when the tax rate was 20 percent.

Putting this all together, the increase in incentives in the highest tax bracket was a whopping 233 percent for a 23 percent cut in tax rates—a ten-to-one benefit/cost ratio—while the increase in incentives in the lowest tax bracket was a mere 7.5 percent for a 30 percent cut in rates—a one-to-four benefit/cost ratio. The lessons here are simple: The higher tax rates are, the greater will be the economic (supply-side) impact of a given percentage reduction in tax rates. Likewise, under a progressive tax structure, an equal across-the-board percentage reduction in tax rates should have its greatest impact in the highest tax bracket and its least impact in the lowest tax bracket.

2. Timing of Tax Cuts

The second and equally important concept regarding tax cuts concerns the timing of those cuts. People in their quest to earn what they can after tax not only can change how much they work, they also can change when they work, when they invest, and when they spend. Lower expected tax rates in the future will reduce taxable economic activity in the present as people try to shift activity out of the relatively higher-taxed present period into the relatively lower-taxed future period. People tend not to shop at a store a week before that store has its well-advertised discount sale. Likewise, in the periods before legislated tax cuts actually take effect, people will defer income and then realize that income when tax rates have fallen to their fullest extent. It has always amazed me how tax cuts don't work until they actually take effect.

When assessing the impact of tax legislation, it is imperative to start the measurement of the tax-cut period after all the tax cuts have been put into effect. As will be obvious when we look at the three major tax-cut periods, and even more so when we look at capital-gains tax cuts, timing is of the essence.

3. Location of Tax Cuts

As a final point, people can also choose where they earn their after-tax income, where they invest their money, and where they spend their money. Regional and country differences in various tax rates matter, as we will see when we look at state and country effects of tax changes.

The Harding/Coolidge Tax Cuts

In 1913, the federal progressive income tax was put into place with a top marginal rate of 7 percent (Figure A-2). Thanks in part to World War I, this tax rate was quickly increased significantly and peaked at 77 percent in 1918. Then, through a series of tax-rate reductions, the Harding/Coolidge tax cuts dropped the top personal marginal income-tax rate to 25 percent in 1925.

While tax-collection data for the National Income and Product Accounts (from the U.S. Bureau of Economic Analysis) don't exist for the 1920s, we do have total federal receipts from the U.S. budget tables. During the four years proceeding 1925 (the year the tax cut was fully enacted), inflation-adjusted revenues declined by an average of 9.2 percent per year (Table A-1). Over the four years following the tax-rate cuts, revenues remained volatile but averaged an inflation-adjusted gain of 0.1 percent per year. The economy responded strongly to the tax cuts, with output nearly doubling and unemployment falling sharply.

Figure A-2 The Top Marginal Personal Income-Tax Rate, 1913–2003

(when applicable, top rate on earned and/or unearned income)

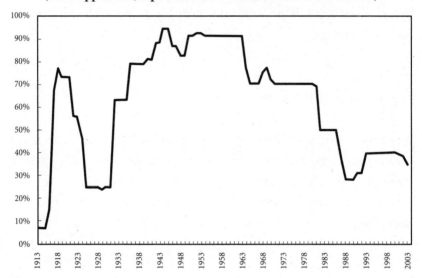

In the 1920s, tax rates on the highest income brackets were reduced the most, which is exactly what economic theory suggests should be done to spur the economy.

But those income classes with lower tax rates were not left out in the cold: The Harding/Coolidge tax-rate cuts did result in reduced tax rates on lower income brackets. Internal Revenue Service data show that the dramatic tax cuts of the 1920s resulted in an increase in the share of total income taxes paid by those making more than $100,000 per year from 29.9 percent in 1920 to 62.2 percent in 1929 (Table A-2). And keep in mind the significance of this increase, given that the 1920s was a decade of falling prices, and therefore a $100,000 threshold in 1929 corresponds to a higher real income threshold than $100,000 did in 1920. The consumer price index *fell* a combined 14.5 percent from 1920 to 1929. In this case, the effects of bracket creep that existed before the federal income-tax brackets were indexed for inflation (in 1985) worked in the opposite direction.

Table A-1 A Look at the Harding/Coolidge Tax Cut

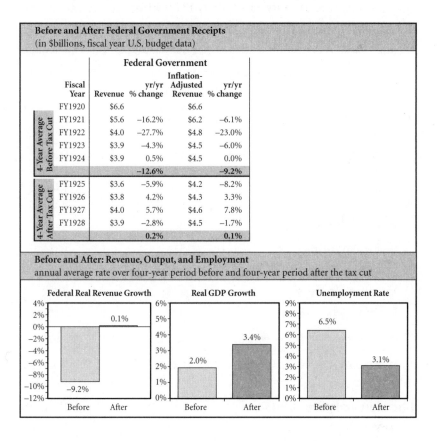

Before and After: Federal Government Receipts
(in $billions, fiscal year U.S. budget data)

	Fiscal Year	Federal Government			
		Revenue	yr/yr % change	Inflation-Adjusted Revenue	yr/yr % change
	FY1920	$6.6		$6.6	
4-Year Average Before Tax Cut	FY1921	$5.6	−16.2%	$6.2	−6.1%
	FY1922	$4.0	−27.7%	$4.8	−23.0%
	FY1923	$3.9	−4.3%	$4.5	−6.0%
	FY1924	$3.9	0.5%	$4.5	0.0%
			−12.6%		−9.2%
4-Year Average After Tax Cut	FY1925	$3.6	−5.9%	$4.2	−8.2%
	FY1926	$3.8	4.2%	$4.3	3.3%
	FY1927	$4.0	5.7%	$4.6	7.8%
	FY1928	$3.9	−2.8%	$4.5	−1.7%
			0.2%		0.1%

Before and After: Revenue, Output, and Employment
annual average rate over four-year period before and four-year period after the tax cut

Federal Real Revenue Growth — Before: −9.2%, After: 0.1%

Real GDP Growth — Before: 2.0%, After: 3.4%

Unemployment Rate — Before: 6.5%, After: 3.1%

Table A-2 Percentage Share of Total Income Taxes
Paid By Income Class: 1920, 1925, and 1929

Income Class	1920	1925	1929
Under $5,000	15.4%	1.9%	0.4%
$5,000–$10,000	9.1%	2.6%	0.9%
$10,000–$25,000	16.0%	10.1%	5.2%
$25,000–$100,000	29.6%	36.6%	27.4%
Over $100,000	29.9%	48.8%	62.2%

Source: Internal Revenue Service.

Perhaps most illustrative of the power of the Harding/Coolidge tax cuts was the increase in GDP, the fall in unemployment, and the improvement in the average American's quality of life over this decade. Table A-3 demonstrates the remarkable increase in American quality of life, as reflected by the percentage of Americans owning items in 1930 that previously only the wealthy (or no one at all) could afford.

Table A-3 Percentage of Americans Owning Selected Items

Item	1920	1930
Autos	26%	60%
Radios	0%	46%
Electric lighting	35%	68%
Washing machines	8%	24%
Vacuum cleaners	9%	30%
Flush toilets	20%	51%

Source: Stanley Lebergott, *Pursuing Happiness: American Consumers in the Twentieth Century.* (Princeton: Princeton University Press, 1993), pp. 102, 113, 130, 137.

The Kennedy Tax Cuts

During the Depression and World War II the top marginal income-tax rate rose steadily, peaking at an incredible 94 percent in 1944 and 1945. The rate remained above 90 percent well into President John F. Kennedy's term in office, which began in 1961. Kennedy's fiscal policy stance made it clear he was a believer in progrowth, supply-side tax measures. Kennedy said it all in January 1963 in the *Economic Report of the President:*

> *Tax reduction thus sets off a process that can bring gains for everyone, gains won by marshalling resources that would otherwise stand idle—workers without jobs and farm and factory capacity without markets. Yet many taxpayers*

seemed prepared to deny the nation the fruits of tax reduction because they question the financial soundness of reducing taxes when the federal budget is already in deficit. Let me make clear why, in today's economy, fiscal prudence and responsibility call for tax reduction even if it temporarily enlarged the federal deficit—why reducing taxes is the best way open to us to increase revenues.

Kennedy further reiterated his beliefs in his *Tax Message to Congress* on January 24, 1963:

In short, this tax program will increase our wealth far more than it increases our public debt. The actual burden of that debt—as measured in relation to our total output—will decline. To continue to increase our debt as a result of inadequate earnings is a sign of weakness. But to borrow prudently in order to invest in a tax revision that will greatly increase our earning power can be a source of strength.

President Kennedy proposed massive tax-rate reductions that passed Congress and went into law after he was assassinated. The 1964 tax cut reduced the top marginal personal income-tax rate from 91 percent to 70 percent by 1965. The cut reduced lower-bracket rates as well. In the four years succeeding the 1965 tax-rate cuts, federal government income-tax revenue, adjusted for inflation, had increased at an average annual rate of 2.1 percent, while total government income-tax revenue (federal plus state and local) had increased 2.6 percent per year (Table A-4). In the four years following the tax cut these two measures of revenue growth rose to 8.6 percent and 9.0 percent, respectively. Government income-tax revenue not only increased in the years following the tax cut, it increased at a much faster rate in spite of the tax cuts.

The Kennedy tax cut set the example that Reagan would follow some seventeen years later. Increasing incentives to work, produce, and invest increased the growth of real GDP in the years following the tax cuts, more people worked, and the tax base expanded. The expenditure side of the budget benefited as well because the unemployment rate was significantly reduced.

Table A-4 A Look at the Kennedy Tax Cut

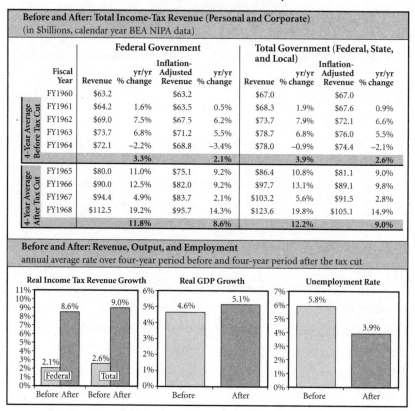

Before and After: Total Income-Tax Revenue (Personal and Corporate)
(in $billions, calendar year BEA NIPA data)

	Fiscal Year	Federal Government				Total Government (Federal, State, and Local)			
		Revenue	yr/yr % change	Inflation-Adjusted Revenue	yr/yr % change	Revenue	yr/yr % change	Inflation-Adjusted Revenue	yr/yr % change
4-Year Average Before Tax Cut	FY1960	$63.2		$63.2		$67.0		$67.0	
	FY1961	$64.2	1.6%	$63.5	0.5%	$68.3	1.9%	$67.6	0.9%
	FY1962	$69.0	7.5%	$67.5	6.2%	$73.7	7.9%	$72.1	6.6%
	FY1963	$73.7	6.8%	$71.2	5.5%	$78.7	6.8%	$76.0	5.5%
	FY1964	$72.1	−2.2%	$68.8	−3.4%	$78.0	−0.9%	$74.4	−2.1%
			3.3%		2.1%		3.9%		2.6%
4-Year Average After Tax Cut	FY1965	$80.0	11.0%	$75.1	9.2%	$86.4	10.8%	$81.1	9.0%
	FY1966	$90.0	12.5%	$82.0	9.2%	$97.7	13.1%	$89.1	9.8%
	FY1967	$94.4	4.9%	$83.7	2.1%	$103.2	5.6%	$91.5	2.8%
	FY1968	$112.5	19.2%	$95.7	14.3%	$123.6	19.8%	$105.1	14.9%
			11.8%		8.6%		12.2%		9.0%

Before and After: Revenue, Output, and Employment
annual average rate over four-year period before and four-year period after the tax cut

Real Income Tax Revenue Growth

Federal: Before 2.1% After 8.6%
Total: Before 2.6% After 9.0%

Real GDP Growth

Before 4.6% After 5.1%

Unemployment Rate

Before 5.8% After 3.9%

In addition, in 1965, one year following the tax cut, personal income-tax revenue data exceeded expectations by the greatest amounts in the highest income classes (Table A-6).

Table A-5 Actual vs. Forecast Federal Budget Receipts, 1964–67

(in $billions)

Fiscal Year	Actual Budget Receipts	Forecast Budget Receipts	Difference	Percentage Actual Revenue Exceeded Forecasts
1964	$112.7	$109.3	+$3.4	3.1%
1965	$116.8	$115.9	+$0.9	0.7%
1966	$130.9	$119.8	+$11.1	9.3%
1967	$149.6	$141.4	+$8.2	5.8%

Source: Congressional Budget Office, *A Review of the Accuracy of Treasury Revenue Forecasts, 1963–1978* (February 1981), p. 4

Table A-6 Actual vs. Forecast Personal Income-Tax Revenue by Income Class, 1965

(calendar year, revenue in $millions)

Adjusted Gross Income Class	Actual Revenue Collected	Forecast Revenue	Percentage Actual Revenue Exceeded Forecasts
$0–$5,000	$4,337	$4,374	−0.8%
$5,000–$10,000	$15,434	$13,213	16.8%
$10,000–$15,000	$10,711	$6,845	56.5%
$15,000–$20,000	$4,188	$2,474	69.3%
$20,000–$50,000	$7,440	$5,104	45.8%
$50,000–$100,000	$3,654	$2,311	58.1%
$100,000+	$3,764	$2,086	80.4%
Total	$49,530	$36,407	36.0%

Source: Estimated revenues calculated from Joseph A. Pechman, "Evaluation of Recent Tax Legislation: Individual Income Tax Provisions of the Revenue Act of 1964," *Journal of Finance*, Vol. 20 (May 1965), p. 268. Actual revenues are from internal Revenue Service, *Statistics of Income—1965, Individual Income Tax Returns*, p. 8.

Testifying before Congress in 1977, Walter Heller, President Kennedy's chairman of the Council of Economic Advisors, summed it all up:

What happened to the tax cut in 1965 is difficult to pin down, but insofar as we are able to isolate it, it did seem to have a tremendously stimulative effect, a multiplied effect on the economy. It was the major factor that led to our running a $3 billion surplus by the middle of 1965 before escalation in Vietnam struck us. It was a $12 billion tax cut, which would be about $33 or $34 billion in today's terms, and within one year the revenues into the Federal Treasury were already above what they had been before the tax cut.

Did the tax cut pay for itself in increased revenues? I think the evidence is very strong that it did.[2]

The Reagan Tax Cuts

In August 1981, Ronald Reagan signed into law the Economic Recovery Tax Act (ERTA, also known as Kemp-Roth). ERTA slashed marginal earned income-tax rates by 25 percent across the board over a three-year period. The highest marginal tax rate on unearned income dropped to 50 percent from 70 percent immediately (the Broadhead Amendment) and the tax rate on capital gains also fell immediately, from 28 percent to 20 percent. Five percentage points of the 25 percent cut went into effect on October 1, 1981. An additional ten percentage points of the cut then went into effect on July 1, 1982, and the final ten percentage points of the cut began on July 1, 1983.

Looking at the cumulative effects of ERTA in terms of tax (calendar) years, the tax cut provided a reduction in tax rates of 1.25 percent through the entirety of 1981, 10 percent through 1982, 20 percent through 1983, and the full 25 percent through 1984.

---

2. Walter Heller, in testimony before the Joint Economic Committee of Congress, 1977, quoted by Bruce Bartlett in the *National Review*, October 27, 1978.

As a provision of ERTA, Reagan also saw to it that the tax brackets were indexed for inflation beginning in 1985.

To properly discern the effects of the tax-rate cuts on the economy, I use the starting date of January 1, 1983, given that the bulk of the cuts were in place on that date. However, a case could be made for a start date of January 1, 1984, the date the full cut was in effect.

These across-the-board marginal tax-rate cuts resulted in higher incentives to work, produce, and invest, and the economy responded (Table A-7). Between 1978 and 1982 the economy grew at a 0.9 percent rate in real terms, but from 1983 to 1986 this growth rate increased to 4.8 percent.

Before the tax cut the economy was choking on high inflation, high interest rates, and high unemployment. All three of these economic bellwethers dropped sharply after the tax cuts. The unemployment rate, which had peaked at 9.7 percent in 1982, began a steady decline, reaching 7.0 percent by 1986 and 5.3 percent when Reagan left office in January 1989.

Inflation-adjusted revenue growth dramatically improved. Over the four years preceding 1983, federal income-tax revenue declined at an average rate of 2.8 percent per year, and total government income-tax revenue declined at an annual rate of 2.6 percent. Between 1983 and 1986 these figures were a positive 2.7 percent and 3.5 percent, respectively.

The most controversial portion of Reagan's tax revolution was the big drop in the highest marginal income-tax rate from 70 percent when he took office to 28 percent in 1988. However, Internal Revenue Service data reveal that tax collections from the wealthy, as measured by personal income taxes paid by top-percentile earners, increased between 1980 and 1988 despite significantly lower tax rates (Table A-8).

Table A-7 Percentage of Total Personal Income Taxes Paid by Percentile of Adjusted Gross Income (AGI)

Calendar Year	Top 1% of AGI	Top 5% of AGI	Top 10% of AGI	Top 25% of AGI	Top 50% of AGI
1980	19.1%	36.8%	49.3%	73.0%	93.0%
1981	17.6%	35.1%	48.0%	72.3%	92.6%
1982	19.0%	36.1%	48.6%	72.5%	92.7%
1983	20.3%	37.3%	49.7%	73.1%	92.8%
1984	21.1%	38.0%	50.6%	73.5%	92.7%
1985	21.8%	38.8%	51.5%	74.1%	92.8%
1986	25.0%	41.8%	54.0%	75.6%	93.4%
1987	24.6%	43.1%	55.5%	76.8%	93.9%
1988	27.5%	45.5%	57.2%	77.8%	94.3%

Source: Internal Revenue Service.

Table A-8 A Look at the Reagan Tax Cut

Before and After: Total Income-Tax Revenue (Personal and Corporate)
(in $billions, calendar year BEA NIPA data)

	Fiscal Year	Federal Government				Total Government (Federal, State, and Local)			
		Revenue	yr/yr % change	Inflation-Adjusted Revenue	yr/yr % change	Revenue	yr/yr % change	Inflation-Adjusted Revenue	yr/yr % change
	FY1978	$260.3		$260.3		$307.4		$307.4	
4-Year Average Before Tax Cut	FY1979	$299.0	14.9%	$268.7	3.2%	$350.8	14.1%	$315.3	2.6%
	FY1980	$320.3	7.1%	$253.5	−5.7%	$377.4	7.6%	$298.7	−5.3%
	FY1981	$356.3	11.2%	$255.6	0.8%	$419.6	11.2%	$301.0	0.8%
	FY1982	$344.0	−3.5%	$232.5	−9.0%	$410.0	−2.3%	$277.1	−7.9%
			7.2%		**−2.8%**		**7.5%**		**−2.6%**
4-Year Average After Tax Cut	FY1983	$347.5	1.0%	$227.6	−2.1%	$421.7	2.9%	$276.2	−0.3%
	FY1984	$376.6	8.4%	$236.5	3.9%	$462.9	9.8%	$290.7	5.2%
	FY1985	$412.3	9.5%	$250.0	5.7%	$504.6	9.0%	$306.0	5.3%
	FY1986	$433.9	5.2%	$258.2	3.3%	$534.0	5.8%	$317.8	3.9%
			6.0%		**2.7%**		**6.8%**		**3.5%**

Before and After: Revenue, Output, and Employment
annual average rate over four-year period before and four-year period after the tax cut

Real Income-Tax Revenue Growth — Federal: Before −2.8%, After 2.7%; Total: Before −2.6%, After 3.5%

Real GDP Growth — Before 0.9%, After 4.8%

Unemployment Rate — Before 7.6%, After 7.8%

ACKNOWLEDGMENTS

It goes without saying that authors get a lot of help—in a variety of forms—when they endeavor to write a book, and we would be remiss to allow this book to be published without expressing our gratitude to everyone who helped make this book a reality. To begin with, a big thank-you to our families—and especially our wives, Traci Laffer and Allison Moore—for putting up with a part-time author in the house.

We'd also like to thank our family, friends, and colleagues for the assistance they lent us in putting our thoughts on paper, particularly Joel Citron, Ron Felmus, Harvey Hammond, David Kretschmer, Ken Petersen, Robert Rowland, Alex Sharp, Bill Shiebler, and Catherine Wood. Additionally, Wayne Winegarden and Ford Scudder deserve a special thank-you for their tireless efforts on our behalf.

Finally, thank you to our team at Pocket Books, including Maggie Crawford, Kate Dresser, Kevin Smith, and Anthony Ziccardi, and our agent, Alexander Hoyt, for working so hard to get this complex project completed.

INDEX

311

corporations (*cont.*)
  stock market performance and, 232
  taxes and, 6, 8, 57, 68–69, 73, 94–96,
    99, 102–3, 105, 115–16, 119, 151, 155,
    162, 165–68, 173, 175–78, 180–81,
    185–88, 190–92, 195–96, 217, 219–
    20, 232, 262–63, 284
  unions and, 83–84, 87
Cox, Michael, 134
creative destruction, 148
credit, 236, 256, 261
credit cards, 280
Cuba, embargo of, 22, 25
currency, currencies, 257–58, 269, 273
  gold and, 264–65
  inflation and, 229, 242, 277
  M1 and, 235, 237
  monetary base and, 250, 257
  money supply and, 245–46
  trade and, 228, 275–77, 279–81
  values of, 9, 227–30, 245–46, 264–66,
    276
customs duties, 179–80, 268

Daschle, Tom, 105
deflation, 246, 257, 261
de Gaulle, Charles, 228
depreciation, 170, 188, 190–91
Diocletian, Emperor of Rome, 5
disabled veterans' compensation, 55
dividends:
  incomes and, 161–62
  increases in, 147
  taxes and, 68, 93, 99–100, 118, 151, 162,
    185, 189, 281
"Do Devaluations Really Help Trade?"
    (Laffer), 228
Doha Round, 27, 271, 287–88
dollar:
  Nixon's Camp David edict and, 4
  stability of, 9, 286–87
  trade and, 275–77, 280–81
  value of, 4, 88, 189, 227–30, 242, 245,
    248–50, 254, 265, 275–76, 278, 280,
    289
Domesday Book, 68–69
Dominican Republic–Central
    America Free Trade Agreement
    (DR-CAFTA), 271
Dow Jones Industrial Average, 111, 234
Dow Jones Spot Commodity Index, 231
Duisenberg, Wim, 282

earmarks, 7, 286
Earned-Income Tax Credit (EITC), 72,
    157
  poverty and, 210*n*, 211, 214
ECB, 282
economic effect, 293–94
Economic Growth and Tax Relief
    Reconciliation Act, 151*n*
Economic Recovery Tax Act (ERTA),
    304–5
economics, economy:
  collapses of, 16, 48, 54, 82, 147, 193,
    255–56, 261–68, 284, 300
  crises in, 283
  fairness in, 131
  free-market, 26
  growth of, 53, 106, 116, 126–27, 129,
    131, 147, 149–51, 168–69, 171, 173,
    175–76, 182–83, 210–11, 221, 237–
    39, 242, 259, 273–74, 279, 281, 284,
    289–90, 297–98
  and rising tide lifting all boats, 129–31
  underground, 194
Edict on Maximum Prices, 5
education:
  and after-tax rates of return, 154
  enterprise zones and, 218
  incomes and, 132, 138, 145–46
  living standards and, 149
  universities and, 185–86
Ehrlichman, John, 2, 5
Einstein, Albert, 91
Eisenhower, Dwight D., 19
Emanuel, Rahm, 104
embargoes:
  adjusting to, 25–26
  Bhagwati theorems on, 23
  energy policy and, 23
  political ineffectiveness of, 22–23, 25
  during wartime, 25–26
Employee Free Choice Act (Card Check),
    6, 87
employment, employers, employees,
    unemployment, 7–8, 26, 53*n*,
    135–43, 148–49, 162, 168–71, 257,
    273, 292–97
  after-tax earnings and, 154, 156, 168,
    173, 296
  and Cash for Clunkers, 62, 64
  consumption and, 62–65, 87, 141
  CPI and, 262, 266–67
  data biases on, 142